Measurement and Evaluation in Early Childhood Education

Measurement and Evaluation in Early Childhood Education

Second Edition

Sue Clark Wortham
The University of Texas at San Antonio

Merrill,
an imprint of Prentice Hall

PRENTICE HALL, UPPER SADDLE RIVER, NEW JERSEY 07458

Library of Congress Cataloging-in-Publication Data
Wortham, Sue Clark
     Measurement and evaluation in early childhood
education / Sue Clark Wortham,—2nd ed.
        p. cm.
     Rev. ed. of: Tests and measurement in early
childhood education. © 1990.
    Includes bibliographical references and index.
    ISBN 0-02-430033-0 (pbk.)
    1. Educational tests and measurements—United States.
2. Psychological tests for children—United States. 3. Ability in
children—United States—Testing. 4. Early childhood education—
United States.   I. Wortham, Sue Clark   Tests and measurement
in early childhood education. II. Title.

LB3051.W64 1995	94-3594
372.12′6—dc20	CIP

Cover photo: Elizabeth Hathon/The Stock Market
Editor: Ann Castel Davis
Production Editors: Laura Messerly and Mary Irvin
Photo Editor: Anne Vega
Text and Cover Designer: Anne Flanagan
Production Buyer: Deidra M. Schwartz
Electronic Text Management: Marilyn Wilson Phelps, Matthew Williams, Jane Lopez,
    Karen L. Bretz

This book was set in Zapf Calligraphic by Prentice Hall and was printed and bound by Book Press.
The cover was printed by Phoenix Color Corp.

Earlier edition, entitled *Tests and Measurement in Early Childhood Education*, © 1990 by Merrill Publishing
Company.

Photo credits: Barbara Schwartz/Prentice Hall and Merrill: pp. 1, 67, 179, 182, 223, 235; Todd Yarring-
ton/Prentice Hall and Merrill: pp. 4, 149; Anne Vega/Prentice Hall and Merrill: 17, 26, 37, 93, 101, 111,
121, 133, 168, 187; Tom Watson/Prentice Hall and Merrill: p. 197

Printed in the United States of America

10 9 8 7 6

ISBN: 0-02-430033-0

PRENTICE-HALL INTERNATIONAL (UK) LIMITED, *LONDON*
PRENTICE-HALL OF AUSTRALIA PTY. LIMITED, *SYDNEY*
PRENTICE-HALL CANADA INC., *TORONTO*
PRENTICE-HALL HISPANOAMERICANA, S.A., *MEXICO*
PRENTICE-HALL OF INDIA PRIVATE LIMITED, *NEW DELHI*
PRENTICE-HALL OF JAPAN, INC., *TOKYO*
PEARSON EDUCATION ASIA PTE. LTD., *SINGAPORE*
EDITORA PRENTICE-HALL DO BRASIL, LTDA., *RIO DE JANEIRO*

Preface

All students preparing to become elementary school teachers take a course in tests and measurements as part of their undergraduate curriculum. Many textbooks for such courses describe both psychological and teacher-designed tests and how they are used to assess and evaluate students.

Students preparing to become teachers of young children—those from infancy through the primary grades—must be prepared to measure or evaluate children who are in the period of development called *early childhood*. Tests and other measurements designed for young children are different from those intended for children in later grades in elementary school. Because infants and children under age eight have developmental limitations different from those of older children, a textbook that includes discussion of measurement and evaluation in the early childhood years must be written from a developmental perspective.

This book is written especially for teachers and future teachers of young children. It includes information not only about standardized tests used in the early childhood years, but also about other types of evaluation and measurement that are developmentally appropriate for younger children, such as observation, checklists and rating scales, and tests and manipulative measures designed by teachers. In this edition the section on informal strategies has been expanded to include performance assessments and systems of reporting performance assessments. A more comprehensive coverage of student-based assessment is provided, with the foundations of informal strategies introduced first in chapters 5 through 7, and in-depth explanation of how these informal strategies support performance assessment and reporting in chapters 8 and 9. Efforts to promote authentic or performance assessment are valid and important; nevertheless, standardized tests in early childhood education continue to be valuable when used appropriately. Thus in this text I seek to inform the reader about all types of measurements and their appropriate use.

An important factor in the measurement of young children is when and how they should be measured and evaluated. This is a controversial issue. The strengths and weaknesses of each type of measurement presented are discussed, as are research on the problems surrounding testing and evaluation in early childhood. Because many sources in the literature and textbooks do not include the limitations as well as merits of assessment techniques, this edition of the text provides an objective perspective on issues surrounding the efficacy and effectiveness of evaluation and reporting strategies.

The book is divided into two parts. The first half is devoted to topics about standardized tests for infants and children in the early childhood years through the primary grades. Following an introductory chapter that gives the historical background of measurement and evaluation in early childhood and an overview of different types of measurement used with young children, the next three chapters cover standardized tests. In chapter 2, "Strategies for Measurement and Evaluation," the differences between standardized tests and informal evaluation measures are described. In chapter 3, "Standardized Tests," information on the process of designing standardized tests and characteristics of dependable tests is provided. In chapter 4, "Using and Reporting Standardized Test Results," how these tests are used with young children is discussed, as well as the issues surrounding the misuse and application of standardized test results with young children.

Informal methods of evaluating children are covered beginning with chapter 5, "Informal Measures: Observation." Observation as a measurement tool is described, including different strategies and purposes for using observation. Checklists and rating scales as assessment and record keeping instruments are discussed in chapter 6, "Informal Measures: Checklists and Rating Scales." Chapter 7, "Informal Measures: Classroom and Teacher-Designed Tests and Assessments," presents the ways in which teachers design their own assessments in early childhood classes to complement the developmental levels of their students. Chapter 7 presents information on how concrete, hands-on assessment tasks are gradually replaced by paper-and-pencil activities as students achieve some competence in reading and writing.

In chapter 8, "Informal Measures: Performance-Based Evaluation," the trend toward more authentic assessment is introduced that focuses on what the child can do with knowledge and skills that have been learned. Different strategies are described for how the child can demonstrate progress and mastery, as well as how they are interrelated and depend on the teacher and child together to conduct an evaluation.

Chapter 9, "Using Informal Strategies to Report Student Progress," covers performance assessments and informal strategies that serve as the foundation for reporting children's progress. Systems for reporting more relevant and authentic types of assessment are explained, as well as why these reporting systems are needed as alternatives to more traditional reporting methods.

Chapter 10, "Putting Measurement and Evaluation in Perspective: Looking Ahead," presents a final look at measurement and evaluation of young children. The process of and purposes for program evaluation are discussed, and a look ahead to challenges for measurement and evaluation in the future is presented. Designing and implementing quality programs for all young children, including those from diverse backgrounds and with disabilities, present ongoing challenges for the development and use of appropriate evaluation measures.

The first edition of this book was initiated at the suggestion of undergraduate students enrolled in a course on tests and measurements in early childhood. During a period of two years, these students worked with tentative materials and initial drafts, providing feedback on content and format. In this second edition I respond to the expressed needs of teachers and graduate students who must understand and use current trends in assessment and put them in perspective within the reality of public schools that are required to use standardized measures.

Graduate students gave generously of their time and expertise during development of the text. Special thanks are due to Sharron Calhoun, Cynthia Cates, Susan Fillinger, Marla MacDonald, Della Meyer, Mary Jo Nelson, Nancy Pfrang, Linda Williams, and Cheryl Workman, who spent many hours studying and discussing each chapter of the first edition.

Graduate students Elizabeth Herring and Gloria Morales provided valuable assistance for the second edition through suggestions for additions and changes and research on additional test resources. Lori Richardson helped edit draft copies. Two colleagues, Cindy Soto and Karen Wellhousen, provided ideas for resources and also edited draft copies.

I would like to thank the reviewers who provided valuable suggestions and feedback during the writing process. Their input helped make this a better book, and I am indebted to them for their assistance. Those who reviewed parts or all of the manuscript are Richard Fiene, Pennsylvania State University-Harrisburg; Darla Springate, Eastern Kentucky University; Tes Mehring, Emporia State University; Susan Kontos, Purdue University; John Johnston, Memphis State University; Ronald Padula, Delaware County Community College; Landace Logan, Emporia State University; and Ruth Hough, Georgia State University.

I especially thank Linda Sullivan, editor at Merrill, for her continuing support and encouragement for this second edition, as well as her suggestions for additions and improvements.

Brief Contents

Contents

Chapter 1

An Overview of Measurement in Early Childhood   1

Chapter 2

Strategies for Measurement and Evaluation   17

Chapter 3

Standardized Tests   37

Chapter 4

Using and Reporting Standardized Test Results   67

Chapter 5

Informal Measures: Observation   93

Chapter 6

Informal Measures: Checklists and Rating Scales   121

Chapter 7

Informal Measures: Classroom and Teacher-Designed Tests and Assessments   149

Chapter 8

Informal Measures: Performance-Based Evaluations   179

Chapter 9

Using Informal Assessment Strategies to Report Student Progress   197

Chapter 10

Putting Measurement and Evaluation in Perspective: Looking Ahead   223

Appendix

A Selected Annotated Bibliography of Evaluation Instruments for Infancy and Early Childhood   241

Measurement and Evaluation in Early Childhood Education

Chapter 1

An Overview of Measurement in Early Childhood

Chapter Objectives

As a result of reading this chapter you will be able to

1. understand the purposes of measurement in early childhood.
2. understand different meanings of the term *measurement*.
3. understand the history of tests and measurement in early childhood.
4. develop an awareness of issues in testing young children.

Throughout elementary and high school, children take many different kinds of tests. Some tests determine their grades for each reporting period; some are achievement tests, IQ tests, or tests for admission to a college or university. Measurement and evaluation, however, are more than the testing that is familiar to us. Furthermore, we may be unaware of the role that measurement and evaluation play with children in the years from birth to eight years of age.

Measurement can mean many things. Goodwin and Goodwin (1982) describe measurement as "the process of determining, through observation or testing, an individual's traits or behaviors, a program's characteristics, or the properties of some other entity, and then assigning a number, rating, or score to that determination" (p. 523). The studying of individuals for measurement purposes begins before birth, with assessments of fetal growth and development. At birth and throughout infancy and early childhood, various methods of measurement are used to evaluate the individual's traits or behaviors. Before a child is able to take a written test, he or she is measured through medical examinations, observation of developmental milestones by parents and other family members, and perhaps screened or evaluated for an early childhood program or service.

Information about measurement, particularly for psychological testing, comes from many sources. All college students preparing to become teachers take courses in educational psychology in which they learn about the characteristics of various tests, how they are administered, and how the results are interpreted.

How is a book on measurement and evaluation of young children different from a textbook prepared for a course in educational psychology? Most textbooks in testing and measurement focus primarily on the psychological and educational testing of school-age children and adults, with some attention to younger individuals. The tests and teacher assessments described usually assume some facility in reading and writing.

Measurement of children from birth through the preschool years is different from measurement of older people. Not only can young children not write or read, but the young developing child also presents different challenges that influence the choice of measurement strategy. Evaluation strategies must be matched with the level of mental, social, and physical development at each stage. Developmental change in young children is rapid, and there is a need to assess whether

EARLY INTERVENTION FOR A CHILD
WITH HEARING IMPAIRMENT

Julio, who is two years old, was born prematurely. He did not have regular checkups during his first year, but he was taken by his mother to a community clinic when he had a cold and fever at about nine months of age.

When she noticed that Julio did not react to normal sounds in the examining room, the clinic doctor stood behind him and clapped her hands near each ear. Because Julio did not turn toward the clapping sounds, the doctor suspected that he had a hearing loss. She arranged for Julio to be examined by an audiologist at an eye, ear, nose, and throat clinic.

Julio was found to have a significant hearing loss in both ears. He was fitted with hearing aids and is attending a special program twice a week for children with hearing deficits. Therapists in the program are teaching Julio to speak. They are also teaching his mother how to make Julio aware of his surroundings and help him develop a vocabulary. Had Julio not received intervention services at an early age, he might have entered school with severe cognitive and learning deficits that would have put him at a higher risk for learning.

development is progressing normally. If development is not normal, the measurement and evaluation procedures used are important in making decisions regarding appropriate intervention services during infancy and the preschool years.

If medical problems, birth defects, or developmental delays in motor, language, cognitive, or social development are discovered during the early, critical periods of development, steps can be taken to correct, minimize, or remediate them before the child enters school. For many developmental deficits or differences, the earlier they are detected and the earlier intervention is planned, the more likely the child will be able to overcome them or compensate for them. For example, if a serious hearing deficit is identified early, the child can learn other methods of communicating and acquiring information.

Besides identifying and correcting developmental problems, measurement of very young children is conducted for other purposes. One purpose is research. Researchers study young children to better understand their behavior or to measure the appropriateness of the experiences that are provided for them.

Measurement of young children is also used to place them in infant or early childhood programs or to provide special services. To ensure that a child receives the best services, careful screening and more extensive testing may be conducted before selecting the combination of intervention programs and other services that will best serve the child.

Program planning is another purpose of measurement. After children have been identified and evaluated for an intervention program or service, measurement results can be used in planning the programs that will serve them. These programs, in turn, can be evaluated to determine their effectiveness.

How were these measurement strategies developed? In the next section I describe how certain movements or factors, especially during this century, have affected the development of testing instruments, procedures, and other measurement techniques that are used with infants and young children.

There are many purposes and strategies for measuring young children.

THE EVOLUTION OF MEASUREMENT AND TESTING WITH YOUNG CHILDREN

Interest in studying young children to understand their growth and development dates back to the initial recognition of childhood as a separate period in the life cycle. Johann Pestalozzi, a pioneer in developing educational programs specifically for children, wrote about the development of his 3½-year-old son in 1774 (Irwin & Bushnell, 1980). Early publications also reflected concern for the proper upbringing and education of young children. *Some Thoughts Concerning Education,* by John Locke, 1699), *Emile* (Rousseau, 1911/1762), and Frederick Froebel's *Education of Man* (1896) were influential in focusing attention on the characteristics and needs of children in the eighteenth and nineteenth centuries. Rousseau believed that human nature was essentially good and that education must allow that goodness to unfold. He stated that more attention should be given to studying the child so that education could be adapted to meet individual needs (Weber, 1984). The study of children, as advocated by Rousseau, did not begin until the late nineteenth and early twentieth centuries.

Scientists throughout the world used observation to measure human behaviors. Ivan Pavlov proposed a theory of conditioning. Alfred Binet developed the concept of a normal mental age by studying memory, attention, and intelligence in children. Binet and Theophile Simon developed an intelligence scale to determine mental age that made it possible to differentiate the abilities of individual children (Weber, 1984). American psychologists expanded these early efforts, developing instruments for various types of measurement.

The study and measurement of young children today has evolved from the child study movement, the development of standardized tests, Head Start and other federal programs funded in the 1960s, and the passage of Public Law 94–142, the Individuals with Disabilities Education Act. All of these movements have generated an interest in measurement or evaluation of young children and contributed to the development of tests and measures designed specifically for this age group.

The Child Study Movement

G. Stanley Hall, Charles Darwin, and Lawrence Frank were leaders in the development of this child study movement that emerged after the turn of the century. Darwin, in suggesting that by studying the development of the infant one could glimpse the development of the human species, initiated the scientific study of the child (Kessen, 1965). Hall developed and extended methods of studying children. After he became president of Clark University in Worcester, Massachusetts, he established a major center for child study. Hall's students—John Dewey, Arnold Gesell, and Lewis Terman—all made major contributions to the study and measurement of children. Dewey advocated educational reform that affected the development of educational programs for young children. Gesell first described the behaviors that emerged in children at each chronological age. Terman became a leader in the development of mental tests (Irwin & Bushnell, 1980).

Research in child rearing and child care was furthered by the establishment of the Laura Spelman Rockefeller Memorial child development grants. Under the leadership of Lawrence Frank, institutes for child development were funded by the Rockefeller grants at Columbia University's Teachers College (New York), the University of Minnesota, the University of California at Berkeley, Arnold Gesell's Clinic of Child Development at Yale University, the Iowa Child Welfare Station, and other locations.

With the establishment of child study at academic centers, preschool children could be observed in group settings, rather than as individuals in the home. With the development of laboratory schools and nursery schools in the home economics departments of colleges and universities, child study research could also include the family in broadening the understanding of child development. Researchers from many disciplines joined in an ongoing child study movement that originated strategies for observing and measuring development. The results of their research led to an abundant literature. Between the 1890s and the 1950s, hundreds of children were studied in academic settings throughout the United States (Weber, 1984). Thus the child study movement has taught us how to use observation and other strategies to measure the child. Investigators today continue to add new knowledge about child development and learning that aids parents, preschool teachers and staff members, and professionals in institutions and agencies that provide services to children and families (Irwin & Bushnell, 1980).

Standardized Tests

Standardized testing also began around 1900. When colleges and universities in the East sought applicants from other areas of the nation in the 1920s, they found the high school transcripts of these students difficult to evaluate. The *Scholastic Aptitude Test* was established to permit fairer comparisons of applicants seeking admission (Cronbach, 1984).

As public schools expanded to offer twelve years of education, a similar phenomenon occurred. To determine the level of instruction, pace of instruction, and grouping of students without regard for socioeconomic class, objective tests were developed (Gardner, 1961). These tests grew out of the need to sort, select, or otherwise make decisions about both children and adults.

The first efforts to design tests were informal. When a psychologist, researcher, or physician needed a method to observe a behavior, he or she developed a procedure to meet those needs. The procedure was often adopted by others with the same needs. When many people wanted to use a particular measurement strategy or test, the developer prepared printed copies for sale. As the demand for tests grew, textbook publishers and firms specializing in test development and production also began to create and/or sell tests (Cronbach, 1984).

American psychologists built on the work of Binet and Simon in developing the intelligence measures described earlier. Binet's instrument, revised by Terman at Stanford University, came to be known as the *Stanford-Binet Intelligence Scale*. Other Americans, particularly educators, welcomed the opportunity to use precise measurements to evaluate learning. Edward Thorndike and his students designed measures to evaluate achievement in reading, mathematics, spelling, and language ability (Weber, 1984). By 1918 more than 100 standardized tests had been designed to measure school achievement (Monroe, 1918).

After World War II the demand for dependable and technically refined tests grew, and people of all ages came to be tested. As individuals and institutions selected and developed their own tests, the use of testing became more centralized. Statewide tests were administered in schools, and tests were increasingly used at the national level.

The expanded use of tests resulted in the establishment of giant corporations that could assemble the resources to develop, publish, score, and report the results of testing to a large clientele. Centralization improved the quality of tests and the establishment of standards for test design. As individual researchers and teams of psychologists continue to design instruments to meet current needs, the high quality of these newer tests can be attributed to the improvements and refinements made over the years and to increased knowledge of test design and validation (Cronbach, 1984).

Head Start and the War on Poverty

Prior to the 1960s, tests for preschool children were developed for use by medical doctors, psychologists, and other professionals serving children. Developmental measures, IQ tests, and specialized tests to measure developmental deficits were generally used for noneducational purposes. Child study researchers tended to use observational or unobtrusive methods to study the individual child or groups of children. School-age children were tested to measure school achievement, but this type of test was rarely used with preschool children.

After the federal government decided to improve the academic performance of lower-class children and those from non-English-speaking backgrounds, test developers moved quickly to develop new measurement and evaluation instruments for these preschool and school-age populations.

In the late 1950s, there was concern about the consistently low academic performance of children from poor homes. As researchers investigated the problem, national interest in improving education led to massive funding for many programs designed to reduce the disparity in achievement between poor and middle-class children. The major program that involved preschool children was Head Start. Models of early childhood programs ranging from highly structured academic, child-centered developmental to more traditional nursery school models were designed and implemented throughout the United States (White, 1973; Zigler & Valentine, 1979).

All programs funded by the federal government had to be evaluated for effectiveness. As a result, new measures were developed to assess individual progress and the programs' effectiveness (Laosa, 1982). The quality of these measures was uneven, as was comparative research designed to compare the overall effectiveness of Head Start. Nevertheless, the measures and strategies developed for use with Head Start projects added valuable resources for the assessment and evaluation of young children (Hoepfner, Stern, & Nummedal, 1971).

Other federally funded programs developed in the 1960s, such as bilingual programs, Title I, the Emergency School Aid Act, Follow Through, and Home Start, were similar in effect to Head Start. The need for measurement strategies and tests to evaluate these programs led to the improvement of existing tests and the development of new tests to evaluate their success accurately.

PL 94–142: Mainstreaming Young Children with Disabilities

Perhaps the most significant law affecting the measurement of children was Public Law (PL) 94-142, the Education for All Handicapped Children Act, passed in 1975. This law, later amended and renamed the Individuals with Disabilities Education Act, guaranteed all children with disabilities the right to an appropriate education in a free public school and placement in the least restrictive learning environment. The law further required the use of nondiscriminatory testing and evaluation of these children (Mehrens & Lehmann, 1984).

The implications of the law were far-reaching. Testing, identification, and placement of students with mental retardation and those with other disabilities were difficult. Existing tests no longer were considered adequate for children with special needs. Classroom teachers had to learn the techniques used to identify students with disabilities and determine how to meet their educational needs (Kaplan & Saccuzzo, 1982)

The law requires that a team of teachers, parents, diagnosticians, school psychologists, medical personnel, and perhaps social workers or representatives of government agencies or institutions be used to identify and place students with disabilities. When appropriate, the child must also be included in the decision-making process. The team screens, tests, and develops an individual educational program (IEP) for each child. Not all team members are involved in every step of the process, but they can influence the decisions made.

The term **mainstreaming** came to define the requirement that the child be placed in the least restrictive environment. This meant that as often as possible the child would be placed with children developing normally, rather than in a segregated classroom for students in special education. How much mainstreaming is beneficial for the individual student? The question has not yet been answered. In addition, the ability of teachers to meet the needs of students with and without disabilities simultaneously in the same classroom is still debated. Nevertheless, classroom teachers are expected to develop and monitor the educational program prescribed for students in special education (Clark, 1976).

The identification and diagnosis of students with disabilities is the most complex aspect of PL 94-142. Many types of children need special education, including students with mental retardation, physical and visual disabilities, speech impairments, auditory disabilities, learning disabilities, emotional disturbances, and students who are gifted. Children may have a combination of disabilities. The identification and comprehensive testing of children to determine what types of disabilities they have and how best to educate them requires a vast array of measurement techniques and instruments. Teachers, school nurses, and other staff members can be involved in initial screening and referral, but the extensive

---

ONE FAMILY'S EXPERIENCE WITH HEAD START

Rosa is a graduate of the Head Start program. For two years she participated in a class housed in the James Brown School, a former inner-city school that had been closed and remodeled for other community services. Two Head Start classrooms were in the building, which was shared with several other community agencies serving low-income families. In addition to learning at James Brown School, Rosa went on many field trips to places including the zoo, the botanical garden, the public library, and a nearby McDonald's.

This year Rosa is a kindergarten student at West Oaks Elementary School with her older brothers, who also attended Head Start. Next year Rosa's younger sister, Luisa, will begin the program. Luisa looks forward to Head Start. She has good memories of the things she observed Rosa doing in the Head Start classroom while visiting the school with her mother.

Luisa's parents are also happy that she will be attending the Head Start program. Luisa's older brothers are good students, which they attribute to the background they received in Head Start. From her work in kindergarten, it appears that Rosa will also do well when she enters first grade.

testing used for diagnosis and prescription requires professionals who have been trained to administer psychological tests (Mehrens & Lehmann, 1984).

Under PL 94-142, all children with disabilities between the ages of three and twenty-one are entitled to free public education. This means that preschool programs must also be provided for children under the age of six. Public schools have implemented early childhood programs for children with disabilities, and Head Start programs are required to include them (Guralnick, 1982). Other institutions and agencies also provide preschool programs for children with and without disabilities.

Meeting the developmental and educational needs of preschool children with disabilities, and at the same time providing mainstreaming, is a complex task. How should these children be grouped for the best intervention services? When children with and without disabilities are grouped together, what are the effects when all of them are progressing through critical periods of development? Not only is identification of preschool children with disabilities more complex, but evaluation of the preschool programs providing intervention services also is difficult (Allen, 1980; Bronfenbrenner, 1975).

Many of the shortcomings of PL 94-142 were addressed in PL 99-457 (Education of the Handicapped Act Amendments), passed in 1986. The newer law authorized two new programs: the Federal Preschool Program and the Early Intervention Program. Under PL 94-142, the state could choose whether to provide services to children with disabilities between the ages of three and five. Under PL 99-457, states must prove that they are meeting the needs of all of these children if they wish to receive federal funds under PL 94-142. The Federal Preschool Program extends the rights of children with disabilities under PL 94-142 to all children with disabilities between the ages of three and five.

The Early Intervention Program established early intervention services for all children between birth and two years of age who are developmentally delayed. At the end of the five-year implementation period, participating states must provide intervention services for all infants and toddlers with disabilities (Morrison, 1988).

How to measure and evaluate young children with disabilities and the programs that serve them is a continuing challenge (Guralnick, 1982). The design of measures to screen, identify, and place preschool children in intervention programs began with the passage of PL 94-142 and was extended under PL 99-457. Many of these instruments and strategies, particularly those dealing with developmental delay, are now also used with preschool programs serving children developing normally, as well as those with developmental delays or disabilities.

As children with disabilities are served in a larger variety of settings such as integrated preschools, Head Start programs, infant intervention programs, and hospitals, early childhood educators from diverse backgrounds are involved in the determination of whether infants and young children are eligible for services for special needs. Early childhood special educators and other practitioners in the field are challenged to be knowledgeable in measurement and evaluation strategies for effective identification, placement, and assessment of young children in integrated early childhood settings (Goodwin & Goodwin, 1993).

CURRENT PRACTICES AND TRENDS IN MEASUREMENT AND EVALUATION IN EARLY CHILDHOOD EDUCATION

The 1980s brought a new reform movement in education, accompanied by a new emphasis on testing. The effort to improve education at all levels included the use of standardized tests to provide accountability for what students are learning. Minimum competency tests, achievement tests, and screening instruments were used to ensure that students from preschool through college reached the desired educational goals and achieved the minimum standards of education that were established locally or by the state education agency.

The increased use of testing at all levels has been criticized, but the testing of young children is of particular concern. Standardized tests and other informal measures are now being used in preschool, kindergarten, and first grade to help determine whether children will be admitted to preschool programs, promoted to first grade or placed in a transitional classroom, or retained. Those who advocate raising standards in education are calling for more stringent policies to improve school achievement. The use of tests with young children for placement purposes has serious implications because it can be developmentally inappropriate for this age group. Decisions made about placement, particularly placement in a transitional class or retention in a grade, can have a strong impact on the self-esteem of young children, particularly their perception of whether they are successful students or failures.

Emerging Practices in Using Inclusion with Children with Disabilities

Specialists in the assessment of young children emphasize that early childhood educators need to be informed about purposes and methods of testing. Meisels, Steele, and Quinn-Leering (1993) remind us that not all tests are bad.

The Americans with Disabilities Act (ADA) passed in 1990 (Stein, 1993) and the amendments to PL 94–142, the Individuals with Disabilities Education Act, have had an additional impact for the education of young children with disabilities. Under ADA all early childhood programs must be prepared to serve children with special needs. Facilities and accommodations for young children including outdoor play environments must be designed, constructed, and altered appropriately to meet the needs of young children with disabilities. The PL 94–142 amendments, passed in 1991, require that the individual educational needs of young children with disabilities must be met in all early childhood programs (Deiner, 1993; Wolery, Strain, & Bailey, 1992). These laws advance the civil rights of young children and have resulted in the inclusion of young children into early childhood programs. As a result, the concept of mainstreaming is being replaced by **integration** or **inclusion**, whereby all young children learn together with the goal that the individual needs of all children will be met (Krick, 1992). The efforts of these programs and their services must be assessed and evaluated to determine whether the needs of children are met effectively.

When reliable, valid screening tests are administered by trained testers, children who are at high risk for failure can be identified and helped through proper intervention. Nevertheless, too much attention has been given to the use of standardized tests, rather than a multidimensional approach that includes informal strategies such as portfolios, teacher report forms, and criterion-referenced assessments in addition to valid screening instruments. This broader view of assessment in early childhood programs is echoed by the organizations that endorsed and supported the Guidelines for Appropriate Curriculum Content and Assessment in Programs Serving Children Ages 3 Through 8, a position statement of the National Association for the Education of Young Children and the National Association of Early Childhood Specialists in State Departments of Education adopted in 1990 (1992). These guidelines proposed that the purpose of assessment is to benefit individual children and to improve early childhood programs. Appropriate assessment should help enhance curriculum choices, help teachers collaborate with parents, and help ensure that the needs of children are addressed appropriately. Rather than being narrowly defined as testing, assessment should link curriculum and instruction with program objectives for young children (Hills, 1992).

Concerns about Testing and Assessment of Young Children with Cultural and Language Differences

A concurrent concern related to current trends and practices in the measurement of young children is the question of how appropriate our tests and measurement strategies are for the diversity in young children attending early childhood programs. Socioeconomic groups are changing dramatically and rapidly in our society, with an expansion of the poorer class and a corresponding shrinking of the middle class (Raymond & McIntosh, 1992). At the same time an increase in nonwhite citizens is expanded by the continuing influx of people from other countries, especially Southeast Asia and Central and South America. Assessment of developmental progress of children from these groups is particularly important if their learning needs are to be identified and addressed. The fairness of existing tests for children who are school-disadvantaged and linguistically and culturally diverse serves as an indicator of the need for alternative assessment strategies for young children (Goodwin & Goodwin, 1993). Appropriate measurement and evaluation strategies that will enhance, rather than diminish, potential of achievement in minority children is a major issue in the 1990s.

Although early childhood specialists, both individuals and organizations, are concerned about the trends in education and the testing of young children, developmentally inappropriate practices continue to expand. Now more than ever, teachers, parents, and other adults active in the care and education of young children need to be informed about the measurement of these children and when and how it should be conducted. This textbook is a resource for such information.

AN OVERVIEW OF TOPICS COVERED IN THIS BOOK

In the chapters that follow, measurement and evaluation are discussed in terms of how they are applied to infants and young children. Basic information is provided about each topic in general, and then the application of the information to young children is explained. Issues regarding each topic are also explored. Thus the background information needed to understand a facet of measurement is presented, as well as the pertinence of the measurement approach when used with young children.

Chapter 2, "Strategies for Measurement and Evaluation," introduces the types of measurement to be presented in later chapters. This chapter briefly discusses the categories of measurement and evaluation strategies used with infants and preschool children and explains why they are used. The strategies are divided into formal, or psychological, tests and informal strategies that include observation, teacher-designed measures, and checklists, and various types of performance assessments.

Chapter 3, "Standardized Tests," describes how standardized tests are designed. People who use these tests must know how they should be constructed and pilot-tested before they are made available to the public. Administration of tests and interpretation of test scores are also covered. Many issues surround the use of standardized tests, particularly with young children. These issues are explained in a discussion of the advantages and disadvantages of using such tests with young children. Also provided are suggestions on how standardized tests should be evaluated and selected. The reader is directed to strategies for determining the quality of these tests by studying the test manual and reading reviews of the test in test review resources.

Standardized tests can be classified as having norm-referenced results, criterion-referenced results, or both. Chapter 4, "Using and Reporting Standardized Test Results," discusses the distinctions between the two types of tests and how each is used with young children. An important part of test administration and interpretation is knowing how to share the information about test results. Teachers must know how to report a child's performance to parents, while school district personnel must report school and district results to school staff, administrators, and the board of education. Also discussed are the advantages and disadvantages of using criterion-referenced and norm-referenced tests.

In chapter 5, "Informal Measures: Observation," the focus shifts from standardized tests to informal means of evaluation. The informal methods are reviewed before exploring the types of observation that can be done to learn about the child's development and behavior. The role of observation in understanding specific areas of development is explained to include physical, social and emotional, cognitive, and language development. Many strengths and weaknesses are inherent in the use of observation; these are discussed, and guidelines for observation are suggested.

Checklists and rating scales are instruments that can be used for evaluation purposes. Chapter 6, "Informal Measures: Checklists and Rating Scales," describes appropriate uses for checklists. It discusses how they can also be used as guides to understanding children's development, to developing curriculum, and to evaluating learning development. The process of checklist design is explained, as well as the strengths and limitations of checklists as measurement and evaluation resources.

Another type of informal measure is discussed in chapter 7, "Informal Measures: Classroom and Teacher-Designed Tests and Assessments." Teacher-conducted assessments designed for preschool children must be task oriented, rather than pencil-and-paper activities; various measures are discussed separately. Designing a teacher-conducted evaluation includes designing test objectives, constructing a table of specifications, organizing the instrument or tasks, and providing for instruction and extensions and correctives.

Chapter 8, "Informal Measures: Performance-Based Evaluation," expands the concept of informal assessment to include performance assessments in which children's progress is evaluated through an activity that permits the child to demonstrate understanding or accomplishment. Sometimes called authentic assessments, performance assessments include teacher-directed activities such as interviews with the child or child-initiated activities in which the child's natural interaction with materials or play activity allows the teacher to observe progress.

Chapter 9, "Using Informal Assessment to Report Student Progress," focuses on alternative reporting systems. The rationale for using an authentic system for reporting is discussed, instead of the traditional report card. The portfolio and narrative reports are described as two strategies that will facilitate a comprehensive summary of development and learning.

Finally, chapter 10, "Putting Measurement and Evaluation in Perspective: Looking Ahead," provides a synthesis of the problems and opportunities involved in the evaluation and assessment of young children. Discussed are the use of early childhood measures for program evaluation and the importance and process of program evaluation as an extension of the measurement of children. Because we are in a period of new influences and directions in early childhood education, measurement and evaluation strategies are again in the forefront in evaluating the effectiveness of schooling. Ongoing issues, as well as the trends, are discussed.

SUMMARY

The measurement of children begins very early in the life span. Newborns are tested for their neonatal status, and infant tests designed to assess development begin the trend for testing and measurement in the early childhood years. Measurement and evaluation in the early childhood years have many purposes; some are beneficial for young children, while others are detrimental.

The advent of measures to assess and evaluate young children's development and learning was at the turn of the century. As the decades passed and the twenty-first century approaches, significant trends in the study of young children and services and programs implemented for young children have driven the need to develop standardized tests and other measures to evaluate children's progress and program effectiveness.

There are issues surrounding the testing of young children. One may question the validity and reliability of standardized tests used with young children, as well as the purposes for administering the tests. In addition are concerns about the appropriateness of administering tests to children who are culturally and linguistically diverse. At the same time, the value of using tests to identify and provide services for children with disabilities continues as a positive purpose for individual testing and evaluation.

KEY TERMS

inclusion
integration
mainstreaming

SUGGESTED ACTIVITY

Review a recent journal article on a topic related to current issues in the testing and assessment of young children. Describe the major points in the article and your response.

REFERENCES

ALLEN, K. E. (1980). Mainstreaming: What have we learned? *Young Children, 35,* 54-63.

BRONFENBRENNER, U. (1975). Is early intervention effective? In B. Z. Friedlander, G. M. Sterritt, & G. E. Kirk (Eds.), *Exceptional infant* (Vol. 2, pp. 449–475). New York: Brunner/Mazel.

CLARK, E. A. (1976). Teacher attitudes toward integration of children with handicaps. *Education and Training of the Mentally Retarded, 11,* 333-335.

CRONBACH, L. J. (1984). *Essentials of psychological testing.* New York: Harper & Row.

DEINER, P. L. (1993). *Resources for teaching children with diverse abilities.* Fort Worth, TX: Harcourt Brace Jovanovich.

FROEBEL, F. (1896). *Education of man.* New York: Appleton.

GARDNER, J. W. (1961). *Excellence: Can we be equal and excellent too?* New York: Harper & Row.

GOODWIN, W. L., & GOODWIN, L. D. (1982). Measuring young children. In B. Spodek (Ed.), *Handbook of research in early childhood education* (pp. 523–563). New York: Free Press.

GOODWIN, W. L., & GOODWIN, L. D. (1993). Young children and measurement: Standardized and nonstandardized instruments in early childhood education. In B. Spodek (Ed.), *Handbook of research on the education of young children* (pp. 441–463). New York: Macmillan.

GURALNICK, M. J. (1982). Mainstreaming young handicapped children: A public policy and ecological systems analysis. In B. Spodek (Ed.), *Handbook of research in early childhood education* (pp. 456-500). New York: Free Press.

HILLS, T. W. (1992). Reaching potentials through appropriate assessment. In S. Bredekamp & T. Rosegrant (Eds.), *Reaching potentials: Appropriate curriculum and assessment for young children* (pp. 43–64). Washington, DC: National Association for the Education of Young Children.

HOEPFNER, R., STERN, C., & NUMMEDAL, S. (Eds.). (1971). *CSE-ECRC preschool/kindergarten test evaluations.* Los Angeles: University of California, Graduate School of Education.

IRWIN, D. M., & BUSHNELL, M. M. (1980). *Observational strategies for child study.* New York: Holt, Rinehart & Winston.

KAPLAN, R. M., & SACCUZZO, D. P. (1982). *Psychological testing principles: Applications and issues.* Belmont, CA: Brooks/Cole.

KESSEN, W. (1965). *The child.* New York: John Wiley.

KRICK, J. C. (1992). All children are special. In B. Neugebauer (Ed.), *Alike and different: Exploring our humanity with young children* (rev. ed., pp. 152–158). Washington, DC: National Association for the Education of Young Children.

LAOSA, L. M. (1982). The sociocultural context of evaluation. In B. Spodek (Ed.), *Handbook of research in early childhood education* (pp. 501-520). New York: Free Press.

LOCKE, J. (1699). *Some thoughts concerning education* (4th ed.). London: A & J Churchill.

MEHRENS, W. A., & LEHMANN, I. J. (1984). *Measurement and evaluation in education and psychology* (3rd ed.). New York: Holt, Rinehart & Winston.

MEISELS, S. J., STEELE, D. M., & QUINN-LEERING, K. (1993). Testing, tracking, and retaining young children: An analysis of research and social policy. In B. Spodek (Ed.), *Handbook of research on the education of young children* (pp. 279–292). New York: Macmillan.

MONROE, W. S. (1918). Existing tests and standards. In G. W. Whipple (Ed.), *The measurement of educational products, 14th yearbook of the National Society for the Study of Education, Part II* (pp. 71-104). Bloomington, IL: Public School Publishing.

MORRISON, G. S. (1988). *Educational development of infants, toddlers, and preschoolers.* Glenview, IL: Scott, Foresman.

NATIONAL ASSOCIATION FOR THE EDUCATION OF YOUNG CHILDREN and the NATIONAL ASSOCIATION OF EARLY CHILDHOOD SPECIALISTS IN STATE DEPARTMENTS OF EDUCATION. (1992). Guidelines for appropriate curriculum content and assessment in programs serving children ages 3 through 8. In S. Bredekamp & T. Rosegrant (Eds.), *Reaching potentials: Appropriate curriculum and assessment for young children* (pp. 9–27). Washington, DC: Authors.

RAYMOND, G., & MCINTOSH, D. K. (1992). The impact of current changes in social structure on early childhood education programs. In B. Neugebauer (Ed.), *Alike and different: Exploring our humanity with young children* (rev. ed., pp. 116–126). Washington, DC: National Association for the Education of Young Children.

ROUSSEAU, J. J. (1911). *Emile or On education* (B. Foxley, Trans.). London: Dent. (Original work published 1762)

STEIN, J. U. (1993). Critical issues: Risk management, informed consent, and participant safety. In S. J. Grosse & D. Thompson (Eds.), *Leisure opportunities for individuals with disabilities: Legal issues* (pp. 37–54). Reston, VA: American Alliance for Health, Physical Education, Recreation, and Dance.

WEBER, E. (1984). *Ideas influencing early childhood education. A theoretical analysis.* New York: Teachers College Press.

WHITE, S. H. (1973). *Federal programs for young children: Review and recommendations* (Vol. 13). Washington, DC: Government Printing Office.

WOLERY, M., STRAIN, P. S., & BAILEY, D. B. (1992). Reaching potentials of children with special needs. In S. Bredekamp & T. Rosegrant (Eds.), *Reaching potentials: Appropriate curriculum and assessment for young children* (pp. 92–112). Washington, DC: National Association for the Education of Young Children.

ZIGLER, E., & VALENTINE, J. (Eds.). (1979). *Project Head Start: A legacy of the War on Poverty.* New York: Free Press.

Chapter 2

Strategies for Measurement and Evaluation

Chapter Objectives

As a result of reading this chapter you will be able to

1. describe various purposes for using measurement and evaluation with infants, preschoolers, and school-age children.
2. explain types of psychological tests and how the results are used.
3. identify tests that are used to evaluate the young child's intellectual ability.
4. understand the differences between formal and informal measures.

What are measurement and evaluation? Why do we need to test or evaluate children in the early childhood years?

We live in a world in which we are interested not only in knowing more about how infants and young children grow and develop but also in having access to tools to help us with problems in a child's development and learning.

Measurement and evaluation are used for various purposes. We may want to learn about individual children. We may conduct an evaluation to measure a young child's development in language or mathematics. When we need to learn more, we may assess the child to describe what he or she has achieved. For example, a preschool teacher may use measurement techniques to assess what concepts a child has learned prior to entering school. Likewise, a student in first grade might be assessed in reading to determine what reading skills have been mastered and what weaknesses exist that indicate a need for additional instruction.

Evaluation strategies may be used for diagnosis. Just as a medical doctor conducts a physical examination of a child to diagnose an illness, psychologists, teachers, and other adults who work with children can conduct an informal or formal assessment to diagnose a developmental delay or identify causes for poor performance in learning.

We also perform measurement and evaluation to gain information about groups of children or the success of programs or other services provided to them. Both formal and informal evaluation techniques may be used to measure a day care or preschool program that serves children with disabilities. Program providers may want to know how the children in the program have benefited from the intervention services they have received. A common example of evaluation of groups of children is standardized achievement tests that are given annually by school districts. In addition to learning about the achievement of each student tested, the school district can evaluate the instructional program by studying group achievement results. Program evaluators can study group results to find areas of strength or weakness in the curriculum at different grade levels.

Just as there are many reasons for measuring and evaluating young children, various methods are available to accomplish our goals. Sometimes we measure the child informally. We might look for characteristics by watching the child's

ASSESSMENT FOR RISK IN DEVELOPMENTAL STATUS

When Sarah was six months old, her teenage mother gave her up for adoption. Because Sarah's father could not be located to agree to release her for adoption, Sarah was placed temporarily in a foster home.

Prior to placement with the foster family, Sarah had lived with her mother in her maternal grandparents' home. In addition to Sarah's mother, six other children were in the family. Both grandparents were employed. Sarah's primary caregiver had been an aunt with mental retardation who was 12 years old.

For the first few days after Sarah was placed in the foster home, she cried when the foster parents tried to feed her. She sat for long periods of time and stared vacantly without reacting to toys or people. She had no established patterns for sleeping and usually fretted off and on during the night.

When Sarah was examined by a pediatrician, she was found to be malnourished, with sores in her mouth from vitamin deficiencies. As determined by the *Denver Developmental Screening Test,* she was developing much more slowly than normal.

A special diet and multivitamins were prescribed for Sarah. Members of the foster family patiently taught her to enjoy eating a varied diet beyond the chocolate milk and cereal that she had been fed previously. Regular times for sleeping at night gradually replaced her erratic sleeping habits. Her foster family spent many hours playing with her, talking with her, and introducing her to various toys.

By the age of eleven months, Sarah had improved greatly. She was alert, ate well, began to walk, and said a few words. Her development was within the normal range, and she was ready for adoption.

Sarah had benefited from being placed in a home where she received good nutrition, guidance in living patterns, and stimulation for cognitive, physical, and social development. Without early intervention, Sarah's delay in development might have become more serious over time. Adaptability to an adoptive home might have been difficult for her and her adoptive parents. If she had been unable to adjust successfully with an adoptive family, she might have spent her childhood years in a series of foster homes, rather than with her adoptive family. She also would have been at risk for learning, beginning in the first years of schooling.

behaviors at play or in a setting arranged for that purpose. A pediatrician may watch a baby walk during an examination to determine whether he or she is progressing normally. In a similar fashion, a teacher may observe a child playing to determine how he or she is using language. A second-grade teacher who constructs a set of subtraction problems to evaluate whether his students have mastered a mathematics objective is also using an **informal test**.

Formal methods, or standardized instruments, are also used for measurement and evaluation. These are more extensive and proven measures for evaluation. Specialists in tests and measurements design and then try out with a large number of children instruments that evaluate the characteristics we have targeted. This process ensures that they can use the information gained each time the test is given to another child or group of children. This type of test is called a **standardized test** because a standard has been set from the results achieved by using the test with children who are representative of the population.

Why are we interested in measuring infants and young children? The most common purpose is to assess development. Soon after a child's birth, the **obstetrician** or **pediatrician** evaluates the newborn by using the *Apgar Scale* (Apgar, 1975) to determine whether he or she is in good health. Thereafter, at regular intervals, parents, doctors, and teachers follow the baby's development by using tests and informal evaluation strategies (Wodrich, 1984). The screening test for phenylketonuria (PKU) may also be administered to detect the presence of the enzyme phenylalanine, which can cause mental retardation if not managed through diet. In addition, there are newborn screening tests for cystic fibrosis and congenital hypothyroidism (Widerstrom, Mowder, & Sandall, 1991).

But what if development is not progressing normally? How can evaluation measures be used to help the young child? In recent years, researchers, medical specialists, and educators have learned how to work with children at increasingly younger ages to minimize the effects of delays in growth or other problems that retard the child's developmental progress. Various strategies and instruments are now available. A **neonatologist** conducts a comprehensive evaluation on a premature baby to determine what therapy should be initiated to improve the infant's chances for survival and optimal development. A young child can be tested for hearing loss or mental retardation. The child who does not speak normally or who is late in speaking is referred to a speech pathologist, who assesses the child's language and prescribes activities to facilitate improved language development.

During a child's infancy and toddler years, child development specialists follow the child's progress and initiate therapy when development is not normal. During the preschool years this effort includes evaluating and predicting whether the child is likely to experience difficulties in learning. Tests and other measures are used to help determine whether the child will develop a **learning disability** and how that disability will affect his or her success in school. Again, when problems are detected, plans are made to work with the child in a timely manner to help him or her overcome as much of the disability as possible before entering school. The child may have a vision problem, difficulty in hearing, or a disability that may interfere with learning to read. The evaluation measures used will assist in identifying the exact nature of the problem. In addition, test results will be used to help determine what kind of intervention will be most successful (Wodrich, 1984).

In the preschool period or even earlier, a different kind of developmental difference may emerge. Parents or other adults who deal with the child may observe that the child demonstrates a learning ability or potential that is much higher than the normal range. A more formal evaluation using a standardized test may confirm these informal observations. Plans then can be made to facilitate the child's development to help him or her achieve full potential for learning.

Although potential for learning may be assessed at a very early age in the child who is gifted or talented, learning aptitude may also be evaluated in the general population during the preschool and primary school years. Educators wish to determine children's learning abilities and needs, as well as the types of programs that will be most beneficial for them. Informal strategies and formal tests are used with individual children and groups of children to assess what and how much they have already learned and to evaluate weak areas that can be given special attention.

COMBATING LIMITATIONS IN VOCABULARY AND CONCEPT DEVELOPMENT

Micah, who is four years old, is the sixth child in a family of seven children. Both of his parents work, and he and his younger brother are cared for by a grandmother during the day. Although Micah's parents are warm and loving, their combined income is barely enough to provide the basic necessities for the family. They are unable to buy books and toys that will enhance Micah's development. Because the family rarely travels outside the immediate neighborhood, Micah has had few experiences that would broaden his knowledge of the larger community.

Fortunately, Micah's family lives in a state that provides a program for four-year-old children who can benefit from a prekindergarten class that stresses language and cognitive development. The program serves all children who come from low-income homes or who exhibit language or cognitive delay.

In response to a letter sent by the school district, Micah's grandmother took him to the school to be tested for the program. Micah's performance on the test showed that he uses a limited expressive vocabulary and lacks many basic concepts. When school begins in late August, Micah will start school with his older brothers and sisters and will be enrolled in the prekindergarten class.

Micah will have the opportunity to play with puzzles, construction toys, and other manipulative objects that will facilitate his cognitive development. Stories will be read and discussed each day, and Micah will be able to look at a variety of books. Micah's teacher will introduce learning experiences that will allow Micah to learn about shapes, colors, numbers, and many other concepts that will provide a foundation for learning in the elementary school grades.

Micah will also travel with his classmates to visit places that will help him learn about the community. They may visit a furniture or grocery store or a bread factory. Visitors to the classroom will add to the students' knowledge about occupations and cultures represented in the community. The children will have opportunities to paint, participate in cooking experiences, and talk about the new things they are learning. They will dictate stories about their experiences and learn many songs and games. When Micah enters kindergarten the following year, he will use the knowledge and language he learned in prekindergarten to help him learn successfully along with his five-year-old peers.

Informal and formal strategies are also used to evaluate the success of programs that serve children, as well as provide indicators for how programs can be improved.

PSYCHOLOGICAL TESTS

Psychological tests are designed to measure individual characteristics. The test may be administered to an individual or to a group. The purpose of psychological tests is to measure abilities, achievements, aptitudes, interests, attitudes, values, and personality characteristics. The results can be used to plan instruction, to study differences between individuals and groups, and for counseling and guidance.

Ability refers to the current level of knowledge or skill in a particular area. Three types of psychological tests—**intelligence tests, achievement tests,** and **aptitude tests**—are categorized as ability tests because they measure facets of ability. Young children are often measured to determine the progress of their development. A measure used with such children may assess ability in motor, language, social, or cognitive skills. The *McCarthy Scales of Children's Abilities* (McCarthy, 1972), for example, has indices for verbal, perceptual/performance, quantitative, cognitive, memory, and motor abilities.

Achievement is related to the extent to which a person has acquired certain information or has mastered identified skills. An achievement test measures ability in that it evaluates the child's achievement related to specific prior instruction. The *Peabody Individual Achievement Test* (Dunn & Markwardt, 1970) is a measure of achievement in mathematics, reading recognition, reading comprehension, spelling, and general information.

Aptitude is the potential to learn or develop proficiency in some area, provided that certain conditions or training is available. An individual may have a high aptitude for music or art. Like achievement tests, aptitude tests also measure learned abilities. An aptitude test measures the results of both general and incidental learning and predicts future learning.

Intelligence tests are ability tests in that they assess overall intellectual functioning. They are also aptitude tests because they assess aptitude for learning and problem solving. The *Stanford-Binet Scale* (Terman & Merrill, 1973) is an example of an intelligence scale that also measures individual aptitude.

Personality tests measure a person's tendency to behave in a particular way. Such tests are used to diagnose children's emotional problems. Because an inventory is used to assess personality characteristics, the test is quite lengthy, usually containing several hundred items in a true-false format. Test items are answered by the parent or child or by both together and are analyzed to determine whether the child has certain personality traits.

Interest inventories are used to determine a person's interest in a certain area or vocation and are not used with very young children. A school-age child may be given a reading interest inventory to provide the teacher with information that will serve as a guide when helping the child select reading material.

Attitudes are also measured in older children and adults, rather than in young children. An **attitude measure** determines how a person is predisposed to think about or behave toward an object, event, institution, type of behavior, or person or group of people. Politicians frequently use such measures to determine the attitudes of voters on controversial issues.

Tests for Infants

Various psychological tests have been constructed for infants and young children. Such tests are challenging because of the child's developmental limitations. Babies are particularly difficult to evaluate because of their short attention span. Their periods of alertness are brief, and they have their own schedules of opportune moments for testing. In addition, developmental changes occur rapidly, making test results unreliable for more than a short time. Generally, because of these limitations, the validity and reliability of infant scales are questionable. The tests are difficult to administer and interpret. Nevertheless, they are useful in evaluating the status of newborns and infants (Wodrich, 1984).

The status of a newborn can be determined by various measures. The *Apgar Scale,* administered 1 minute and 5 minutes after birth, assesses the health of the newborn by evaluating the heart rate, respiratory effort, muscle tone, body color, and reflex irritability. Each characteristic is scored on a scale of 0–2. A score of 7–10 indicates the infant is in good condition; a score of 5 may indicate developmental difficulties. A score of 3 or below is very serious and indicates an emergency concerning the infant's survival (Santrock, 1988). The *Brazelton Neonatal Behavior Scale,* another neonatal measure (Als, Tronick, Lester, & Brazelton, 1979), measures temperamental differences, nervous system functions, and the capacity of the neonate to interact. Its purpose is to locate mild neurological dysfunctions and variations in temperament. A newer scale, the *Neonatal Behavioral Assessment Scale (NBAS)* (Brazelton, 1984) is used with newborns from the first day of life through the end of the first month. In this test the infant's competence is measured through behavioral items. In addition to identifying the infant's performance, if administered with the parents present, it can be used to help parents understand their infant's signals and skills. This knowledge of child development generally and their baby's competence specifically can facilitate improvement in parenting skills (Widerstrom et al., 1991).

An adaptation of the NBAS to assess preterm infants came through the design of the *Assessment of Preterm Infant's Behavior (APIB)* (Als, Lester, Tronick, & Brazelton, 1982). It includes many of the items in the NBAS, but refined them to be able to observe the preterm infant's functioning (Als, 1986).

Infant development scales go beyond measuring neonatal status to focus on development from one month to two years. The *Gesell Developmental Schedules* (Yang, 1979) were the first scales devised to measure infant development. Gesell designed them to detect infants who were delayed in development and might need special services. *The Bayley Scales of Infant Development* (Bayley, 1933) were designed to learn about the infant's intelligence, rather than overall development. Although the Gesell and Bayley instruments are difficult and tedious to administer because of their length, the *Denver Developmental Screening Test* (Frankenburg, Dodds, Fandal, Kazuk, & Cohrs, 1975) is a simple instrument designed to identify children who are likely to have significant delays and need early identification and intervention. Figure 2.1 presents information about some neonatal and infant tests; Figure 2.2 provides examples of items on the revised form of this test.

Tests for Preschool Children

Psychologists have designed a variety of tests to evaluate development and to detect developmental problems during the preschool years. Just as the testing of infants and toddlers presents challenges to test administrators because of the children's developmental limitations, the evaluation of preschool children under six years of age must also be conducted with their developmental characteristics in

NAME	LEVEL	TYPE	PURPOSE
Apgar Scale	Neonate	Birth Status	Assess health of the new-born infant
Brazelton Neonatal Assessment Scale	Neonate	Neonatal status	Locate mild neurological dysfunctions and variations in temperament
Neonate Behavioral Assessment Scale	First Month		Identify the infant's ability to modulate its behavioral systems in response to external stimuli
Assessment of Preterm Infants' Behavior (APIB)	Preterm infants	Preterm development	Identify current status. Identify intervention targets
Bayley Scales of Infant Development	Infant	Intelligence	Diagnose developmental delays in infants
Gesell Developmental Schedules	Infant	Development	Detect developmental delays
Denver Developmental Screening Test–Revised	1 month–6 years	Developmental screening	Identify significant developmental delays

Figure 2.1
Neonatal and infant tests.

mind. Instruments that assess characteristics used to identify developmental delays or to diagnose sources of disabilities that put the young child at risk for learning are administered to one child at a time. Test items are concrete tasks or activities that match the child's ability to respond; nevertheless, validity and reliability are affected by such factors as the child's limited attention span and willingness to attempt to respond to the examiner.

Preschool intelligence tests and adaptive behavior scales are used to diagnose mental retardation. Although intelligence measures during the preschool years are generally unreliable because children's IQs can change enormously between early childhood and adolescence, they are used with young children to measure learning potential.

The *Stanford-Binet Intelligence Scale* (Terman & Merrill, 1973), the original IQ test, was designed to assess general thinking or problem-solving ability. It is valuable in answering questions about developmental delay and retardation. Conversely, the *McCarthy Scales of Children's Abilities* (McCarthy, 1972) is useful in identifying mild retardation and learning disabilities. Another instrument, the

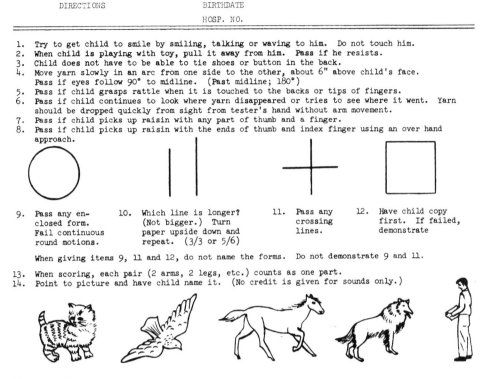

DIRECTIONS

DATE
NAME
BIRTHDATE
HOSP. NO.

1. Try to get child to smile by smiling, talking or waving to him. Do not touch him.
2. When child is playing with toy, pull it away from him. **Pass** if he resists.
3. Child does not have to be able to tie shoes or button in the back.
4. Move yarn slowly in an arc from one side to the other, about 6" above child's face.
   Pass if eyes follow 90° to midline. (Past midline; 180°)
5. Pass if child grasps rattle when it is touched to the backs or tips of fingers.
6. Pass if child continues to look where yarn disappeared or tries to see where it went. Yarn
   should be dropped quickly from sight from tester's hand without arm movement.
7. Pass if child picks up raisin with any part of thumb and a finger.
8. Pass if child picks up raisin with the ends of thumb and index finger using an over hand
   approach.

9. Pass any en-
   closed form.
   Fail continuous
   round motions.

10. Which line is longer?
    (Not bigger.) Turn
    paper upside down and
    repeat. (3/3 or 5/6)

11. Pass any
    crossing
    lines.

12. Have child copy
    first. If failed,
    demonstrate

When giving items 9, 11 and 12, do not name the forms. Do not demonstrate 9 and 11.

13. When scoring, each pair (2 arms, 2 legs, etc.) counts as one part.
14. Point to picture and have child name it. (No credit is given for sounds only.)

Figure 2.2
Denver Developmental Screening Test: examples of test items.
Source: Frankenburg et al., 1975

Wechsler Preschool and Primary Scale of Intelligence (Wechsler, 1967), is useful in identifying signs of uneven development.

Measures of adaptive behavior assess possible developmental problems related to learning disabilities. Adaptive behavior instruments attempt to measure how well the young child has mastered everyday living tasks such as toileting and feeding.

The *Vineland Social Maturity Scale* (Doll, 1965) assesses the everyday behavior of the child that indicates the level of development. The *Developmental Indicators for the Assessment of Learning-Revised* (DIAL-R) (Mardel-Czundowski & Goldenberg, 1983) can be used to screen a child for overall developmental delay, and the AAMD (American Association on Mental Deficiency) *Adaptive Behavior Scale* (Lambert, 1984) assesses adaptive behavior, but also measures other categories, such as language development and socialization. Figure 2.3 provides a sample of behaviors assessed with the *AAMD Adaptive Behavior Scale.* Figure 2.4 presents the characteristics of preschool tests.

Preschool tests that identify developmental delays are administered to one child at a time.

Tests for School-Age Children

For the child old enough to attend preschool and elementary school, many tests are available for use by teachers, school psychologists, program evaluators, and other personnel with responsibilities for students and the early childhood curriculum. In addition to preschool programs for children with disabilities, many states conduct programs for four-year-old and kindergarten children as well. Although individual tests are available for some purposes in these programs, group testing is also used. Group tests require the child to use paper and pencil; therefore, test results may be affected by the child's ability to respond in this manner. Test validity and reliability may be affected by the child's ability both to respond in a group setting and to use a pencil to find and mark responses on the test. As students move into the primary grades, these factors become less important.

Many preschool programs are designed for children at high risk for learning disabilities. Available are bilingual programs for children whose first language is not English, intervention programs for children with a physical or mental disability, and preschool programs for children from low-income homes who lack the early childhood experiences that predict successful learning. These programs may include a screening instrument to determine which children are eligible. Thus the *Bilingual Syntax Measure* (Burt, Dulay, & Hernandez, 1976) is a standardized test that can be used to screen children for language ability and dominance; the *Wechsler Intelligence Scale for Children—Revised* (WISC—R) (Wechsler, 1974) and the *Bender Gestalt Test* (Bender, 1946) may be administered to a preschool or

Figure 2.3
AAMD Adaptive Behavior Scale: examples of behaviors.

DOMAIN 1
Independent Functioning

(A) Eating Subdomain

ITEM 1   **Use of Table Utensils**
                                        (Circle only one)
                    Uses knife and fork correctly and neatly 6
                    Uses table knife for cutting and spreading 5
                    Feeds self with spoon and fork, neatly 4
                    Feeds self with spoon and fork,
                                    considerable spilling 3
                    Feeds self with spoon, neatly 2
            Feeds self with spoon, considerable spilling 1
            Feeds self with fingers, or must be fed 0

ITEM 2   **Eating in Public**
                                        (Circle only one)
                    Orders complete meals in restaurants 3
        Orders simple meals like hamburgers and hot dogs 2
            Orders soft drinks at soda fountains or canteens 1
                    Does not order at public eating places 0

ITEM 3   **Drinking**
                                        (Circle only one)
        Drinks without spilling, holding glass in one hand 3
            Drinks from cup or glass unassisted, neatly 2
                    Drinks from cup or glass unassisted,
                                    considerable spilling 1
        Does not drink from cup or glass unassisted 0

ITEM 4   **Table Manners**
                                        (Circle all that apply)
                    Swallows food without chewing 1
                    Chews food with mouth open 1
                    Drops food on table or floor 1
            Uses napkin incorrectly or not at all 1
                    Talks with mouth full 1
                    Takes food off others' plates 1
                    Eats too fast or too slow 1
                    Plays in food with fingers 1 | 8 |
                    Has no problem with the above 0
        Does not demonstrate the above, e.g., because
            he or she is bedfast or has liquid food only 8

(A)   **SUBDOMAIN TOTAL** (Add Items 1–4)

Source: Lambert, 1984

school-age child with disabilities by a school psychologist or school diagnostician to determine whether the child needs educational services in a program for early childhood children with disabilities. Poor performance on the *Bender Gestalt Test* by a school-age child indicates the need for further study of the child (Cronbach, 1984). The *Peabody Picture Vocabulary Test—Revised* (Dunn & Dunn, 1981) provides information on a child's language ability that can help determine whether a child will benefit from a language enrichment program.

NAME	LEVEL	TYPE	PURPOSE
Stanford-Binet Intelligence Scale	Ages 2–adult	Global intelligence	To detect delays and mental retardation
McCarthy Scales of Children's Abilities	Ages 2½–8	Intelligence	To identify and diagnose delays in cognitive and noncognitive areas through subtests
Wechsler Preschool and Primary Scale of Intelligence	Ages 4–6	Intelligence	To identify signs of uneven development; to detect overall delay
Vineland Social Maturity Scale	Ages 1–25	Adaptive behavior	To assess whether the child has mastered living skills expected for the age level in terms of everyday behavior
AAMD Adaptive Behavior Scale	Ages 3–16	Adaptive behavior	Assesses adaptive behavior in terms of personal independence and development; can be compared to norms for children developing normally, with retardation, and with severe retardation
Developmental Indicators for the Assessment of Learning–Revised	Ages 2–5	Developmental	Assesses motor, language, and cognitive development

Figure 2.4
Preschool tests.

Achievement tests are useful when making decisions about instruction. If a child is exhibiting learning difficulties, a psychologist might administer the *Peabody Individual Achievement Test* (Dunn & Markwardt, 1970) or the *Wide Range Achievement Test* (Jastak & Jastak, 1978) to gain information about specific learning disabilities. *The Early School Inventory* (Nurss & McGauvran, 1976), the *Boehm Test of Basic Concepts—Revised* (Boehm, 1986), or the *Circus* (Anderson & Bogatz, 1974, 1976, 1979) might be administered by the teacher to young children to determine their need for instruction in basic concepts or to assess successful learning of concepts previously taught.

Primary-grade teachers also may need specific information about a child having difficulties in the classroom. Diagnostic tests such as the *Brigance Diagnostic*

Inventory of Basic Skills (Brigance, 1976), the *Diagnostic Reading Scales* (Spache, 1981), or the *Battelle Developmental Inventory* (Newborg, Stork, Wnek, Guidubaldi, & Svinicki, 1984) can be administered by classroom teachers to pinpoint skills in which students need additional instruction. The *Battelle Developmental Inventory*, for example, can be used to identify developmental strengths and weaknesses in infant, preschool, and primary children. It can also be used as a screening measure to identify children who might be "at risk" for developmental delays. Figure 2.5 gives an example of items on self-concept and peer interaction in the Personal-Social Domain on the *Battelle Developmental Inventory*. Figure 2.6 presents information about tests used with school-age children.

Group achievement tests are used to evaluate individual achievement, group achievement, and program effectiveness. A school district may administer achievement tests every year to determine each student's progress, as well as to gain diagnostic information on the child's need for future instruction. The same test results can be used at the district level to give information on student progress between and within schools and to determine the effectiveness of the district's instructional program.

Instructional effectiveness may also be evaluated at the state or national level. A state agency may administer statewide achievement tests to work toward establishing a standard of instructional effectiveness in all schools within the state. Test results can identify school districts that both exceed and fall below the set standard. Indicators of poor instructional areas in many school districts will pinpoint weaknesses in the state's instructional program and facilitate specific types of improvement. National assessments are made periodically to pinpoint strengths and weaknesses in the educational progress of American children in different subject areas. These findings frequently are compared with achievement results of students in other countries.

INFORMAL EVALUATION STRATEGIES

Standardized tests are not the only tools available for evaluation and assessment. Various types of informal instruments and strategies to determine development and learning are available as well.

School districts often use informal tests or evaluation strategies developed by local teachers or staff members. In early childhood programs an informal screening test may be administered to preschool children at registration to determine their instructional needs. Likewise, the speech teacher may use a simple screening instrument to evaluate the child's language development or possible speech difficulties.

Observation

One of the most valuable ways to become aware of the individual characteristics of young children is through observation. Developmental indicators in early childhood are more likely to be noted from children's behavior in natural circumstances than from a designed evaluation or instrument. Adults who observe children as

PERSONAL-SOCIAL DOMAIN (cont.)

Basal = a score of 2 on two consecutive items at an age level
Ceiling = a score of 0 on two consecutive items at an age level

Subdomain: Self-Concept

Suggested Starting Points (age in months)	Test Item	Score (circle one score per item)	Comments
0–5	PS 31. Shows awareness of his/her hands	2 1 0	
6–11	PS 32. Responds to his/her name	2 1 0	
18–23	PS 33. Expresses ownership or possession	2 1 0	
	PS 34. Identifies self in mirror	2 1 0	
24–35	PS 35. Shows pride in achievements	2 1 0	
	PS 36. Knows his/her first name	2 1 0	
	PS 37. Uses pronoun or his/her name to refer to self	2 1 0	
	PS 38. Speaks positively of self	2 1 0	
	PS 39. Knows his/her age	2 1 0	
36–47	PS 40. Calls attention to his/her performance	2 1 0	
	PS 41. Knows his/her first and last names	2 1 0	
48–59	PS 42. Asserts self in socially acceptable ways	2 1 0	
60–71	PS 43. Performs for others	2 1 0	
	PS 44. Demonstrates ability to "show and tell" without major discomfort	2 1 0	

+ ___sum___ ___sum___ = [ ] Subdomain Score

Subdomain: Peer Interaction

Suggested Starting Points (age in months)	Test Item	Score (circle one score per item)	Comments
12–17	PS 45. Initiates social contacts with peers in play	2 1 0	
	PS 46. Imitates another child or children at play	2 1 0	
18–23	PS 47. Plays independently in company of peers	2 1 0	
	PS 48. Plays alongside another child	2 1 0	
24–35	PS 49. Participates in group play	2 1 0	
	PS 50. Shares property with others	2 1 0	
36–47	PS 51. Interacts with peers	2 1 0	
48–59	PS 52. Has special friends	2 1 0	
	PS 53. Chooses his/her own friends	2 1 0	
	PS 54. Plays cooperatively with peers	2 1 0	
	PS 55. Cooperates in group activities	2 1 0	
	PS 56. Takes turns and shares	2 1 0	
60–71	PS 57. Initiates social contacts and interactions with peers	2 1 0	
	PS 58. Participates in competitive play activities	2 1 0	
	PS 59. Uses peers as resources	2 1 0	
	PS 60. Gives ideas to other children as well as going along with their ideas	2 1 0	
72–83	PS 61. Serves as leader in peer relationships	2 1 0	

+ ___sum___ ___sum___ = [ ] Subdomain Score

Figure 2.5
Battelle Developmental Inventory: examples of self-concept and peer interaction items.
Source: Battelle Developmental Inventory. DLM Teaching Resources

NAME	LEVEL	TYPE	PURPOSE
Bilingual Syntax Measure	Kindergarten–Grade 2	Language	To determine language dominance
Wechsler Intelligence Scale for Children–Revised	Ages 6½–16½	Intelligence	To diagnose mental retardation and learning disability; includes verbal and performance subscales
Bender Gestalt Test	Ages 4–10	Visual motor functioning	To assess perceptual skills and hand-eye coordination, identify learning disabilities
Peabody Picture Vocabulary Test–Revised	Ages 2½–18	Vocabulary	To measure receptive vocabulary for standard American English
Peabody Individual Achievement Test	Kindergarten–Grade 12	Individual achievement	To assess achievement in mathematics, reading, spelling, and general information
Metropolitan Early School Inventory	Kindergarten	Development	To assess physical cognitive, language, and social-emotional development
Boehm Test of Basic Concepts–Revised	Kindergarten–Grade 2	Cognitive ability	To screen for beginning school concepts
Circus	Preschool–Grade 3	Achievement Program evaluation	To assess developmental skills and knowledge
Brigance Diagnostic Inventory of Basic Skills	Kindergarten–Grade 6	Academic achievement	To assess academic skills and diagnose learning difficulties in language, math, and reading
Spache Diagnostic Reading Scales	Grade 1–8 reading levels	Diagnostic reading test	To locate reading problems and plan remedial instruction
Battelle Developmental Inventory	Birth–8 years	Comprehensive developmental assessment	To identify child's strengths and weaknesses and plan for intervention or instruction

Figure 2.6
School-age tests.

they play and work in individual or group activities are able to determine progress in all categories of development. The child who shows evidence of emerging proso-cial skills by playing successfully in the playground is demonstrating significant growth in social development. Children who struggle to balance materials on both sides of a balance scale demonstrate visible signs of cognitive growth. Physical development can be evaluated by the observation of children using playground equipment. Because young children learn best through active involvement with their environment, evaluation of learning may be assessed most appropriately by observation of the child during periods of activity. Observation records can be used to plan instruction, to report progress in various areas of development, and to keep track of progress in mastery of preschool curriculum objectives.

Teacher-Designed Measures

Teachers have always used tests that they have devised to measure the level of learning after instruction. Early childhood teachers are more likely to use concrete tasks or oral questions for informal assessment with young children. Teachers fre-quently incorporate evaluation with instruction or learning experiences. Activities and games can be used both to teach and to evaluate what the child has learned. Evaluation can also be conducted through learning centers or as part of a teacher-directed lesson. Although pencil-and-paper tests are also a teacher-designed mea-sure, they should not be used until children are comfortable with writing.

Checklists

Developmental checklists or other forms of learning objective sequences are used at all levels of preschool, elementary, and secondary schools. Often referred to as a **scope** or **sequence of skills,** a checklist is a list of the learning objectives established for areas of learning and development at a particular age, grade level, or content area.

Skills continuums are available from many sources. The teacher may construct one, or a school district may distribute checklists for each grade level. Educational textbook publishers frequently include a skills continuum for teachers to use as an instructional guide with the textbook they have selected. State education agencies now publish objectives to be used by all school districts in the state. For example, the Texas Education Agency has distributed comprehensive skills continuums commonly referred to as *Essential Elements* (Texas Education Agency, 1985) for every grade level and subject area taught in Texas public schools. The Essential Elements serve as an educational framework to ensure that all school districts in Texas adhere to certain instructional goals and objectives in the curriculum.

Performance Assessments

Additional forms of informal assessments focus on more meaningful types of evaluation of student learning. Sometimes named **performance assessments** or **authentic assessments** (Goodwin & Goodwin, 1993), these evaluation measures use strategies that permit the child to demonstrate his or her understanding of a concept or mastery of a skill. The evaluation might take the form of a teacher-directed **interview** in which a dialogue with the child would reveal the child's thinking and understanding. Other procedures might include games, **directed assignments,** or a **contract** between the teacher and the student.

Processes for reporting student progress related to outcome-based or authentic assessments are also intended to communicate learning and development from a meaningful perspective. Traditional report cards and standardized test results do not necessarily reflect accurately the student's progress. **Portfolios** with samples of student work are one type of reporting of progress that is compatible with outcome-based assessment. A detailed narrative or **narrative report** of the student's progress developed by the teacher is another process that enables the teacher to describe the nature of the child's activities that have resulted in achievement and learning.

SUMMARY

For many reasons, we need to be able to evaluate the growth and development of young children. Specialists who work with children from various perspectives have devised formal and informal measures that can be used with newborns, as well as later in the early childhood years. Members of the medical profession, psychologists, educators, and parents all have interest and concern for knowing that the young child is developing at a normal rate. If development deviates from acceptable progress in some way, tests and other evaluation strategies are available to study the child and to help in devising early intervention measures that can minimize or eliminate the developmental problem.

REVIEW QUESTIONS

1. Describe several purposes for measuring and evaluating infants and young children.
2. What professionals test young children?
3. How can a young child's development be atypical? Give examples.
4. What are the differences between achievement tests, aptitude tests, and intelligence tests? Give examples.
5. Why are infant neonatal scales administered? Infant development scales?
6. What is the purpose of preschool intelligence tests? How are adaptive scales used? Give examples.
7. Why do schools administer tests to preschool children? Describe the purposes.
8. Name preschool tests that teachers can administer and tests that school psychologists must administer.
9. How do schools use group achievement tests? State education agencies? National agencies?
10. How are informal measures different from psychological or standardized tests?
11. Why is observation an important evaluation method to use with young children?

KEY TERMS

achievement test

aptitude test

attitude measure

authentic assessment

contract

developmental checklist

directed assignment

informal test

intelligence test

interest inventory

interview

learning disability

narrative report

neonatologist

obstetrician

pediatrician

performance assessment

personality test

portfolio

psychological test

scope (sequence of skills)

standardized test

SUGGESTED ACTIVITIES

1. Examine two developmental tests for infants or young children discussed in the chapter. Describe the similarities and differences between the two measures.

2. Examine two achievement tests used with preschool or primary children. Describe the similarities and differences between the two measures.

REFERENCES

ALS, H. (1986). Assessing the neurobehavioral development of the premature infant in the environment of the neonatal intensive care unit: A syntactive model of neonatal behavioral organization. *Physical and Occupational Therapy in Pediatrics, 6,* 3–53.

ALS, H., TRONICK, E., LESTER, B. M., & BRAZELTON, T. B. (1979). Specific neonatal measures: The Brazelton Neonatal Behavioral Assessment Scale. In J. D. Osofsky (Ed.), *Handbook of infant development* (pp. 185–215). New York: John Wiley.

ALS, H., LESTER, B. M., TRONICK, E. C., & BRAZELTON, T. B. (1982). Towards a research for the assessment of preterm infants' behavior (APIB). In H. E. Fitzgerald, B. M. Lester, & M. W. Yogman (Eds.), *Theory and research in behavioral pediatrics* (Vol. 1, pp. 1–35). New York: Plenum.

ANDERSON, S. B., & BOGATZ, G. A. (1974). *Circus manual and technical report.* Monterey, CA: CTB/McGraw-Hill.

ANDERSON, S. B., & BOGATZ, G. A. (1976). *Circus manual and technical report.* Monterey, CA: CTB/McGraw-Hill.

ANDERSON, S. B., & BOGATZ, G. A. (1979). *Circus manual and technical report.* Monterey, CA: CTB/McGraw-Hill.

APGAR, V. (1975). A proposal for a new method of evaluation of a newborn infant. *Anesthesia and Analgesia, 32,* 260–267.

BAYLEY, N. (1933). *The California First-Year Mental Scale.* Berkeley: University of California Press.

BENDER, L. (1946). *Bender Gestalt Test: Cards and manual of instructions.* New York: American Orthopsychiatric Association.

BOEHM, A. (1986). *Boehm Test of Basic Concepts—Revised. Preschool Edition.* San Antonio: Psychological Corp.

BRAZELTON, T. B. (1984). *Neonatal Behavioral Assessment Scale* (2nd ed.). Philadelphia: J. B. Lippincott.

BRIGANCE, A. H. (1976). *Brigance Diagnostic Inventory of Basic Skills.* Woburn, MA: Curriculum Associates.

BURT, M. K., DULAY, H. C., & HERNANDEZ, E. C. (1976). *Bilingual Syntax Measure.* Orlando, FL: Harcourt Brace Jovanovich.

CRONBACH, L. J. (1984). *Essentials of psychological testing.* New York: Harper & Row.

DOLL, E. A. (1965). *Vineland Social Maturity Scale: Condensed manual of directions.* Circle Pines, MN: American Guidance Service.

DUNN, L. M., & DUNN, L. (1981). *Peabody Picture Vocabulary Test—Revised.* Circle Pines, MN: American Guidance Service.

DUNN, L. M., & MARKWARDT, F. C. (1970). *Peabody Individual Achievement Test.* Circle Pines, MN: American Guidance Service.

FRANKENBURG, W. K., DODDS, J. B., FANDAL, A. W., KAZUK, E., & COHRS, M. (1975). *Denver Developmental Screening Test: Reference manual.* Denver: University of Colorado Medical Center.

GOODWIN, W. L., & GOODWIN, L. D. (1993). Young children and measurement: Standardized and nonstandardized instruments in early childhood education. In B. Spodek (Ed.), *Handbook of research on the education of young children* (pp. 441–463). New York: Macmillan.

JASTAK, J. F., & JASTAK, S. (1978). *The Wide Range Achievement Test: Manual of instructions.* Wilmington, DE: Jastak Associates.

LAMBERT, N. (1984). *Diagnostic and technical manual: AAMD Adaptive Behavior Scale, School Edition.* Monterey, CA: CTB/McGraw-Hill.

MARDELL-CZUNDOWSKI, C. D., & GOLDENBERG, D. S. (1983). *Developmental Indicators for the Assessment of Learning—Revised (DIAL—R).* Edison, NJ: Childcraft Education Corp.

MCCARTHY, D. (1972). *Manual for the McCarthy Scales of Children's Abilities.* New York: Psychological Corp.

NEWBORG, J., STORK, J. R., WNEK, L., GUIDUBALDI, J., & SVINICKI, J. (1984). *Battelle Developmental Inventory.* Allen, TX: Teaching Resources.

NURSS, J. R., & MCGAUVRAN, M. E. (1976). *Early School Inventory.* Orlando, FL: Harcourt Brace Jovanovich.

SANTROCK, J. W. (1988). *Children.* Dubuque, IA: William C. Brown.

SPACHE, G. D. (1981). *Diagnostic Reading Scales: Examiner's manual.* Monterey, CA: CTB/McGraw-Hill.

TERMAN, L. M., & MERRILL, M. A. (1973). *Stanford-Binet Intelligence Scale: Manual for the third revision, Form L-M.* Boston: Houghton Mifflin.

TEXAS EDUCATION AGENCY. (1985). *State Board of Education rules for curriculum: Principles, standards, and procedures for accreditation of school districts.* Austin: Author.

WECHSLER, D. (1967). *Wechsler Preschool and Primary Scale of Intelligence: Manual.* New York: Psychological Corp.

WECHSLER, D. (1974). *Manual for the Wechsler Intelligence Scale for Children—Revised.* New York: Psychological Corp.

WIDERSTROM, A. H., MOWDER, B. A., & SANDALL, S. R. (1991). *At-risk and handicapped newborns and infants.* Englewood Cliffs, NJ: Prentice-Hall.

WODRICH, D. (1984). *Children's psychological testing.* Baltimore: Paul H. Brooks.

YANG, R. K. (1979). Early infant assessment: An overview. In J. D. Osofsky (Ed.), *Handbook of infant development* (pp. 000–000). New York: John Wiley.

Chapter 3

Standardized Tests

Chapter Objectives

As a result of reading this chapter you will be able to

1. understand the process of standardized test design.
2. understand the differences between test validity and test reliability.
3. understand how test scores are interpreted and reported.
4. understand the advantages and disadvantages of standardized testing.
5. understand the difficulties in using standardized tests with young children.
6. be able to use resources and strategies for selecting and evaluating standardized tests.
7. understand issues in selecting and using standardized tests.

In chapter 2 various methods and purposes for measuring and evaluating infants and young children were discussed. We differentiated between formal measures and informal methods of measurement. Psychological tests and some educational tests are considered formal instruments because they have been standardized.

How are standardized tests different from other kinds of measures? What are their advantages? In this chapter we discuss how standardized tests are designed and tried out to measure the desired characteristics. Test validity and reliability are explained, as well as their effect on the dependability of the test.

People who use standardized tests with young children must be able to interpret the results. To understand more clearly how scores on a test are translated into meaningful information, raw scores and standard scores are described. The normal curve and its role in interpreting test scores also are explained.

STEPS IN STANDARDIZED TEST DESIGN

Test designers follow a series of steps when constructing a new test. These steps ensure that the test achieves its goals and purposes. In planning a test, the developers first specify the purpose of the test. Next they determine the test format. As actual test design begins, they formulate objectives; write, try out, and analyze test items; and assemble the final test form. After the final test form is administered, the developers establish norms and determine the validity and reliability of the test. As a final step they develop a test manual containing procedures for administering the test and statistical information on standardization results.

Specifying the Purpose of the Test

Every standardized test should have a clearly defined purpose. The description of the test's purpose is the framework for the construction of the test. It also allows evaluation of the instrument when design and construction steps are completed. *The Standards for Educational and Psychological Tests and Manuals* (American Psychological Association [APA], 1974) has established the standards for including the test's purpose in the test manual. The standards are as follows:

> B2. The test manual should state explicitly the purpose and applications for which the test is recommended. (p. 14)
>
> B3. The test manual should describe clearly the psychological, educational and other reasoning underlying the test and the nature of the characteristic it is intended to measure. (p. 15)

Test designers should be able to explain what construct or characteristics the test will measure, how the test results will be used, and who will take the test or to whom it will be administered.

The population for whom the test is intended is a major factor in test design. Tests constructed for infants and young children are very different from tests designed for adults. As test developers consider the composition and characteristics of the children for whom they are designing the test, they must include variables such as age, intellectual or educational level, socioeconomic background, cultural background, and whether or not the young child is able to read.

Determining Test Format

Test format decisions are based on determinations made about the purpose of the test and the characteristics of the test takers. The test format results from the developer's decision on how test items will be presented and how the test taker will respond (Brown, 1983). One consideration is whether the test will be verbal or written. Although adults are most familiar with written tests, infants and young children are unable to read or write. Tests designed for very young children usually are presented orally by a test administrator. An alternative is to use a psychomotor response; the child is given an object to manipulate or is asked to perform a physical task.

For older children, high school students, and adults, other test formats are possible. Test takers may respond to an alternative-choice written test such as one with true-false, **multiple-choice,** or matching items. The test may be given as a **group test,** rather than administered as an **individual test** to one person at a time. Short-answer and essay items are also possibilities.

After the test designers have selected the format most appropriate for the test's purpose and for the group to be tested, actual test construction begins. Experimental test forms are assembled after defining test objectives and writing test items for each objective.

Developing Experimental Forms

In preparing preliminary test forms, developers use the test purpose description as their guide. Test content is now delimited. If an achievement test for school children is to be written, for example, curriculum is analyzed to ensure that the

PURPOSE OF AND RATIONALE FOR SELECTED TESTS

The test developers of the *K-ABC Kaufman Assessment Battery for Children* (Kaufman & Kaufman, 1983) state the test's purpose as follows:

> The K-ABC is intended for psychological and clinical assessment, evaluation of learning-disabled and other exceptional children, educational planning and placement, minority group assessment, preschool assessment, neuropsychological assessment, and research. (p. 2)

Information about the expected uses of the *Peabody Picture Vocabulary Test—Revised Manual, Forms L and M* (Dunn & Dunn, 1981) includes school, clinical, vocational, and research uses. Part of the school use description follows:

> Since the PPVT-R is a reasonably good measure of scholastic aptitude for subjects where the language of the home is Standard English, it should also be useful as an initial *screening device* in scanning for bright, low ability, and language impaired children who may need special attention. Too, it should be helpful in identifying underachievers, when used in conjunction with a measure of school achievement. (p. 3)

The California Achievement Tests, Forms E and F (1985) are described as follows:

> This latest edition of the California Achievement Tests will continue to provide the accurate measurement in the basic skills for which the CAT series has been noted. It will continue, for example, to serve well the measurement and evaluation of such programs as Chapter I, ECIA. This new, improved, and augmented test battery will also be of special value to those schools seeking an assessment system that will help them work toward, and achieve greater excellence. CAT E & F will thus meet the full range of information requirements of today's schools. (p. 4)

test will reflect the instructional program. If the achievement test is to be designed for national use, then textbook series, syllabi, and curricular materials are studied to check that test objectives will accurately reflect curriculum trends. Teachers and curriculum experts will be consulted to review the content outlines and behavioral objectives that serve as reference points for test items.

The process of developing good test items involves writing, editing, trying out, and rewriting or revising test items. Before being tried out, each item for an achievement test may be reviewed and rewritten by test writers, teachers, and other experts in the field. Many more items than will be used are written because many will be eliminated in the editing and rewriting stages (Burrill, 1980).

A preliminary test is assembled so that the selected test items can be tried out with a sample of students. The experimental test forms resemble the final form. Instructions are written for administering the test. The test may have more questions than will be used in the final form because many questions will be revised or eliminated after the tryout. The sample of people selected to take the preliminary test is similar to the population that will take the final form of the test.

The tryout of the preliminary test form is described as *item tryout and analysis.* **Item analysis** involves studying three characteristics of each test question: difficulty level, discrimination, and grade progression in difficulty. The *difficulty level* of a question refers to how many test takers in the tryout group answered the question correctly. *Discrimination* of each question involves the extent to which the question distinguishes between test takers who did well or poorly on the test. Test takers who did well should have been more successful in responding to an item than test takers who did poorly. The item differentiates between people who have greater or less knowledge or ability. The *grade progression of difficulty* refers to tests that are taken by students in different grades in school. If a test question has good grade progression of difficulty, a greater percentage of students should answer it correctly in each successively higher grade (Burrill, 1980).

Assembling the Test

After item analysis is completed, the final form of the test is assembled. As a result of item analysis, test items have been reexamined, rewritten, or eliminated. Test questions or required behaviors to measure each test objective are selected for the test. If more than one test form is to be used, developers must ensure that alternate forms are **equivalent** in content and difficulty. Test directions are made final with instructions for both test takers and test administrators. In addition, information for test administrators includes details about the testing environment and testing procedures.

Standardizing the Test

Although test construction is complete when the final form is assembled and printed, the test has not yet been standardized. The final test form must be administered to another, larger sample of test takers to acquire norm data. **Norms** provide the tool whereby children's test performance can be compared with the performance of a reference group.

A reference group that represents the children for whom the test has been designed is selected to take the test for the purpose of establishing norms. The performance of the reference or sample group on the final test form during the standardization process will be used to evaluate the test scores of individuals and/or groups who take the test in the future.

The norming group is chosen to reflect the makeup of the population for whom the test is designed. If a national school achievement test is being developed, the standardization sample will consist of children from all sections of the country to include such variables as gender, age, community size, geographic area, and socioeconomic and ethnic factors. For other types of tests, different characteristics may be used to match the norming sample with future populations to be tested.

Various kinds of norms can be established during the standardization process. Raw scores of sample test takers are converted into derived scores or standard scores for purposes of comparison. Standard scores are achieved by calculating the **raw score,** or the number of items answered correctly, into a score that can be used to establish a norm. Various types of standard scores can be used to compare the people selected to standardize the test with future populations who will be given the test. Each type of **grade norm** allows test users to interpret a child's test scores in comparison with the scores of children used to norm the test (Burrill, 1980). For example, an age score is established by determining the norms for age groups when the test is given to the norming sample. The age norms describe the average performance of children of various ages. Likewise, grade norms or grade equivalent norms are established by determining the average scores made by children at different grade levels in the norming group (Brown, 1983).

Developing the Test Manual

The final step in test design is development of the test manual. The test developer describes the purpose of the test, the development of the test, and the standardization procedures. Information on test validity and reliability is also included to give test users information on the dependability of the test. When explaining standardization information in the users' manual, test developers will describe the method used to select the norming group. The number of individuals included in standardizing the test is reported, as well as the geographic areas, types of communities, socioeconomic groups, and ethnic groups they represent.

Validity and Reliability

Norm information is important for establishing confidence in analyzing and interpreting the significance of test scores. Test users also need information demonstrating that the test will be valuable for the intended purposes. Therefore, the test manual must provide information on validity and reliability. Both types of dependability indicators are equally important in determining the quality of the test. **Validity** is the degree to which the test serves the purpose for which it will be used; **reliability** is the extent to which a test is stable or consistent. Test validity can be determined through content validity, criterion-related validity, or construct validity.

When first designing a test, the developers describe its purpose. Test objectives or the test outlines provide the framework for the content of the test. When a manual provides information on **content validity**, the test developers are defining the degree to which the test items measured the test objectives and fulfilled the purpose of the test. Thus, for example, on an achievement test, content validity is the extent to which the content of the test represents an adequate sampling of the instructional program it is intended to cover.

Criterion-related validity is related to the validity of an aptitude test. Rather than analyzing course content, test items focus on skills or tasks that predict future success in some area. The estimates of predictive validity are concerned with stability over time. For example, an **intelligence quotient (IQ)** test might be predictive of school achievement. Likewise, the *Scholastic Aptitude Test* scores may predict whether high school students will be successful in college. Validity is predictive because the criteria for success are the future grades the student will earn in college or the student's future grade point average.

Criterion-related validity may be **concurrent validity**, rather than predictive validity. Instead of using a future measure to determine validity, current measures are used. The outside criterion is assessed when the test is standardized. The developer of an intelligence test may cite an existing intelligence test as the criterion to measure validity. The developer administers both intelligence tests to the sample group. If the new test scores correlate highly with scores on the existing test, they may be used to establish concurrent validity.

If a test measures an abstract psychological trait, the users' manual will describe how the sample group was tested to establish construct validity. **Construct validity** is the extent to which a test measures a relatively abstract psychological trait such as personality, verbal ability, or mechanical aptitude. Rather than examine test items developed from test objectives, one examines construct validity by comparing test results with the variables that explain the behaviors. For example, suppose the construct is believed to include certain behavioral characteristics, such as sociability or honesty. An instrument's construct validity can be checked by analyzing how the trait is affected by changing conditions. Alternatively, an instrument may measure level of anxiety; its construct validity is determined by creating experiments to find out what conditions affect anxiety (Gronlund, 1990).

Construct validity is necessary when measuring creativity. To have construct validity, the test designed to measure creativity must differentiate the behavior of creative people from that of uncreative people (Mehrens & Lehmann, 1984).

The validity of a test is the extent to which the test measures what it is designed to measure. Test users, however, are also interested in a test's dependability or stability in measuring behaviors. Test developers, therefore, also establish and report on the reliability of the instrument as part of the standardization process.

Test reliability is related to test item discrimination. When test items are analyzed after the initial item tryout, they are examined for discrimination power. After the final test form is administered to a norming sample, the items are analyzed again to ensure that the instrument is fairly reliable. The whole test is analyzed, rather than individual test items. The test manual will report the test's reliability as determined by using alternate-form, split-half, or test-retest reliability measures. A test's reliability coefficient describes the degree to which a test is free from error of measurement. If **alternate-form reliability** strategies are used, test developers construct two equivalent forms of the final test. Both forms are administered to the norming group within a short period. The correlation between the results on the two different forms measures the coefficient of reliability.

If a **split-half reliability** coefficient is used to establish reliability, the norming group is administered a single test, and scores on one-half of the test are correlated with scores on the other half of the test. Split-half reliability is determined from the contents of the single test. A test with split-half reliability is also considered to have **internal consistency;** that is, the items on each half of the test are positively intercorrelated in measuring the same characteristics.

Test-retest reliability is also derived from the administration of a single test form. In this case, however, the test is administered to the norming group and then is administered again after a short interval. The two sets of scores are compared to determine whether they were consistent in measuring the test objectives.

Standard Error of Measurement

No matter how well designed, no test is completely free from error. Although there is a hypothetical **true score,** in reality it does not exist. The reliability of the test depends on how large the **standard error** of measurement is after analysis of the chosen method of determining reliability. If the reliability correlations are poor, the standard error of measurement will be large. The larger the standard error of measurement, the less reliable the test. Standard error of measurement is the estimate of the amount of variation that can be expected in test scores as a result of reliability correlations.

Several variables that are present during standardization affect test reliability. First is the size of the population sample. Generally, the larger the population sample, the more reliable the test will be. Second is the length of the test. Longer tests are usually more reliable than shorter tests. Longer tests have more test items, resulting in a better sample of behaviors. The more items that measure a behavior, the better the estimate of the true score and the greater the reliability.

A third variable that can affect standard error of measurement is the range of test scores obtained from the norming group. The wider the spread of scores, the more reliably the test can distinguish between them. Thus, the range of the scores demonstrates how well the test discriminates between good and poor students (Gronlund, 1990).

INTERPRETING TEST SCORES

A child's performance on a standardized test is meaningless until it can be compared with other scores in a useful way. The raw score must be translated into a score that reports how well that child's performance compared with those of other children who took the same test. In describing the standardization process, we have discussed how norms are set for comparing individual or group test scores on the basis of the scores made by a norming sample. Although several different scoring systems have been established for translating and interpreting raw scores, the bell-shaped normal curve is the graph on which the distribution of scores is arranged by using some type of standard score.

The Normal Curve

The normal curve (Figure 3.1) represents the ideal **normal distribution** of test scores of groups of people, as well as the distribution of many other human characteristics. Physical and psychological traits are distributed in a bell-shaped frequency polygon, with most scores clustered toward the center of the curve. If, for example, we were to chart the heights of all adult men in the United States, most heights would be grouped around a mean height, with fewer distributed toward very short and very tall heights.

Ideally, group test scores have a similar distribution, and the normal curve can be used as a reference for understanding individual test scores. Any numerical

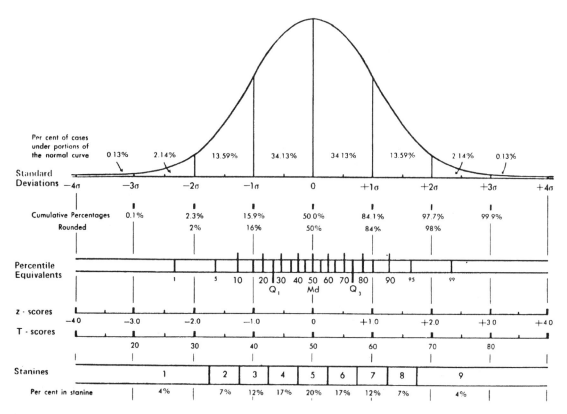

Figure 3.1
Normal curve.

scale can be used with the normal curve to demonstrate the range of scores on a test instrument.

The midpoint of the curve is the **mean.** Because the curve represents the total number of scores in the distribution of scores on a test, the mean divides the curve into two halves. As many scores are distributed above the mean as below it.

The normal curve is used to describe or pinpoint an individual's performance on a standardized test. Derived scores are used to specify where the individual score falls on the curve and how far above or below the mean the score falls (Cronbach, 1984).

Standard Deviations

The normal curve is divided further into eight equal sections called **standard deviations** (designated by a sigma, **s**). Standard deviations are used to calculate how an individual scored, compared with the scores of the norming group on a standardized test. Standard deviations describe how test scores are dispersed around the mean. For example, an individual score that is one standard deviation above the mean indicates that the individual scored higher than the mean of test scores on the norming sample. Further, the individual scored higher than about 84 percent of the individuals who normed the test. If we look at the percentage of scores in each standard deviation, we find that about 68 percent of the scores are found between one standard deviation below the mean and one standard deviation above the mean. The percentage of scores in each successive standard deviation above and below the mean decreases sharply beyond one standard deviation. When raw scores are transformed into percentiles, or standard scores, standard deviations further explain individual scores compared to the normal distribution of scores (Brown, 1983).

All scoring scales are drawn parallel to the baseline of the normal curve. Each uses the deviation from the mean as the reference to compare an individual score with the mean score of a group. In the next section the transformation of raw scores into standard scores is explained in terms of percentile ranks, stanines, and Z scores and T scores as illustrated in Figure 3.1.

Percentile Ranks and Stanines

After a test is standardized, percentile ranks and stanines may be used as the measures of comparison between the norming sample and individual test scores. Figure 3.1 shows how **percentile ranks** are arrived at by looking at cumulative percentages and percentile equivalents under the normal curve. We already understand that a percentage of the total distribution of scores is arranged within each standard deviation on the normal curve, with a smaller percentage located in each deviation as we move away from the mean. These percentages can also be understood in a cumulative fashion. Beginning at the negative end of the curve, percentages in each standard deviation can be added together. At the mean, the cumulative percentage is 50 percent, while 99.9 percent is reached at three standard deviations above the mean.

Percentile equivalents are derived from the accumulated percentages. If the cumulative percentages represent the percentage of test scores falling into standard deviations along the normal curve, **percentiles** represent a point on the normal curve below which a percentage of test scores are distributed. A score at the 40th percentile equals or surpasses 40 percent of the scores on the test being used.

After a percentile rank norm is established for a standardized test, the developers determine how the distribution of scores acquired from the norming sample are arranged on the normal curve. The distribution is calculated by standard deviations and percentiles. Future test users can then use these norms as measures of comparison to interpret individual or group scores in comparison with the scores of the original norming group.

Stanines provide another way to understand the distribution of scores. As shown in Figure 3.1, stanines divide into nine groups the norm population represented by the normal scale. Except for Stanine 9, the top, and Stanine 1, the bottom, each stanine represents one-half of a standard deviation. Stanines provide a helpful way to compare cumulative percentages and percentile ranks on the normal curve. One can look at the percentage of scores distributed in each stanine and understand how the percentile rank is correlated with the overall distribution. In reporting group test scores, the stanine rank of an individual score provides a measure of how the individual ranked within the group of test takers (Seashore, 1980).

Z Scores and T Scores

Some standardized test results are reported in terms of Z scores or T scores because they provide a simple way to locate an individual score along the normal curve. **Z scores** and **T scores** are called **standard scores** because they report how many standard deviations a person's transformed raw score is located above or below the mean on the normal curve.

Z scores are considered to be the most basic of all standard scores and the building blocks for other standard scores. They are used to determine how far above or below the mean a score is located in standard deviation units. Percentile ranks are understood by looking at where cumulative percentages fall on the normal curve. Z scores make a similar comparison; however, with Z scores the standard deviations are used as the criteria for determining where an individual score falls. Z scores are parallel to standard deviations in that the mean is at the center of the normal distribution; if a score falls within one standard deviation above the mean, the Z score will be +1. If the score falls two standard deviations below the mean, the Z score will be –2.

T scores also report scores that are parallel to standard deviations on the normal curve. Like percentiles, T scores are cumulative along the curve. T scores range from 0 to 100, with a range of 10 points from one standard deviation to the next. T scores are almost the same as Z scores: Z scores have a mean of 0 and a standard deviation of 1.0, while T scores have a mean of 50 and a standard deviation of 10 (Hopkins, Stanley, & Hopkins, 1990; Kubiszyn & Borich, 1987). Various standardized tests use T scores. The *McCarthy Scales of Children's Abilities* (McCarthy, 1972) report T scores, as do IQ tests such as the *Stanford-Binet Test* (Terman & Merrill, 1973).

CONSIDERATIONS IN CHOOSING AND EVALUATING TESTS

Whenever a private school, public school district, preschool, or child care center decides to use a test to evaluate children, one must decide how to select the best test for that purpose. Those charged with the responsibility for selecting the test must determine the relevant questions to ask about the test. Brown (1983) identifies various factors that must be considered by test users: (1) the purpose of the testing, (2) what characteristics are to be measured, (3) how the test results will be used, (4) the qualifications of the people who will interpret the scores and use the results, and (5) any practical constraints (pp. 449–450).

All of these factors are important in selecting tests for young children. Because of the developmental limitations of young test takers, test formats must be compatible with their ability to respond. Developmental limitations include short attention span, undeveloped fine motor skills, inability to use reading skills for test responses, and poor performance on group tests. Limitations in training and experience in those who administer the test are factors in test selection.

Other relevant concerns, particularly in selecting tests for young children, are the costs involved, testing time, and ease of scoring and using test results (Cronbach, 1984). The test must be reasonable in cost, and the time needed to administer the test should be suitable for young children.

A major issue is whether the test has quality. Is it a good test to use with the children? The person searching for an appropriate test will want to examine the test manual for indications of how well the test was designed and normed. The test manual should include information on the following:

1. *The purpose of the test.* The statement of purpose should include the rationale for the test, the characteristics the test is designed to measure, and the uses for the test.
2. *Test design.* The procedures and rationale for selecting test items and on the development and trial of test forms should be explained.
3. *Establishment of validity and reliability.* The description should describe the procedures used to establish validity and reliability to include sufficient data on validity, reliability, and norms.
4. *Test administration and scoring.* Specific information should be given on how to administer and score the test and to interpret test results. Information should be adequate for users to determine whether the test is practical and suitable for their purposes. Potential problems should be pointed out that can be encountered when administering and scoring the test (Kaplan & Saccuzo, 1982). See Figure 3.2 for questions that should be answered in a test manual, including an acceptable coefficient of reliability.

Test users need extensive training in tests and measurements to interpret a test manual adequately. For many users the explanations and data reported in test manuals are complex and difficult to understand. A reader may have difficulty in deciding whether the reliability coefficient is adequate, whether the size and demographic characteristics of the norming population are appropriate, or whether test content and format are suitable for the intended uses. To obtain additional help in understanding the suitability of the test, test users will want to consult resources for test standards and reviews. The *Standards for Educational and Psychological Tests and Manuals* (APA, 1974) includes standards for tests, manuals, and reports. It also includes standards for reliability and validity, as well as information that should be included on the use of tests. A less technical resource is *Guidelines for Test Use: A Commentary on the Standards for Educational and Psychological Tests* (Brown, 1980).

Other sources identify, describe, and evaluate published tests. *Tests in Print II* (Buros, 1974) is a comprehensive bibliography of almost 2,500 tests. The tests are listed by type, and basic information is given about each test. The *Eighth Mental*

Checklist of questions that should be answered in the test manual

---

Standardization Sample

1. How many subjects were used to establish the reliability, validity, and norms for the test?
2. What were the demographic and personal characteristics of these subjects? Are they similar to those of the group you will give the test to?

Reliability

1. What methods were used to estimate the reliability of the test?
2. Is the reliability high enough for your purposes (usually .90 or above for tests used to make decisions about individuals and .70 or above for research purposes)?

Validity

1. Is there evidence that the test is meaningful for your purposes?
2. What specific criteria was the test validated against?

Scoring

1. Are scoring keys available?
2. If the test can be scored by machine, how much does it cost and what sort of report is offered?

Practical Considerations

1. How long does it take to administer the test?
2. Does the test require reading? If so, is it at the right level for the people you will test?
3. How much training is required for the test administrator? How can the training be obtained?

Figure 3.2
Questions about test manuals.
Source: Kaplan and Saccuzzo, 1982

Measurements Yearbook (Buros, 1978) includes test information and sources of information about test construction, validation, and use. Critical reviews of the tests are included.

A resource that is particularly helpful to persons without a background in test design at a technical level is *Test Critiques, Volumes I–VII* (Keyser & Sweetland, 1984–1987). It includes information about test design and use, as well as a critique of the tests. Other resources for test evaluation and selection are particularly suitable for users of early childhood tests. Readers who desire more information on sourcebooks are directed to "Measuring Young Children" (Goodwin & Goodwin, 1982). Additional information on standardized tests used with young children is located in the appendix.

Brown (1980) summarized the steps in selecting and evaluating tests as follows:

1. Outline your general requirements: the purpose of testing, the characteristics to be measured, and the nature of the group to be tested. Consider also the qualifications of test users and practical considerations.
2. Identify what tests are available that appear to meet your needs. Here sources such as *Tests in Print,* the *Mental Measurement Yearbooks,* test publishers' catalogs, and test compilations will be most helpful.
3. Obtain further information about these tests from texts, journals, reference books, and consultation with people who have used this type of test.
4. Select the most promising tests. Obtain sample (specimen sets) of these tests.
5. Make a detailed evaluation of these tests, keeping in mind the unique requirements of your situation. On the basis of these evaluations, select the test(s) to be used.
6. If at all possible, conduct an experimental tryout of the test before putting it to use.
7. Use the test. Constantly monitor and evaluate its usefulness and effectiveness. (p. 463)

ADVANTAGES OF STANDARDIZED TESTS

Standardized tests can be described as measuring instruments. Each test is constructed, administered, and scored to measure some human characteristic. An individual's responses to the test items provide samples of his or her behavior that can be scored and evaluated according to an established standard. In contrast to informal strategies, standardized tests have unique qualities that are advantageous for measuring human behavior. Among these characteristics are uniformity in test administration, quantifiable scores, norm referencing, and validity and reliability.

Uniformity in Test Administration

Standardized tests have precise administration procedures. Because the results should be dependable, test designers must be sure that all persons who give the test to children will follow instructions exactly. Whether the test is being given in Wisconsin or in Florida, the procedures are the same. Informal methods are less specific; the examiner uses personal strategies for assessment.

Quantifiable Scores

Standardized tests are quantifiable because they have numerical scores. The correct answers are totaled to determine the raw score. The raw score is then translated into a derived score so that the child's performance on the test can be compared with the performance of other test takers. The derived-score can be interpreted to evaluate the child's performance when compared to the established standard.

ISSUES IN SELECTING AND USING STANDARDIZED TESTS

The Wayland Consolidated School District selected a standardized achievement test to be used in April of each year at every grade level in the district. After administering the test for three years, school administrators were concerned: Although the test results in the intermediate and higher grades had been satisfactory, achievement in reading in the primary grades had been consistently disappointing in each of the three years.

Because the Wayland District is a small rural school district, funds for testing are limited. The test selected was chosen partially because of the moderate cost of purchase and scoring.

Primary-grade teachers and their principals decided to ask the school district counselor who coordinated the testing program to help them determine the cause of the poor reading scores. When reading objectives for the test were examined, the problem became clear.

Whereas the primary teachers were following a reading program that focused on emergent literacy, or a natural approach to reading, the test emphasized phonics more strongly than reading comprehension.

Wayland School District officials considered the dilemma. Should they change to a different testing program or make modifications in the reading program? Either choice would be costly, and neither would be a complete solution to the problem.

The school counselor investigated other achievement tests, only to discover that they, too, tested for phonics skills. After more discussion, teachers and administrators decided to continue using the test they had and to supplement their current reading program with phonics instruction. The issue would be reconsidered after test manufacturers revised their tests.

Norm Referencing

Norm referencing refers to the process of developing a standard for interpreting test scores on a standardized test. To compare a child's performance on a test with the performance of other children, a norm group is selected. The test is administered to that group to determine what normal performance is. The norm group's test responses will result in a range of scores with which a child's performance can be compared.

Validity and Reliability

Unlike informal evaluation and measurement strategies, standardized tests have established dependability through determination of validity and reliability. Reliability is the test's ability to measure the child's characteristics accurately under different conditions. If the child were given the test more than once, would the results be similar?

Validity establishes whether a test measures the characteristics it was designed to measure. If the test is designed to measure intelligence, does it actually yield results that show the child's level of intelligence?

Tests that have proven reliability and validity are dependable. They can be administered to many children, either individually or as a group, and children's scores can be interpreted with confidence that the results accurately reflect each child's behaviors or characteristics.

Validity, reliability, norm referencing, and other test characteristics that contribute to the effectiveness of the standardized test result from careful and thorough test design. Each step in test construction has the goal of producing a dependable test to measure a human characteristic accurately.

DISADVANTAGES OF STANDARDIZED TESTS

Although standardized tests are carefully designed and standardized before they are used with children, they are not necessarily the best method of evaluating young children. Standardized tests have weaknesses, and many educators have concerns about schools' increasing reliance on the tests' results. Specific issues about the use of standardized tests with young children focus on validity and reliability, difficulties in administering standardized tests to preschool and primary school-age children, inappropriate use of test results, and the need to improve standardized tests.

Concerns About the Increased Use of Standardized Tests

Use of standardized testing in public education has increased in recent years. The movement for educational reform, combined with concern about accountability, has resulted in massive spending for test development and implementation. State education agencies have mandated the use of state-level achievement tests for elementary and secondary schools to compare achievement among school districts. Some states use minimum-competency tests for high school graduation and admission to teacher education programs.

Ironically, standardized tests are increasingly challenged at this time. Efforts to reexamine their use began in the late 1970s and continued in the 1980s. In 1972 the National Education Association (NEA) proposed a national moratorium on standardized testing, including intelligence, achievement, and aptitude tests (National Education Association, 1972). In 1977 the NEA issued a report after studying standardized tests. Although the report stated that some testing was necessary and that some measures had reliability and validity, it was critical of test content, types of test items, and specific tests (NEA, 1977).

Other organizations expressed similar concerns (National School Boards Association [NSBA], 1977; Oakland & Laosa, 1977). The Council for Basic Education (Weber, 1977) expressed concern about several types of standardized tests used in public schools, including group IQ tests, reading readiness tests, achievement tests, and college admission tests.

The Association for Childhood Education International and the National Association of Elementary School Principals (Perrone, 1976–1978) issued a position paper questioning the usefulness and accuracy of standardized tests with children. A particular concern was the use of test results to place children in special education or remedial programs. The high proportion of children from low socioeconomic and minority populations who were placed in special education or low-track programs was thought to be closely related to test results.

More recently, criticism has focused on government-mandated standardized testing in the schools and its impact on teachers and students. Educators have expressed doubts about the usefulness of the increase in testing (Perrone, 1981) and have deplored the control that testing has imposed on instruction (Durkin, 1987). Calfee (1987) states that government-mandated tests now dictate the curriculum in elementary schools. Labeled by some as *measurement-driven instruction,* such testing is both touted as a cost-effective method for improving the quality of public education (Popham, 1987) and criticized as a process that reduces education to learning bits of information (Bracey, 1987).

Regardless of efforts to question and change the practices of administering standardized tests, use of these tests is increasing (Goodwin & Goodwin, 1993). In the 1986–87 academic year, it was estimated that 105 million tests were administered to 40 million students, about 2.5 tests per student (Neill & Medina, 1989). National support for the continuing use is attributed to various trends that include political origins, accountability, and a desire for national standards. The public desires testing to support equal opportunity, efficiency in schooling, and visible national standards for education (Resnick, 1981). Shanker (1990) proposes that tests enable the American public to determine whether the investment in American education is getting the desired results. Kamii (1990) reports that school boards and legislators at all levels direct that tests be given for accountability related to election votes. Test scores are used to indicate how well schools are functioning. Baker (1989) believes that test scores are a means for policymakers to communicate that they "mean business" in expectations for improvement in student achievement.

Limitations of Standardized Tests

The report *Uses and Abuses of Standardized Testing in the Schools,* by the Council for Basic Education (CBE) (Weber, 1977), describes weaknesses and limitations of standardized tests. The limitations include limited test content, inaccuracy of norms such as **grade equivalent** scores, and inappropriate use of test results. Many achievement tests stress reading and mathematics skills and give little or no emphasis to other subjects taught in elementary schools. A fundamental weakness is that the achievement tests fail to measure important outcomes such as interest in learning, initiative, self-discipline, and skills in the arts. Two important skills—writing and speaking—are excluded from the tests. Because test results may be used for promotion, class assignment, and assignment to special programs such as gifted or special education programs, Weber doubts that the tests are more accurate than teacher assessments.

Norm scores are also considered inadequate. Weber points out that a student's grade equivalent scores could vary from test to test. In addition, on some tests, the grade equivalent score could vary by as much as a year as a result of the answers to a few questions.

Despite these concerns about standardized tests, the long-term campaign to reduce their use has failed. Educational reforms responding to calls for excellence in education have resulted in increased reliance on standardized testing (National Association for the Education of Young Children [NAEYC], 1988). As school districts are pressured by state agencies to improve students' achievement, administrators, in turn, raise their expectations of teachers in individual schools that are reflected in achievement test scores at the end of the school year. Teachers then put pressure on their students in preparation to do well on the test. Overuse of testing and excessive reliance on test results have caused renewed concern about the limitations of standardized tests.

Group test scores can be misleading because it is difficult to ensure that achievement tests are administered correctly by classroom teachers. Because teachers and educational programs frequently are evaluated on the basis of achievement test results, coaching or other forms of assistance can occur. As a result, group test scores should be analyzed with some skepticism.

Another limitation of group scores on achievement tests is related to variables outside school instruction, including socioeconomic conditions and how much money a school district can commit for instruction. One issue is the fairness of tests for children from school-disadvantaged backgrounds. The possibility of bias related to socioeconomic status in standardized tests causes concern about whether they are good measures (Goodwin & Goodwin, 1993). These and other factors can affect group scores regardless of the quality of instruction.

An additional criticism of standardized tests is the presence of cultural bias. These tests have been studied to determine whether test items discriminate against any minority group. Although test developers have worked diligently in recent years to eliminate cultural bias, it is still a concern because all students have not had an equal opportunity to acquire the skills and knowledge being tested in many standardized tests. Further, the concern is that lower performance by minorities can be linked to language and social factors (Duran, 1989). Guilmet (1983) found such a bias in comparing scores on a standardized preschool test between Navajo children and day care children in Los Angeles. The Navajo children had lower scores, particularly the youngest ones who lived in the least acculturated households. Guilmet concluded that testing all children with the same instrument, regardless of the cultural background, is misleading when assessing and understanding the abilities of individual children.

Test designers have found it impossible to develop a culture-free test. Instead, they have tried to develop test items that do not favor specific geographical regions and to use vocabulary that is not offensive to a cultural group or that favors specific groups. They also tried not to use pictures or language that over- or underrepresents or stereotypes a gender group.

Test forms are examined for ethnic bias or selection bias that would favor some group in predicting success on a test such as a reading readiness test. Efforts to eliminate bias in the development of a new battery of measures for Head Start reflects the difficulty in achieving the desired results. Despite the inclusion of Head Start parents, an advisory panel of measurement experts from different ethnic groups, and various reviews during the test development process, the measures that resulted were criticized as still being an achievement test approach (Cordes, 1985; Goodwin & Goodwin, 1993).

An issue in the use of standardized achievement tests is the difference between the purpose of the tests and how teachers actually use test results. Salmon-Cox (1981) analyzed the usefulness of standardized achievement test scores to classroom teachers. Salmon-Cox found that although tests are thought to determine curriculum, teachers actually use their own judgment or interaction and observation skills to assess student performance or skill levels. Durkin (1987) reports that although the *Stanford Early Achievement Test* (Madden & Gardner, 1969, 1971) should have been used to assess student progress, teachers and administrators have a different perception of their purpose. They believe that the tests are for providing information for the child's permanent folder or for selecting children for a transitional class.

Because standardized tests take years to develop and norm, there is at present a discrepancy between what is measured on the tests and current theory about how children learn. One such mismatch is in the area of mathematics. Whereas current theory about how children learn mathematics in the primary grades stresses a Piagetian approach to acquisition of concepts about numbers, tests reflect outdated instructional methods. Whereas current theory advocates the child's construction of concepts through active interaction with materials, achievement tests measure knowledge of numerals (Kamii, 1985a, 1985b).

Current theory in reading instruction stresses a whole-language or emergent literacy approach. Current methods use the child's initiative and developmental progress in an integrated approach that includes oral language, writing, reading, and comprehension. Standardized tests, by contrast, measure more traditional reading instruction that emphasizes phonics, word recognition, and isolated skill acquisition (Farr & Carey, 1986; Teale, 1988; Teale, Hiebert, & Chittenden, 1987; Valencia & Pearson, 1987).

ISSUES IN USING STANDARDIZED TEST RESULTS WITH YOUNG CHILDREN

Many people have serious doubts about the use of standardized tests with preschool and elementary school children. Early childhood educators and specialists are divided in their position on the use of this type of evaluation. Some are opposed to any use of standardized tests with young children. Others state that there is a place for the information they provide, particularly if the test can be improved.

Concerns about Validity and Reliability

The younger the child, the more difficult it is to develop valid and reliable instruments for measurement. Early childhood educators are cautious in using standardized tests with young children because accuracy is important if developmentally appropriate planning is to follow. In the *Position Statement on Developmentally Appropriate Practice in Early Childhood Programs Serving Children from Birth Through Age 8* (NAEYC, 1986), the National Association for the Education of Young Children (NAEYC) proposed that valid instruments for young children are extremely rare.

Cryan (1986) describes difficulties with standardized tests as potentially a plague. Among other concerns, Cryan states that test scores may result in labeling, that they are subject to error, and that norming populations can be used inappropriately when comparing children from dissimilar populations. Cryan also suggests that standardized tests are often the least appropriate measure.

The issues of validity and reliability in standardized tests developed for the early childhood years are addressed more specifically in the *Position Statement on Standardized Testing of Young Children 3 Through 8 Years of Age* (NAEYC, 1988). Reliability and validity are declared to be difficult to obtain in standardized tests, in part, because of the nature of development in young children. Due to the rapidity of developmental change and individual variations in growth and development, results from a single administration of a screening instrument must be confirmed with other periodic screening and assessment methods. Shepard and Smith (1986) propose that developmental inconsistencies in four- and five-year-old children should result in demands for evidence of validity in early childhood tests. For example, the authors state that no existing readiness test is sufficiently accurate to justify placing children in special programs such as transition classes. Specifically, the *Gesell School Readiness Test* (Ilg, Ames, & Gillespie, 1978) was declared to lack the standards of the American Psychological Association for validity, reliability, or normative information (Shepard & Smith, 1986).

The NAEYC position statement on standardized testing also addresses the issue of content validity. The test selected to measure the content of the early childhood program must be accurate. The statement proposes that not using a standardized instrument would be better than using a program to fit the test. Another difficulty related to content validity is the fact that tests for young children measure only cognitive objectives. Important content areas such as social competence, self-esteem, and creativity are omitted (Katz, 1985).

The testing program implemented by the state of Georgia in 1988 is described by Meisels, Steele, and Quinn-Leering (1993) as an example of testing that was problematic in terms of validity and reliability. A test was desired that would determine the readiness of children for first and fourth grades. A modified form of the *California Achievement Test* was designed for this purpose. The modification of the test was piloted only in Georgia, without specific validity data. In addition, the modified test was composed of only the three subtests of visual recognition, sound recognition, and mathematical concepts. The authors questioned the reliability and validity of the three assessment procedures and reported that, fortunately, Georgia subsequently dropped this testing practice.

Goodwin and Goodwin (1982, 1993) describe how quality data should be provided in test manuals regarding validity, reliability, and usability. The authors state that manuals of measures for young children are often deficient in adequate technical quality data. They also cite the cost of these tests as a deterrent to their use in large scale testing programs involving large numbers of young children.

USING INAPPROPRIATE TEACHING MATERIALS AND STANDARDIZED TESTS

Mary Alice Wilson is a beginning kindergarten teacher. Although this was her first year to teach, she was not without teaching experience. Mary Alice attended college in the 1960s, taught school for two years, and then married. She resigned her teaching position after the first of her two children was born. To help meet college expenses for her oldest son, who will soon be graduating from high school, Mary Alice returned to a nearby university to renew her teaching credentials in preschool and elementary education. Although she felt confident about her teaching ability, she was not prepared for the changes that had taken place in the schools.

In September, Mary Alice was hired to teach a kindergarten class of children from low-income homes. To her surprise, she found that she was expected to teach first-grade academic skills with the extensive use of workbook materials. Because this practice was not compatible with her understanding of the active learning style of preschool children, Mary Alice asked why the children were required to use paper-and-pencil learning strategies. In response to Mary Alice's concerns about the use of developmentally inappropriate practices, the principal told her

that it was a response to the school district's policy to upgrade the curriculum and raise achievement standards. The principal agreed that the children were being taught inappropriately but was unable to intervene.

In October, Mary Alice was required to administer a standardized test to her students that required them to be able to mark or "bubble in" the correct answer on a multiple-choice answer sheet. Because Mary Alice knew that her students were unable to follow the instructions for performing appropriately on the test, much less to find the place to mark their answers, she and the students found the experience distressing. Mary Alice felt helpless, unable to determine what was best for the students in her classroom.

Mary Alice's frustration about what she considered to be unsound practice in teaching young children, and the stress her students were experiencing as a result of the school district's policies for instruction and testing, led her to resign in late November. She decided to work as a substitute teacher while determining whether she would be able to teach preschool children under current policies and practices.

Difficulties in Administering Tests to Young Children

Usability is affected when standardized tests are administered to young children. The size of the test group, as well as the length of time required for testing, can be a problem. Reliability is affected when young children are tested in large groups. More time is required, however, when test groups are small.

There are other reasons why time is a problem when testing young children. Some instruments are lengthy, requiring young children to remain attentive beyond their developmental capacities. Evans (1974) also reports that young children in some early intervention programs are given too many tests. This criticism is echoed by Perrone (1981) in an article titled "Testing, Testing and More Testing."

The NAEYC *Position Statement on Standardized Testing of Young Children 3 Through 8 Years of Age* (1988) states that young children should be tested by individuals who are not only qualified to administer the tests but also knowledgeable about the developmental needs of young children. The statement summarizes the problems encountered by young children who are given standardized tests:

> Too often, standardized tests are administered to children in large groups, in unfamiliar environments, by strange people, perhaps during the first few days at a new school or under other stressful conditions. During such test administrations, children are asked to perform unfamiliar tasks, for no reason that they can understand. For test results to be valid, tests are best administered to children individually in familiar, comfortable circumstances by adults whom the child has come to know and trust and who are also qualified to administer the tests. (p. 46)

Misapplication of Test Results

A serious issue in the use of standardized tests is misapplication of test results. In question is the use of tests to keep children out of school, to place children in special education programs, to place preschool children in transitional classes that result in their spending two years in a pre-first-grade program, or to use test results for purposes not intended by test designers.

The Georgia plan for kindergarten testing described above serves an example of misapplication of test results. The purpose of the test was to fulfill a policy that required every child to pass a readiness test or else repeat kindergarten. Despite the doubtful qualities of the modified *CAT* test, it was to be used to retain children in kindergarten (Meisels et al., 1993).

The CBE's report (Weber, 1977) states that the use of standardized tests for promotion, class assignment, and placement in special programs was inappropriate. With the recent emphasis on testing to provide accountability in learning and instruction, standardized tests have been used increasingly to place preschool children. As school district boards of education and school administrators deal with the pressure to have their students attain higher scores on achievement tests, more young children are being kept in kindergarten for an extra year or placed in transitional or "developmental" classes prior to first grade so that their test scores will be higher in the primary grades. This practice is increasing as schools establish minimum standards for promotion. A study reported by the National Academy of Sciences and National Association of State Boards of Education (Gnezda & Bolig, 1988) records the existence of kindergarten testing in more than thirty states. In addition, six states require first-grade readiness testing, while thirty-seven states report first-grade testing at the local level.

Contrary to popular belief, retention in kindergarten, placement in a transitional first grade, and retention in first grade are not effective. Although parents and educators tend to believe that such placements are a solution for immaturity (Byrnes & Yamamoto, 1984), authors of a review of the research on retention (Holmes & Matthews, 1984) concluded that children make progress during the year that they repeat a grade, but not as much progress as children who are promoted. Similar results were found between children who were placed in a prekindergarten or a transitional first grade because they were not "ready." The author of a review of research on such transitional placements (Gredler, 1984) determined that children in such placements were no more successful than retention in a grade. In addition, Bell (1972) found that the self-esteem of children placed in transition classes was lower than that of children who were not retained. In a review of fifteen controlled studies, Shepard (1989) indicated no difference between children who were identified as unready and who spent an extra year before first grade and those who went on to first grade. Shepard questioned both the practice of retention and validity of the tests used to identify and place children (Shepard & Graue, 1993).

The use of standardized tests with young children for placement in pre-first grade or special education programs is a cause of major concern. One issue is the misuse of tests for placement purposes. The NAEYC position paper on the use of standardized tests urges test users to evaluate and carefully select tests only for the purposes for which they were intended (NAEYC, 1988). Shepard and Graue (1993) express concern about the use of individual intelligence tests, developmental screening measures, and school readiness tests for making decisions about school entry. They point out that developmental tests and IQ tests do not differentiate between limited intelligence and limited opportunities to learn. Like readiness tests, IQ tests and developmental measures should not be used to determine school entry.

Meisels (1986) explains the differences between readiness tests and developmental screening tests. Readiness tests such as the *Metropolitan Readiness Test* (Nurss & McGauvran, 1976) and the *Gesell School Readiness Test* (Ilg & Ames, 1972) assess a child's current level of achievement and should not be used as a predictor of success in school. Shepard and Smith (1986) and Shepard and Graue (1993) propose that the *Gesell School Readiness Test* measures the same things as IQ tests, although the claim is made that it measures developmental age.

The use of developmental screening tests was recommended to predict quickly whether a child could profit from a special education placement if such tests have predictive validity, developmental content, and normative standardization (Meisels, 1987; Meisels et al., 1993). Meisels considers the *Early Screening Inventory* (Meisels & Wiske, 1983), the *McCarthy Screening Test* (McCarthy, 1978), and the *Minneapolis Preschool Screening Inventory* (Lichtenstein, 1980) to have excellent reliability and predictive validity. Nevertheless, Meisels states that developmental screening tests should be used to identify children who need further evaluation. The NAEYC position paper on the use of standardized tests (1988) further recommends that decisions on such issues as enrollment, retention, and placement in special classes should never be based on a single test score. Other sources of information, including systematic observation and samples of children's work, should be a part of the evaluation process.

Thurlow, O'Sullivan, and Ysseldyke (1986) also question the technical adequacy of tests being used to identify children for early education programs for children with disabilities. They report that a survey of model programs for such children found that only one-sixth of the tests used for screening purposes had appropriate validity, reliability, and norming samples.

In summary, misuse of standardized tests with young children is primarily related to retention. In addition to the doubtful wisdom of retaining children in kindergarten, the tests being used for retention or placement decisions are used inappropriately. Readiness tests are intended to assess a child's current level of achievement; they are not predictive of future academic success. Developmental screening tests are used to identify children who may be in need of special education services; moreover, the tests describe a child's potential to acquire skills, but not whether he or she should be retained. Intelligence tests are used primarily for identification of children whose ability is very low or very high. They are used for placement for special education services, and students' past learning experiences influence measurement results. When standardized tests are used for appropriate identification and diagnostic purposes with young children, they should have validity and reliability for those purposes.

The Need for Improvements in Standardized Tests

Not all writers would eliminate standardized tests. Cryan (1986) recommends the use of all types of informal and formal measurement strategies. When to use which type of measurement is the issue. Although he advocates teacher-designed evaluation strategies, Cryan also asserts that standardized tests are appropriate when there is a need to evaluate curriculum areas common to many groups of students.

Goodwin and Goodwin (1982, 1993) also indicate standardized tests have a role in measuring young children. They believe that many early childhood educators are not opposed to the use of standardized tests per se, but rather to specific tests. According to these authors, teacher intuition for evaluation can be biased. Systematic measurement and evaluation can have advantages. Although Goodwin and Goodwin describe the shortcomings of standardized tests used with young children, they assert that more is needed than informal measures and teacher observations. Moreover, the future of assessment of young children is linked with the expansion of educational services for young children with disabilities. The need for appropriate instruments to identify at-risk children and to plan programs for remediation will continue pressures for valid and reliable instruments.

SUMMARY

Standardized tests, despite their shortcomings, are useful for test users. Because they have been carefully developed through a series of steps that ensure their dependability, educational institutions in particular use them to measure students' characteristics. Good standardized tests are normed by using many individuals from various backgrounds who live in different parts of the United States. As a result, the tests also accurately measure the population to which they are given.

The normal curve is used as the standard reference for interpreting norm-referenced scores on a standardized test. The distribution of test scores can be compared to the normal curve and interpreted by using percentiles, stanines, or standard scores. In this manner, individual performance on a test can be interpreted by comparison with the norms established by testing a sample group.

Although the process of developing a standardized test may seem to be unnecessarily tedious, good test design requires careful planning and attention to each step. The ultimate validity and reliability of the test result from attention to design details, beginning with the definition of the test's purpose and ending with the description of technical data about the test's construction in the users' manual.

Much is known about the development and use of standardized tests, particularly achievement tests; nevertheless, there is disagreement over whether and when they should be used as an educational tool. This is particularly true in formal testing of young children.

Standardized tests used with young children need continued improvement, but whether they are useful for developmentally appropriate educational programs for young children will not be easily determined. Test developers and early childhood specialists must continue to study the nature of assessment and evaluation and seek to improve strategies for effective measurement of young children.

REVIEW QUESTIONS

1. What are the advantages of using tests that have been standardized?
2. What is meant by quantifiable scores?
3. Describe norm referencing.
4. Why does a test need to have validity? Reliability? Can you have one without the other?
5. Why is description of a test's purpose important? How does test purpose affect test design?
6. List some factors that test developers must consider before starting to develop a test.
7. What are the best test formats to use with preschool children?
8. How are experimental test forms used?
9. What is meant by item tryout and analysis? What is accomplished during this procedure?
10. Discuss three types of item analysis.
11. What kinds of information are acquired when a test is standardized?
12. How is a norming population selected?
13. Explain content validity, criterion-related validity, and construct validity.
14. Explain alternate-form reliability, split-half reliability, and test-retest reliability.
15. Why does every test have a standard error of measurement?
16. Why is a normal curve used to chart the distribution of test scores?
17. What is the function of the mean on the normal curve?
18. How do standard deviations serve as reference points when interpreting test scores?
19. How are percentile ranks and stanines used with standardized test scores?
20. Why are Z scores and T scores useful?
21. List some strengths of standardized tests.
22. How can standardized tests be criticized? Describe some weaknesses.
23. Why are standardized tests not very effective for use with preschool children?
24. How do developmental problems affect test administration in early childhood classes?
25. Describe some ways that standardized tests designed for young children can be improved.

KEY TERMS

alternate-form reliability	norms
concurrent validity	percentile
construct validity	percentile rank
content validity	raw score
criterion-related validity	reliability
equivalent form	split-half reliability
grade equivalent	standard deviation
grade norms	standard error
group test	standard score
individual test	stanine
intelligence quotient (IQ)	T score
internal consistency	test-retest validity
item analysis	true score
mean	validity
multiple choice	Z score
normal distribution	

SUGGESTED ACTIVITIES

1. Interview a kindergarten teacher in a public school to determine whether standardized tests are administered to kindergarten children. If tests are used, find out what tests are given and the purpose for test results. If standardized tests are not administered, find out the school's position on the use of standardized tests with young children under the age of eight.

2. Review current news sources on issues related to testing. Cut out articles in print media and write down information from television or radio news programs.

3. Learn how to administer a standardized test such as the *Peabody Picture Vocabulary Test—Revised* and administer it to two preschool children. Be sure you use a test that is suitable to be given by teachers without extensive training. Evaluate the test results and write a report describing what you learned, including the following: (1) the process of test administration, (2) the similarities and differences in the two children tested, and (3) difficulties you had in administering the test.

REFERENCES

AMERICAN PSYCHOLOGICAL ASSOCIATION (APA). (1974). *Standards for educational and psychological tests and manuals.* Washington, DC: Author.

BAKER, E. L. (1989). Mandated tests: Educational reform or quality indicator? In B. R. Gifford (Ed.), *Test policy and test performance: Education, language, and culture* (pp. 3–23). Boston: Kluwer.

BELL, M. (1972). *A study of the readiness room program in a small school district in suburban Detroit, Michigan.* Unpublished doctoral dissertation, Wayne State University, Detroit.

BRACEY, G. W. (1987). Measurement-driven instruction: Catchy phrase, dangerous practice. *Phi Delta Kappan, 68,* 683–686.

BROWN, E. G. (1980). *Guidelines for test use: A commentary on the standards for educational and psychological tests.* Washington, DC: National Council on Measurement in Education.

BROWN, E. G. (1983). *Principles of educational and psychological testing* (3rd ed.). New York: CBS College Publishing.

BUROS, O. K. (1974). *Tests in print II.* Highland Park, NJ: Gryphon.

BUROS, O. K. (Ed.). (1978). *The eighth mental measurements yearbook.* Highland Park, NJ: Gryphon.

BURRILL, L. E. (1980). *How a standardized achievement test is built.* Test Service Notebook 125. New York: Psychological Corp.

BYRNES, D., & YAMAMOTO, K. (1984). *Grade retention: Views of parents, teachers, and principals.* Logan: Utah State University Press.

CALFEE, R. C. (1987). The school as a context for assessment of literacy. *The Reading Teacher, 40,* 738–743.

CALIFORNIA ACHIEVEMENT TESTS, FORMS E AND F EXAMINATION MATERIALS. (1985). Monterey, CA: CTB/McGraw-Hill.

CORDES, C. (1985, December). New Head Start battery criticized. *APA Monitor,* p. 33.

CRONBACH, L. J. (1984). *Essentials of psychological testing.* New York: Harper & Row.

CRYAN, J. R. (1986). Evaluation: Plague or promise? *Childhood Education, 62,* 344–350.

DUNN, L., & DUNN, L. (1981). *Manual forms L and M. Peabody Picture Vocabulary Test-Revised.* Circle Pines, MN: American Guidance Service.

DURAN, R. P. (1989). Testing of linguistic minorities. In R. L. Linn (Ed.), *Educational measurement* (3rd ed., pp. 573–587). New York: Macmillan.

DURKIN, D. (1987). Testing in the kindergarten. *The Reading Teacher, 40,* 766–770.

EVANS, E. D. (1974). Measurement practices in early childhood education. In R. W. Colvin & E. M. Zaffire (Eds.), *Preschool education: A handbook for the training of early childhood educators.* New York: Springer Verlag.

FARR, R., & CAREY, R. (1986). *Reading: What can be measured?* Newark, DE: International Reading Association.

GNEZDA, M. T., & BOLIG, R. (1988). *A national survey of public school testing of prekindergarten and kindergarten.* Washington, DC: National Academy of Sciences.

GOODWIN, W. L., & GOODWIN, L. D. (1982). Measuring young children. In B. Spodek (Ed.), *Handbook of research in early childhood education* (pp. 523–563). New York: Free Press.

GOODWIN, W. L., & GOODWIN, L. D. (1993). Young children and measurement: Standardized and nonstandardized instruments in early childhood education. In B. Spodek (Ed.), *Handbook of research on the education of young children* (pp. 441–465). New York: Macmillan.

GREDLER, G. R. (1984). Transition classes: A viable alternative for the at-risk child? *Psychology in the Schools, 21,* 463–470.

GRONLUND, N. E. (1990). *Measurement and evaluation in teaching* (6th ed.). New York: Macmillan.

GUILMET, G. M. (1983). The inappropriateness of standard testing in a culturally heterogeneous milieu: A Navajo example. ERIC, ED 261830.

HOLMES, C. T., & MATTHEWS, K. M. (1984). The effects of nonpromotion on elementary and junior high school pupils: A meta-analysis. *Review of Educational Research, 54,* 225–236.

HOPKINS, K. D., STANLEY, J. C., & HOPKINS, B. R. (1990). *Educational and psychological measurement and evaluation* (7th ed.). Englewood Cliffs, NJ: Prentice-Hall.

ILG, F. L., & AMES, L. B. (1972). *School readiness.* New York: Harper & Row.

ILG, F. L., AMES, L. B., & GILLESPIE, C. (1978). *Gesell School Readiness Test Kit.* Rosemont, NJ: Programs for Education Publishers.

KAMII, C. (1985a). Leading primary education toward excellence: Beyond worksheets and drill. *Young Children, 40,* 3–9.

KAMII, C. (1985b). *Young children reinvent arithmetic.* New York: Teachers College Press.

KAMII, C. (1990). *Achievement testing in the early grades: The games grown-ups play.* Washington, DC: National Association of the Education of Young Children.

KAPLAN, R. M., & SACCUZO, D. P. (1982). *Psychological testing principles, applications and issues.* Monterey, CA: Brooks/Cole.

KATZ, L. (1985). Dispositions in early childhood education. *ERIC/EECE Bulletin, 18,* 1, 3.

KAUFMAN, A., & KAUFMAN, N. (1983). *K-ABC Kaufman Assessment Battery for Children sampler manual.* Circle Pines, MN: American Guidance Service.

KEYSER, D. J., & SWEETLAND, R. C. (1984–1987). *Test critiques* (Vols. I–VII). Kansas City, MO: Test Corporation of America.

KUBISZYN, T., & BORICH, G. (1987). *Educational testing and measurement. Classroom application and practice* (2nd ed.). Glenview, IL: Scott, Foresman.

LICHTENSTEIN, R. (1980). *The Minneapolis Preschool Screening Inventory.* Minneapolis: Minneapolis Public Schools.

MADDEN, R., & GARDNER, E. F. (1969). *Stanford Early Achievement Test: Directions for administering Levels I and II.* Orlando, FL: Harcourt Brace Jovanovich.

MADDEN, R., & GARDNER, E. F. (1971). *Stanford Early Achievement Test: Directions for administering Levels I and II.* Orlando, FL: Harcourt Brace Jovanovich.

MCCARTHY, D. (1972). *Manual for the McCarthy's Scales of Children's Abilities.* New York: Psychological Corporation.

MCCARTHY, D. (1978). *The McCarthy Screening Test.* New York: Psychological Corp.

MEHRENS, W. A., & LEHMANN, I. J. (1984). *Measurement and evaluation in education and psychology.* New York: Holt, Rinehart & Winston.

MEISELS, S. J. (1986). Testing four- and five-year-olds: Response to Salzer and to Shepard and Smith. *Educational Leadership, 44,* 90–92.

MEISELS, S. J. (1987). Uses and abuses of developmental screening and school readiness testing. *Young Children, 42,* 4–6, 68–73.

MEISELS, S. J., STEELE, D. M., & QUINN-LEERING, K. (1993). Testing, tracking, and retaining young children: An analysis of research and social policy. In B. Spodek (Ed.), *Handbook of research on the education of young children* (pp. 279–292). New York: Macmillan.

MEISELS, S. J., & WISKE, M. S. (1983). *The Early Screening Inventory.* New York: Teachers College Press.

NATIONAL ASSOCIATION FOR THE EDUCATION OF YOUNG CHILDREN (NAEYC). (1986). Position statement on developmentally appropriate practice in early childhood programs serving children from birth through age 8. *Young Children, 41,* 3–19.

NATIONAL ASSOCIATION FOR THE EDUCATION OF YOUNG CHILDREN (NAEYC). (1988). Position statement on standardized testing of young children 3 through 8 years of age. *Young Children, 43,* 42–47.

NATIONAL EDUCATION ASSOCIATION (NEA). (1972). Moratorium on standard testing. *Today's Education,* 6(1), 41.

NATIONAL EDUCATION ASSOCIATION (NEA). (1977). *Standardized testing issues: Teachers' perspectives.* Washington, DC: Author.

NATIONAL SCHOOL BOARDS ASSOCIATION (NSBA). (1977). *Standardized achievement testing.* Washington, DC: Author.

NEILL, D. M., & MEDIAN, N. J. (1989). Standardized testing: Harmful to educational health. *Phi Delta Kappan, 70,* 688–697.

NURSS, J. R., & MCGAUVRAN, M. E. (1976). *Metropolitan Readiness Tests.* Orlando, FL: Harcourt Brace Jovanovich.

OAKLAND, I., & LAOSA, L. M. (1977). Professional, legislative, and judicial influences on psychoeducational assessment practices in schools. In T. Oakland (Ed.), *Psychological and educational assessment of minority children* (pp. 21–51). New York: Bruner/Mazel.

PERRONE, V. (1976–1978). *On standardized testing and evaluation.* Association for Childhood Education International. Reprint CE-9/1976–78. Wheaton, MD: Association for Childhood Education International.

PERRONE, V. (1981). Testing, testing and more testing. *Childhood Education, 58,* 76–80.

POPHAM, W. J. (1987). The merits of measurement-driven instruction. *Phi Delta Kappan, 68,* 679–682.

RESNICK, D. P. (1981). Testing in America: A supportive environment. *Phi Delta Kappan, 62,* 625–628.

SALMON-COX, L. (1981). Teachers and standardized achievement tests: What's really happening? *Phi Delta Kappan, 62,* 631–633.

SEASHORE, H. C. (1980). *Methods of expressing test scores.* Test Service Notebook 148. New York: Psychological Corp.

SHANKER, A. (1990). The social and educational dilemmas of test use. In *The uses of standardized tests in American education: Proceedings of the 1989 Fiftieth ETS Invitational Conference* (pp. 1–13). Princeton, NJ: Educational Testing Service.

SHEPARD, L. A. (1989). A review of research on kindergarten retention. In L. A. Shepard & M. L. Smith (Eds.), *Flunking grades: Research and policies on retention* (pp. 64–78). London: Falmer.

SHEPARD, L. A., & GRAUE, M. E. (1993). The morass of school readiness screening: Research on test use and test validity. In B. Spodek (Ed.), *Handbook of research on the education of young children* (pp. 293–305). New York: Macmillan.

SHEPARD, L. A., & SMITH, M. L. (1986). Synthesis of research on school readiness and kindergarten retention. *Education Leadership, 44,* 78–86.

TEALE, W. (1988). Developmentally appropriate assessment of reading and writing in the early childhood classroom. *Elementary School Journal, 89,* 173–183.

TEALE, W., HIEBERT, E., & CHITTENDEN, E. (1987). Assessing young children's literacy development. *The Reading Teacher, 40,* 772–776.

TERMAN, L. M., & MERRILL, M. A. (1973). *Stanford-Binet Intelligence Scale: Manual for the third revision forms L-M.* Boston: Houghton Mifflin.

THURLOW, M. L., O'SULLIVAN, P. J., & YSSELDYKE, J. E. (1986). Early screening for special education: How accurate? *Educational Leadership, 44,* 93–95.

VALENCIA, S., & PEARSON, P. (1987). Reading assessment: Time for a change. *The Reading Teacher, 40,* 726–4732.

WEBER, G. (1977). *Uses and abuses of standardized testing in the schools.* Washington, DC: Council for Basic Education.

Chapter 4

Using and Reporting Standardized Test Results

Chapter Objectives

As a result of reading this chapter you will be able to

1. explain the difference between norm-referenced and criterion-referenced tests.
2. list common characteristics of norm-referenced and criterion-referenced tests.
3. explain the advantages of using tests that have been standardized.
4. describe how individual and group test results are used to report student progress and program effectiveness.
5. discuss the advantages and disadvantages of using norm-referenced and criterion-referenced tests with young children.

Tests are administered to young children to acquire beneficial information about them. In Chapter 3 we discussed how standardized tests are planned, designed, and standardized. We considered how the normal curve is used as a reference for translating test scores and comparing individual scores with a norm.

In this chapter we discuss more about using information from children's test scores. In the process of standardizing a test, developers establish the norms that make test score interpretation useful. We not only take a more detailed look at norm-referenced tests but also study how another type of standardized test—the criterion-referenced test—is used to meet the learning needs of young children. Group test scores can be used to analyze and improve curriculum and instruction at various levels within a school district; individual test scores can be used by the classroom teacher to organize appropriate learning experiences for individual students or the class as a whole.

We also discuss how individual and group test results are used to report student progress and program effectiveness. Test results are important to teachers, school district administrators, parents, and school boards. Results are reported to each in a context that provides meaningful interpretation of the test. Finally we consider the disadvantages and advantages of using norm- and criterion-referenced tests with young children.

USES OF NORM-REFERENCED AND CRITERION-REFERENCED TESTS

Distinctions between Norm-Referenced and Criterion-Referenced Tests

Norm-referenced and criterion-referenced tests are both standardized instruments. Some standardized tests are designed for norm-referenced results, and others for criterion-referenced results. The current trend is to design tests that are both norm and criterion referenced. The two types of tests have different purposes, and test items are used differently when measuring student learning or achievement. **Norm-referenced tests** provide information on how the performance of an individual compares with that of others. The individual's standing is compared with that of a known group. The person's percentile rank is obtained to determine the relative standing in a norm group by recording what percentage of the group obtained the same score or a lower score.

In contrast, **criterion-referenced tests** provide information on how the individual performed on some standard or objective. These test results allow users to interpret what an individual can do without considering the performance of others. Criterion-referenced tests are designed to measure the results of instruction; they determine the individual's performance on specific behavioral or instructional objectives (Wilson, 1980). Gronlund (1990) describes the difference between the two types of tests as the ends of a continuum: "The norm-referenced test, at one end, emphasizes *discrimination* among pupils, and the criterion-referenced test, at the other end, emphasizes *description* of performance" (p. 15).

Regardless of whether tests are norm-referenced or criterion-referenced, the process of their design and development are as described in chapter 3. They are constructed and standardized through all of the steps that will result in validity and reliability. It is also possible that norm-referenced and criterion-referenced tests have not been standardized; however, it is criterion-referenced tests that are more often nonstandardized (Goodwin & Goodwin, 1993). It is equally important that criterion-referenced tests have validity and reliability if they are to be used to make decisions about young children.

A case in point is the *Brigance K and 1 Screen for Kindergarten and First Grade*, (Brigance, 1982) which is used to deny entry into kindergarten or to place children into a second year of kindergarten. The test is criticized because it has no empirical data to support its use (Gnezda & Bolig, 1988). Shepard and Graue (1993) report that reviews of the *Brigance* frequently accept the author's assertion that validity and reliability are not needed because the test is criterion-referenced. Shepard and Graue propose that there is a difference between using the *Brigance* to plan instruction for the classroom and using it for placement into special education or into a second year of kindergarten. Norms and validity data are essential if a test is used for placement purposes. Therefore, potential users are warned not to use the *Brigance* for placement purposes (Boehm, 1985).

Norm-referenced and criterion-referenced tests have characteristics in common. Gronlund (1990) describes those common characteristics as follows:

1. Both require a relevant and representative sample of test items.
2. Both require specification of the achievement domain to be measured.
3. Both use the same type of test items.
4. Both use the same rules for item writing (except for item difficulty).
5. Both are judged by the same qualities of goodness (validity and reliability).
6. Both are useful in educational measurement. (p. 14)

Both tests measure what students have learned; nevertheless, the objectives for measurement are different. The norm-referenced test is broad in content. Many aspects of the content are measured. Because the test is concerned with overall achievement, only a small sample of behaviors for each objective can be assessed. The criterion-referenced test focuses on mastery of objectives. Each objective has many test questions to determine whether the objective has been mastered.

Goodwin and Goodwin (1993) further clarify the differences between norm-referenced and criterion-referenced measures. They describe norms as numerical descriptions of the test performance of the test takers. The raw scores of individual test takers are converted into derived scores so that they can be compared with the scores of other test takers. No goal or standard is involved. Criterion-referenced tests make no comparisons among test takers. Test scores are used to determine whether individual students have met a level of performance or absolute standard. If they have met the standard on an objective, they have "passed" or "mastered" the objective. The purpose of test results is to determine how many of the test objectives have been mastered.

An achievement test in mathematics provides a good example. The norm-referenced test for the first grade may have items on addition, subtraction, sets, and all other areas included in the mathematics curriculum. Test items are written to sample the student's overall performance in first-grade mathematics. The student's total raw score then is transformed to compare overall achievement with the test norms. On the criterion-referenced test, student performance on individual curriculum objectives is important. Test items are written to measure whether the child has mastered a particular learning objective in subtraction, addition, or other components of the mathematics curriculum (Goodwin & Goodwin, 1982).

Another difference between norm-referenced and criterion-referenced tests also relates to differences in test items. In a norm-referenced instrument, test items must cover a wide range of difficulty. Because the test is intended to discriminate between the performance of students and groups of students, the difficulty of test items will range above the grade level for which the test is intended. Test items designed primarily for criterion-referenced purposes are written specifically for learning tasks. Easy items are not omitted, and the intent is to evaluate how well the student has learned the objectives for one grade level (Wilson, 1980).

New standardized tests have been developed with dual referencing; that is, they are designed for both norm-referenced and criterion-referenced assessment. Although it is difficult to develop a single test that works equally well for both types of measurement, obtaining both kinds of performance results is helpful to educators. Compromises in test construction are offset by more effective use of the test (Gronlund, 1990). It should be noted that some criterion-referenced tests have not been standardized. This does not imply that they are not well designed and useful, but readers should be aware of this condition.

Uses of Norm-Referenced Measurement with Preschool Children

Norm-referenced test scores are used to measure individual achievement within a designated group. Norms are not standards to be reached; they are numerical descriptions of the test performance of a group of students. Norms can be established at a national level or at a local level. Norm-referenced tests commonly are used to measure school achievement, intelligence, aptitude, and personality traits. Formal tests are administered at the preschool level to identify children who need or can benefit from special instruction, as well as to determine the success of an early childhood program.

Measures of intelligence such as the *Wechsler Preschool and Primary Scale of Intelligence* (Wechsler, 1967) and the *Wechsler Intelligence Scale for Children—Revised* (Wechsler, 1974) are norm-referenced instruments that allow test examiners to differentiate the skills or knowledge of the students who are tested. Preschool intelligence tests may be used to identify students for a class for children with learning disabilities, as well as to qualify children for a preschool gifted program. They may be used with any children for whom an intelligence measure is deemed necessary.

Norm-referenced tests are used with preschool children to measure their present level of knowledge, skills, or performance. In federally funded programs such as Head Start, a norm-referenced measure may be used to evaluate the learning acquired by the children as a result of the program. The *Peabody Picture Vocabulary Test—Revised* (Dunn & Dunn, 1981) provides a measure for language development. The *Boehm Test of Basic Concepts* (Boehm, 1971) and the *Learning Accomplishment Profile* (Sanford, 1974) assess the child's abilities and skills, including the acquisition of concepts.

Uses of Norm-Referenced Measurement with School-Age Children

After children enter primary school, achievement tests are the most frequently administered norm-referenced test. Locally developed achievement tests, as well as state and national tests, can be given in order to measure and analyze individual and group performance resulting from the educational program. Children experiencing difficulties in school are evaluated with screening and diagnostic tests, but all students take achievement tests as early as kindergarten, more frequently beginning in first grade.

Norm-referenced test results are used for more general comparisons of group test results. One such use is to assess achievement level in subject areas. The achievement of a single class in a school, all classes of a certain grade level in the school, all schools with the grade level in a school district, and all schools within a state with that grade level can be studied to determine general progress in one or more subject areas. The results of batteries of tests can be analyzed for trends in achievement.

In a similar type of analysis, components of an instructional program can be studied by using group test scores. If a new instructional program is to be tried, or if an existing method is to be evaluated to help decide whether changes are needed, an achievement test can be used to investigate the effectiveness of the program. Particular areas of weakness and strength can be pinpointed, and decisions and plans can be made to improve weak components in the curriculum.

Uses of Criterion-Referenced Measurement with Preschool Children

Criterion-referenced test scores are used to describe individual performance on specific objectives. Criterion-referenced measures de-emphasize distinctions between individual performances; rather, they indicate whether the individual has mastered the objectives that were tested. Criterion-referenced tests are used for developmental screening, **diagnostic evaluation,** and instructional planning.

In the preschool years, developmental and diagnostic assessment are the criterion-referenced tests used most frequently. Although **developmental screening** is used primarily to identify children who might profit from early education intervention or from special services before kindergarten or first grade, it is used also as a checkpoint for children who are developing normally. Figure 4.1 is an example of a developmental scale to measure social development (Alpern, Boll, & Shearer, 1984).

Many screening tests have been developed as a result of Public Law 94-142, the Individuals with Disabilities Education Act, which required children with disabilities to be placed in the "least restrictive environment" possible. As described by Meisels, "Early childhood developmental screening is a brief assessment procedure designed to identify children who, because of the risk of a possible learning problem or handicapping condition, should proceed to a more intensive level of diagnostic assessment" (1985, p. 1). Thus developmental surveys assess affective, cognitive, and psychomotor characteristics to determine whether further testing and evaluation are needed to identify disabilities and strategies for remediation.

Various screening tests have been developed for the preschool child. The *Denver Developmental Screening Test—Revised* (Frankenburg, Dodds, Fandal, Kajuk, & Cohr, 1975) is commonly used by pediatricians and other medical professionals. The *Early Screening Inventory* (Meisels & Wiske, 1983) and the *McCarthy Scales of Children's Abilities* (McCarthy, 1972, 1978) are also used for screening purposes. Figure 4.2 shows some of the criterion-referenced screening items on the *Early Screening Inventory* (Meisels & Wiske, 1983).

When children have a developmental problem that should be investigated beyond screening procedures, diagnostic evaluation may be needed. The purposes of this assessment are to identify a child's strengths and weaknesses and, ultimately, to suggest strategies for remediation. An example of a diagnostic evaluation instrument that can be used with preschool children is the *Kaufman Assessment Battery for Children* (Kaufman & Kaufman, 1983).

Uses of Criterion-Referenced Measurement with School-Age Children

Diagnostic evaluation measures are also used with school-age children. Intelligence batteries and diagnostic tests in academic content areas are used with students who demonstrate learning difficulties. In addition, criterion-referenced results are used for instructional planning with children at all levels of learning needs and achievement.

TODDLER II: 2-1 to 2-6 years
(25–30 months)
Basal Credit 30 months

Does the child name his/her own sex or tell the sex of others? Child may pass by showing he/she knows that certain clothes, activities, or toys usually go with one sex or another.

Does the child like to help the parents around the house? Does the child enjoy such activities as picking things up from the floor, putting raked leaves in a basket, dusting, setting or clearing the table?

TODDLER III: 2-7 to 3-0 years
(31–36 months)
Basal Credit 36 months

Does the child follow the rules in group games run by an adult? Such rules might mean being able to sit in a circle, follow directions, imitate a leader, or do the same things as the rest of the group.

Is the child able to take turns? Although some help may be needed, the child understands the idea of waiting for someone else to go first *and* allows others to go first 75% of the time.

PRESCHOOLER I: 3-1 to 3-6 years
(37–42 months)
Basal Credit 42 months

Does the child play group games with other children such as tag, hide-and-seek, hopscotch, jump rope, or marbles without needing constant supervision by an adult?

Is the child able to keep "working" for at least *30 minutes* with a similar-aged child on a *single task* such as block building, sand or mud play, or playing store, school, or house?

PRESCHOOLER II: 3-7 to 4-6 years
(43–54 months)
Basal Credit 54 months

Does the child draw a person so that an adult could tell what was drawn? It need not be a whole person, but there should be a head *and* body, *or* a head *and* eyes, nose, or mouth which any adult could recognize.

Is the child allowed to play in his/her own neighborhood without being watched by an adult? This does not mean the child is allowed to cross the street alone.

Figure 4.1
Developmental Profile II (DPII) Social Developmental Age Scale.

Appendix A

Early Screening Inventory
S. J. Meisels and M. S. Wiske

═══ **SCORE SHEET** ═══

Child's name _____   School _____

Date of screening _____ / _____ / _____   Teacher _____
            year *month* *day*

Date of birth _____ / _____ / _____   Screener _____
       year *month* *day*

Current age _____ / _____   Sex: male _____ female _____   Parent questionnaire completed? yes _____ no _____
      years *months*

I. INITIAL SCREENING ITEMS	Pass	Fail	Refuse	Total Points Possible	Total Points Received	Comments
A. Draw a Person (5 parts)				1		
B. Name or Other Letters						
II. VISUAL-MOTOR/ADAPTIVE						
A. Copy Forms						
1. Copy ○				1		
2. Copy +				1		
3. Copy □				1		
4. Copy △				1		

ISBN 0-8077-6080-3 (kit)
ISBN 0-8077-6083-8 (refill)

II. VISUAL-MOTOR/ADAPTIVE (continued) B. Visual Sequential Memory	Pass	Fail	Refuse	Total Points Possible	Total Points Received	Comments
1. + ○				0		
2. ○ + □				1		
or + □ ○ (if fail)				1		
C. Block Building						
Gate (screen)				3		
or Gate (imitate) (if fail)				2		
or Bridge (screen) (if fail)				1		
III. LANGUAGE AND COGNITION						
A. Number Concept						
1. Count 10 blocks				2		
or Count 5 blocks (if fail)				1		
2. How many altogether?				1		

B. Verbal Expression	Name	Color	Shape	Use	Other	Comments
Ball						
Button						
Block						
Car						

Total Score for Verbal Expression _____   Points Received (0–3)

0–5 = 0 pts.;
6–20 = 1 pt.;
21–35 = 2 pts.;
36 + = 3 pts.

Figure 4.2

Early Screening Inventory: example of a developmental screening instrument.

Source: Meisels and Wiske, 1983

Criterion-referenced scores on achievement tests are used to describe individual performance. Reports of individual performance are then used for instructional planning. Individual performance can also be used in teaching groups of children with the same instructional needs.

Mastery testing is a common criterion-referenced measure. Instructional objectives are assessed. After mastery on a test objective has been achieved, instruction proceeds with a new objective. In the case of an achievement test, performance results may be charted to show which objectives have been mastered by the test taker and which ones need further attention. This result can be used in planning instruction for a group of students. In a similar manner, individualized instruction can be initiated as a result of criterion-referenced test results. Figure 4.3 gives the prereading behavioral objectives that are assessed on the *California Achievement Test (CAT)* (1977).

In **individualized instruction,** students are taught singly on the basis of personal needs, rather than in large groups. Instead of planning learning activities for the class as a whole, the teacher diversifies instruction on the basis of the progress of each student. Instructional groups of different sizes are formed, and the pace of instruction is differentiated on the basis of individual progress. Criterion-referenced tests are one source of information for individualized instruction.

Test	Category Objective
Listening for information	1. School vocabulary 2. Spaced/direction/location 3. Relationships—facts/concepts
Letter forms	4. Match uppercase/lowercase
Letter names	5. Recognize uppercase/lowercase
Letter sounds	6. Long vowels (picture/letter) 7. Short vowels (picture/letter) 8. Single consonants (picture/letter)
Visual discrimination	9. Match shapes 10. Match three-letter words 11. Match five- and six-letter words
Sound matching	12. Identical words (oral) 13. Medial short vowels (oral words) 14. Initial consonants (oral words) 15. Final consonants (oral words) 16. Consonant clusters/digraphs (oral words)

Figure 4.3
California Achievement Test: examples of objectives used in a criterion-referenced test.
Source: California Achievement Tests: Tests Coordinator's Handbook, Forms C and D, 1977

Minimum-competency testing also uses criterion-referenced test results. In minimum-competency testing a minimum standard is set regarding competence in achieving test objectives. Individual test scores are interpreted to screen for test takers who have reached or exceeded the established level of competency. Many states have instituted minimum-competency tests for students at the elementary school level whose results help determine promotion or retention.

On a larger scale, criterion-referenced test scores are used for broad surveys of educational accomplishment. Group achievement on a local, state, or national level is assessed to better understand educational progress. The achievement of very large groups of children is analyzed to assess strengths and weaknesses in instruction beyond the level of an individual school district. For example, students tested on a national achievement test in reading were found to be stronger in word identification skills than in comprehension skills. After such information is acquired at a state or national level, curriculum resources and teaching practices can be investigated to correct the problem. In addition to the *California Achievement Test*, other achievement tests include criterion-referenced information: the *Comprehensive Tests of Basic Skills* (1974) and the *Stanford Early Achievement Test* (Madden & Gardner, 1969, 1971).

ADVANTAGES AND DISADVANTAGES OF USING NORM-REFERENCED AND CRITERION-REFERENCED TESTS WITH YOUNG CHILDREN

In chapter 3 we discussed some of the concerns about using standardized tests with young children. Particularly controversial is the practice of using developmental tests to postpone kindergarten attendance or to require a child to spend two years in school before entering first grade (Durkin, 1987). When considering norm-referenced and criterion-referenced tests specifically, advantages accrue when the correct kind of test is administered for an appropriate purpose.

Developmental tests are beneficial when they are used to screen preschool children at risk for academic failure in elementary school. Screening tests can quickly identify such children and indicate whether a child should undergo more intensive evaluation to identify and remediate a learning disability (Meisels, 1985). The earlier such disabilities are identified and intervention is begun, the more likely it is that the child will be able to overcome the disability before entering elementary school.

Norm-referenced and criterion-referenced achievement tests can provide valuable information regarding the effectiveness of curriculum and instruction. At the beginning of the school year, such tests can show what children know in relation to an instructional program (Durkin, 1987). Likewise, achievement tests administered at the end of the school year can demonstrate how well children learned the content of the program. Teachers can use the test results to determine how to reteach or change program content and/or instructional methods. In other words,

USING ACHIEVEMENT TEST RESULTS TO
IMPROVE TEACHING AND LEARNING

The school board in Lucky analyzed the yearly report on school achievement in their community. Results indicated that students achieved at the national norm through the third grade but that thereafter scores tended to drop off steadily among some groups of students. Minority student scores dropped more significantly than the scores of Anglo students. Students from low-income homes did less well than those from middle-income homes.

The teachers in the elementary schools studied the criterion-referenced test results to discover whether certain objectives on the results were weak. Consistent indicators of weakness were found in reading comprehension and in problem solving in mathematics. As a group, students in the school district were stronger in word attack skills in reading and computation in mathematics than they were in higher-order skills that involved analysis and synthesis.

A committee of teachers at each grade level was assigned to search instructional resources to find supplementary materials that would strengthen teaching in those areas. The committees were particularly interested in finding materials that would involve the students in applying what they were learning in mathe-

matics and allow students to engage in meaningful reading experiences.

The grade-level committees first searched through reading and math materials available in their own classrooms. They then surveyed materials available through the school district's central resource center. Finally they traveled to a regional educational service center, where an educational consultant assisted them in locating additional resources that addressed their students' needs in mathematics and reading. The consultant also worked with the committees in designing workshops to share materials and teaching strategies with the other teachers at each grade level.

The second year after the supplementary materials were included, a small improvement was noted in the test scores. Another gain occurred in the third year.

Now, each year, a committee of teachers studies test results to see where the students are encountering difficulty in order to determine whether the instructional program should be modified. The committee is especially attentive to those students who are likely to have lower scores. The school board is pleased with the steady improvement in elementary achievement scores.

teachers can use test results to evaluate their program and to make changes to meet the instructional needs of their students more effectively. Goodwin and Goodwin (1982) state that for many early childhood educators, instructional planning is the only justification for testing young children.

Unfortunately, when Durkin (1987) studied the testing practices of fifteen school districts, she did not find that test results were used to determine the appropriateness of the instructional program. To the contrary, programs were "cast in stone" (p. 769), and children had to adapt to the programs. La Crosse (1970) reports that teachers rely more on their intuition than on measurement data.

As discussed in chapter 3, Meisels (1987) is particularly concerned about the misuse of screening and readiness tests with young children. He states that readiness tests should be used for curriculum planning but that they are frequently used as developmental screening tests to identify children in need of intervention or special services. Meisels points out that individual readiness tests do not have a strong predictive relationship to outcome measures.

There are other disadvantages or difficulties in using norm-referenced and criterion-referenced tests. Screening tests for early identification and possible reversal of developmental disabilities have been used in compliance with the mandates of PL 94–142. Nevertheless, Goodwin and Driscoll (1980) believe that implementation of the law has been difficult.

Some of the problems occurred because the law failed to specify how the screening was to be conducted. As a result, procedures vary and screening and diagnosis are often combined into one process, which can cause ambiguity and confusion.

Another disadvantage is that well-trained personnel are not always available for screening and diagnosis. In addition, there is no consistency in classification and remediation of children with disabilities who move from state to state. Finally, although many tests have been developed for screening and diagnosis, their quality varies.

When and how norm- and criterion-referenced tests should be used with young children is a current issue facing educators associated with early childhood programs. Goodlad, Klein, and Novotny (1973) determined that most early childhood education programs do not use a systematic program for evaluation. In the Position Statement on Developmentally Appropriate Practice in Early Childhood Programs Serving Children from Birth Through Age 8 (National Association for the Education of Young Children [NAEYC], 1986), the following statement was made regarding evaluation or assessment of young children:

> A. Decisions that have a major impact on children such as enrollment, retention, or placement are made on the basis of a single developmental screening device, but consider other relevant information, particularly observation by teachers and parents. (p. 16)

Other issues associated with the use of standardized tests with young children are related to the suitability of achievement tests in the early elementary grades and measurement-driven instruction, or teaching to the test. The major concern about achievement tests in the early grades is whether they are productive. Kamii and Kamii (1990) and Perrone (1990) argue that achievement tests do not measure true learning because they overlook the child's construction of knowledge and internal thinking. In addition, the continuing use of standardized tests encourages developmentally inappropriate practices in curriculum and induces students to become motivated by the desire to obtain acceptable test scores. Teachers are pressured to teach to the test and to use teaching practices that will enhance test scores (Shepard & Graue, 1993). Leinwand (1990, p. 98) summarized the negative effects of using standardized achievement testing with young children. He proposed that such tests have served to

MISUSE OF ACHIEVEMENT TEST RESULTS

Livingston School District, a large urban district, implemented a program for gifted and talented students in response to a mandate by the state education agency. Because funds were very limited, only a few of the students who were eligible could be served at each grade level. To be fair to the students and to avoid complaints from parents, it was decided to use achievement test results as the main criterion for selection. Students' names were ranked in alphabetical order according to their percentile rank on the test.

In the second grade fifteen students were selected. Freddie Marcus was sixteenth on the list. Although he had the same percentile rank as both students above him on the list, he was not included in the program because his last name fell later in the alphabet than theirs.

After the second-grade teachers received the results of the test and the subsequent list of students selected for the program, Freddie's teacher questioned why he was not included. The building principal did not think that she could be flexible in determining the number of students who would be served and decided against including Freddie.

At the next monthly meeting of building teachers, Freddie's teacher asked to discuss the selection process for the gifted and talented program. She questioned the use of a single standardized test to select students, particularly because characteristics of giftedness and different kinds of talent were to be considered. She also asked that flexibility be built into the selection process to include students like Freddie.

The building principal formed a committee of teachers to study the problem and to suggest methods for improving the program and the selection process within the budget limitations. The committee offered a process of teacher observation and questionnaires filled in by parents to be added to the standardized test in selecting students for the program. The committee also suggested that the teacher trained for the gifted and talented program provide classroom teachers with suggestions for developing experiences for a broader group of students within their own classrooms.

perpetuate narrowly focused instruction with a preponderance of one-right-answer drill and practice

foster a more formal and abstract approach to basic skills than is developmentally appropriate for many children

accelerate curriculum downward as more and more teachers try to prepare more and more students for items less and less appropriate for a particular grade level

be a distinct and powerful disincentive for making curriculum improvement because few (at any level) can risk a drop in test scores

narrow the entire program to teaching first those skills covered by the test, often to the exclusion of other, perhaps more important skills

Obviously, educators in early childhood education need to be more informed about the use of standardized tests and informal measures for the evaluation of young children. Informal methods, including observation, are addressed in chapter 5.

REPORTING STANDARDIZED TEST RESULTS

After a standardized test has been administered and scored and individual and group scores have been interpreted, test users can use the information to report not only to professionals within the school district but also to the parents of the students. Reporting originates with individual test results, which then are combined and recombined with the scores of other individuals to form class, school, and district reports.

Individual Test Record

The individual test record in Figure 4.4 is from the *Stanford Diagnostic Reading Test (SDRT)* (Karlsen & Gardner, 1984). The hypothetical student is Robin J. Phillips, who is in the third grade. The test was administered in October, the second month of the school year. Because the *SDRT* is both a norm-referenced and a criterion referenced test, both kinds of scores are reported. In Figure 4.4, norm-referenced scores are located under the heading "Subtests and Totals"; the criterion-referenced or content-referenced information is presented under the heading "Skills Analysis."

Norm-Referenced and Criterion-Referenced Scores

The individual test record includes the subtests or content areas of the test battery. The subtests are Auditory Vocabulary, Auditory Discrimination, Phonetic Analysis, Structural Analysis, and Reading Comprehension. Within each subtest the raw score, scaled score, and grade equivalent are reported. The **scaled score** is a continuous score over all grade levels. It indicates the student's progress on the continuum for each category. In addition, the stanine(s), percentile rank (PR), and percentile bands are included for each subtest.

The "Skills Analysis" section of the test record shows Robin's achievement in individual skills categories within the subtests. The skills measured on the *SDRT* are Vocabulary, Auditory Discrimination, Phonetic Analysis, Structural Analysis, and Reading Comprehension. Robin's teacher, Adrienne Kirby, can study Robin's progress in the skill categories by comparing his raw scores with the number of correct responses possible for each skill. Further, information is provided in the "Progress Indicator" (PI) columns. If the score is under the plus (+) side of the column, it indicates that the raw score is at or above the PI cutoff. If the score is under the minus (-) side of the column, it indicates that Robin scored below the PI cutoff. The PI cutoff score provides additional data on how the PI decision is determined.

Class Reports

Individual test records for students in a classroom can be analyzed for a report on the achievement of the class as a whole (Figure 4.5). The class record sheet of the *Stanford Diagnostic Reading Test* (Karlsen, Madden, & Gardner, 1976) lists the

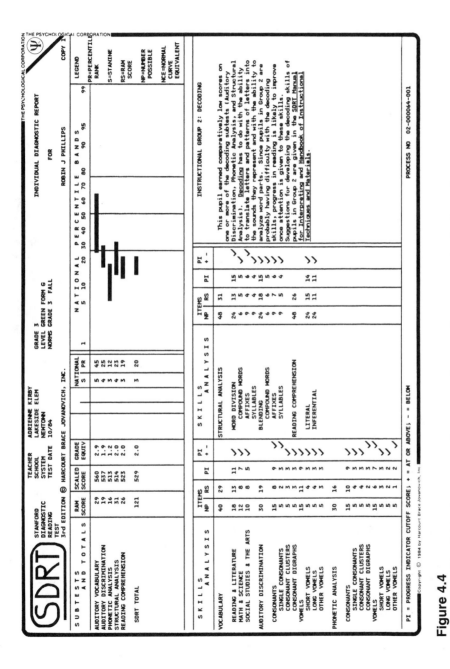

Figure 4.4

Examples of individual test records: norm-referenced scores and criterion-referenced scores.

Source: Stanford Diagnostic Reading Test: Third Edition. Copyright © 1984 by Harcourt Brace Jovanovich, Inc. Reprinted by permission. All rights reserved.

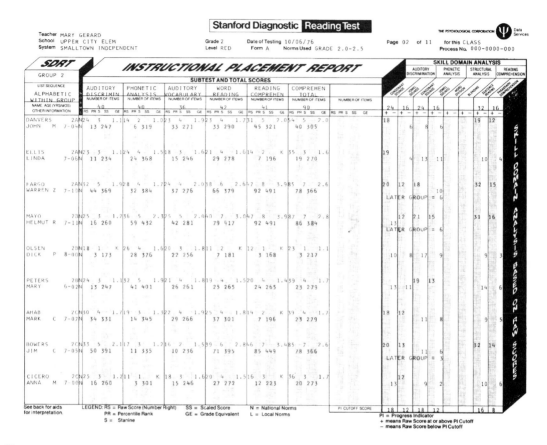

Figure 4.5

Example of a class report.

Source: Stanford Diagnostic Reading Test: Third Edition. Copyright © 1984 by Harcourt Brace Jovanovich, Inc. Reprinted by permission. All rights reserved.

norm-referenced and criterion-referenced scores for each student. In the class report, the teacher can study the norm-referenced achievement scores for each student. In addition, the criterion-referenced information shows the number of students who scored above or below the PI cutoff in each skill category. The teacher can study the Progress Indicators in each Skill Domain category to determine which students need additional instruction in that category. If large numbers of students show nonmastery of certain skills, the curriculum can be studied to make appropriate changes in instruction.

School and District Reports

Summaries of class reports can be grouped to form school and district reports. Both norm-referenced and criterion-referenced information can be organized in a useful form for building principals, school district evaluators, superintendents, and governing boards. Achievement reports can be studied by grade level across a school or among all the schools in the district serving a grade level. Instructional strengths and weaknesses can be analyzed by content areas, as well as by school and by grade level. Achievement can be compared over several years to determine long-term improvement or decline in achievement. Each type of analysis must take into account the error of measurement on the test so that realistic conclusions are drawn from the study of test results.

REPORTING TEST RESULTS TO PARENTS

Parents have the right to know about their child's performance in school, and schools have the responsibility to keep parents informed. One method used to report student learning is the standardized achievement test. The school should report the test results in a manner that is helpful to the parents.

Statistical data that are part of standardized test reports can be confusing to parents. Because of the seeming complexity of test reports, it is important to give parents an opportunity to meet with the teacher for an explanation of their child's test results. Test results can be discussed in a parent-teacher conference.

The classroom teacher has the major responsibility for explaining standardized test results to parents. The teacher not only knows the child from working with him or her every day but also is aware of the kinds of information individual parents will understand and want to acquire. Because parents differ in their educational background and experience with standardized tests, teachers often find it helpful to explain both the value and the limitations of the test scores. For some parents the teacher will describe the test results in terms of what the child can and cannot do, rather than in terms of numerical scores. Parents may also benefit from knowing why the test was chosen and how the results will be used.

It may be helpful for parents to understand how the criterion-referenced test results may be used to plan appropriate learning experiences for their child. For example, the teacher may use test results to suggest activities that the parent can use at home to help the child.

The teacher may also wish to discuss the comparison of test scores of various children, particularly siblings. Parents can be reassured that individual differences in test scores result from many variables. Comparing test scores made by different children is neither accurate nor useful.

Once children enter the primary grades, parents are eager to know how well their child is progressing and whether the child is achieving as well as he or she should be at that grade level. Analysis of the results of a standardized achievement test can provide the information parents need; however, care should be used in interpreting standard scores and other norms used to report the test results. Grade equivalents, percentile ranks, and stanines are the norms most commonly reported to parents from standardized achievement tests. Each can be confusing and must be interpreted carefully so that parents will not misunderstand the implications of the information.

Grade Equivalents

Grade equivalents are a method of interpreting achievement scores in norm-referenced tests, of making comparisons about achievement levels of students at particular grade levels. After a test is given at a particular grade level, it is compared with test results from one grade below and one grade above the grade. Grade equivalents compared with those two grades are made from obtained scores. Scores in grade equivalent tables beyond one grade level above or below are likely to have been estimated only; they represent relative degrees of performance. Moreover, they provide no information on specific skills or deficiencies. In addition, grade equivalents are only averages, not specific to a child. They also are not comparable across school subjects. A grade equivalent score in math may mean something different from the same grade equivalent score in reading (Kubiszyn & Borich, 1987).

Some test publishers recommend that grade equivalents not be used to report to parents because these are the most easily misunderstood norm. If these norms are reported, parents should be given a complete explanation of their meaning.

Parents can understand that a grade equivalent is the grade level reported, in years and months, of the average or mean score of the norming group. Comparing individual test scores with the grade equivalent scores is one way to determine whether a student scored above or below the mean. Parents can misunderstand that grade equivalent scores are not an indicator of the grade-level work that the child is capable of doing. Rather, these scores indicate that the child made the same number of correct responses as the children in the norming group at the grade level in the grade equivalent score. The test score indicates whether the child performed above or below average, but it does not show grade placement in school. Because parents find it difficult to understand the norm comparison made with grade equivalents, percentile ranks and stanines are more effectively used in reporting student performance.

Percentile Ranks

Percentiles and percentile ranks are explained in chapter 3 as reflecting a student's score as related to the normal curve. The percentile rank results from the position of that score on the normal curve, as compared with the test scores of other test takers. The individual percentile rank reflects how many test takers placed at or below that individual's rank on the normal curve.

To understand percentile rank, the parent first must learn about the norming sample used to standardize the test. Then they can understand that their child's percentile score indicates the percentage of students in the norm group who got the same or a lower score on the test. Parents also need to recognize that the percentile rank has nothing to do with the percentage of questions answered correctly on the test. Finally, parents cannot assume that the child's percentile rank refs to the child's standing compared with that of other children in his or her class or school.

Stanines

Stanines are explained in chapter 3 as a type of standard score used to compare performance on the normal curve. Stanines are determined by dividing the curve into nine portions that reflect where fixed percentages of scores fall. Thus the stanines clustered at the center of the normal curve represent the highest percentages of scores, while the stanines one or more standard deviations above or below the mean reflect much lower percentages of scores.

Teachers may use stanines to describe a student's performance on a standardized achievement test. Because the child's performance can be compared both locally and nationally by using stanines, it may be the best norm to use with parents. Parents should be told that a stanine is a nine-unit scale in which a score of 5 indicates average performance. The nine stanines can be used to describe a student's performance even if the parent is not clear about the reference between stanines and the normal curve. *On Telling Parents About Test Results: Test Service Notebook 154* (1980), by the Psychological Corporation, describes student performance in terms of stanines as follows:

9   Very superior
8   Superior
7   Considerably above average
6   Slightly above average
5   Average
4   Slightly below average
3   Considerably below average
2   Poor
1   Very poor (p. 4)

Some parents find this description of their child's achievement easier to understand than either the grade equivalent or the percentile rank. They can have a clear picture of whether the child is performing adequately or may need help with school work. Figure 4.6, the individual test report for the *Peabody Picture Vocabulary Test—Revised* (Dunn & Dunn, 1981), shows how test scores can be reported to parents by using a standard score, percentile rank, and stanine. In this example, the child achieved a percentile rank of 30 percent derived from the standard score of 92. The score placed the child in the fourth stanine, or slightly below average when compared with the norm. At the primary school level, the individual child's test results on the *Stanford Diagnostic Reading Test* (Karlsen et al., 1976) are reported in stanines on the student's test booklet (Figure 4.7). The student, Susan, ranked in the fifth or sixth stanine on all parts of the subtest, placing her at the average or slightly above average on the test. An exception was the test on auditory vocabulary, where she ranked in the ninth or highest stanine.

TRUE SCORE CONFIDENCE BAND

Obtained Test Scores

Mark the obtained standard score equivalent on the top scale. Then draw a heavy, straight, vertical line through it, and across the three scales. This line will extend through the three obtained deviation-type test scores. Depending upon the obtained standard score, shade in a band on both sides of the vertical line, using the schedule to the right. An example is given in Figure 1.4 of the Manual.

Obtained Standard Score	AREA TO SHADE Left of line	AREA TO SHADE Right of line	Obtained Standard Score	AREA TO SHADE Left of line	AREA TO SHADE Right of line
Below 65	0	14	100-109	7	7
65-74	2	12	110-114	8	6
75-84	4	10	115-124	10	4
85-89	6	8	125-134	12	2
90-99	7	7	135 & above	14	0

This shaded area provides a confidence band: the range of scores within which the subject's true scores can be expected to fall 68 times in 100. (These band width values are based on a median standard error of measurement (SEM) of ± 7, with the band widths made increasingly asymmetrical toward the extremes to allow for *regression to the mean.*) See Part I of the Manual and the Technical Supplement for more precise values and a discussion of SEM confidence bands. Also see the Manual for a discussion of how to calculate the true score confidence band for the *age equivalent.*

Raw score . . . . (141)
(from page 4)

Standard score equivalent . . . . [92]
(from Table 1, Appendix A)

Percentile rank . . . . [30]
(from Table 3, Appendix A)

Stanine . . . . [4]
(from Table 3, Appendix A)

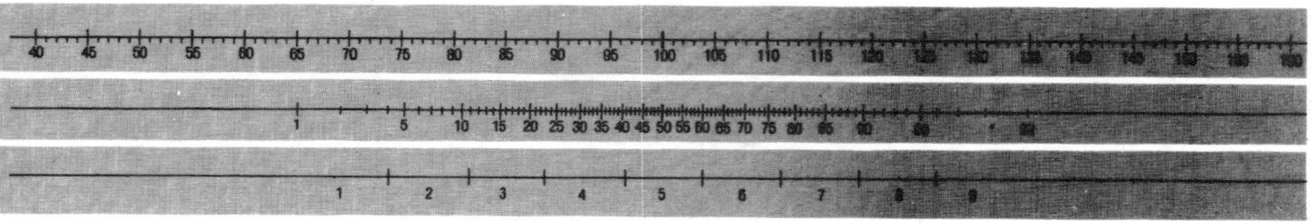

Age equivalent . . . . ⟨16-1⟩
(from Table 4, Appendix A)

EXTREMELY LOW SCORE | MODERATELY LOW SCORE | LOW | HIGH AVERAGE SCORE | MODERATELY HIGH SCORE | EXTREMELY HIGH SCORE

Data from Other Tests

Test	Date	Results
PPVT–R FORM M		

Observations

Briefly describe the subject's test behavior, such as interest in task, quickness of response, signs of perseveration, work habits, etc.:

2

Performance Evaluation

This standardized test provides an *estimate* only of this individual's hearing vocabulary in Standard English, as compared with a cross-section of U.S.A. persons of the same age. Do you believe the performance of this subject represents fairly her or his true ability in this area? ______Yes ______No
If not, cite reasons such as rapport problems, poor testing situation, hearing or vision loss, visual-perceptual disorder, test too easy or too hard (automatic basal or ceiling used), etc.

Recommendations

Examiner's signature

3

Figure 4.6
Peabody Picture Vocabulary Test—Revised: individual test report.
Source: Dunn and Dunn, 1981

	TEST 2	TEST 3	TEST 1	TEST 4	TEST 5	TESTS 4 + 5
	Auditory Discrim-ination	Phonetic Analysis (Parts A + B)	Auditory Vocabulary	Word Reading	Reading Compre-hension (Parts A + B)	Compre-hension Total
Raw Score	32	34	35	33	31	64
S T A N I N E	9 8 7 6 **⑤** 4 3 2 1	9 8 7 6 **⑤** 4 3 2 1	**⑨** 8 7 6 5 4 3 2 1	9 8 7 **⑥** 5 4 3 2 1	9 8 7 6 **⑤** 4 3 2 1	9 8 7 6 **⑤** 4 3 2 1

Pupil Information Box

Name Susan

Teacher_____Grade_____

School_____

City_____State_____

Today's Date_____ month   day   year

Date of Birth_____ month   day   year

Figure 4.7
Stanford Diagnostic Reading Test: primary grade individual record.

Source: Stanford Diagnostic Reading Test: Third Edition. Copyright © 1984 by Harcourt Brace Jovanovich, Inc. Reproduced by permission. All rights reserved.

REPORTING ACHIEVEMENT ON CRITERION-REFERENCED OBJECTIVES

Information on criterion-referenced objectives helps parents see how their child is progressing on specific objectives on a standardized test. The teacher can explain how the objectives are related to the curriculum and how mastery of the objectives is determined. Parents may also be interested in knowing what plans are being made to address nonmastery items and how criterion-referenced tests are similar to teacher-made tests. The *Stanford Diagnostic Reading Test* results, illustrated in Figure 4.7, also exemplify how performance on specific objectives can be reported and explained to parents.

Susan was tested in the categories of Auditory Discrimination, Phonetic Analysis, Auditory Vocabulary, Word Reading, and Reading Comprehension. As her test profile reveals, she scored in the ninth stanine in Auditory Vocabulary, her strongest area. She was close to the mean in the remaining subtests but was weakest in Auditory Discrimination and Reading Comprehension. It is in these areas that her teacher may wish to provide additional help to increase her overall ability in reading.

We have considered some of the people associated with a child's standardized achievement test and how test results are reported to them. Although we have discussed why teachers, parents, school administrators, and school boards need information on achievement test results, we can summarize information on reporting test results by listing how each group can use the information reported.

USES OF STANDARDIZED ACHIEVEMENT TEST SCORES

School Staff

The school staff uses standardized achievement test scores for the following purposes:

To provide information on learning achievement or progress and data for cumulative folders

To provide a longitudinal comparison of the student's progress over a series of grades

To provide the next teacher with one indication of the student's achievement

To provide diagnostic information from criterion-referenced data

To provide an evaluation of the curriculum and instruction that can be used to improve the instructional program

School Administrators

School administrators use standardized achievement test scores for the following purposes:

To compare the school district's achievement with national norms

To provide a record of districtwide progress in subject areas such as reading and mathematics during a school year

To provide longitudinal information on district achievement during a period of years

To provide an analysis of strengths and weaknesses in the curriculum and instruction within the district

Board of Education

The board of education uses standardized achievement test scores for the following purposes:

To provide data on school achievement compared with national norms

To provide an analysis of achievement in individual schools or programs

To provide an analysis of instructional strengths and weaknesses in district schools

Parents

Parents use standardized achievement test scores for the following purposes:

To understand the child's achievement compared with national norms

To understand how the child's progress compares with the progress of other children in the same grade

To learn the child's strengths and weaknesses on individual objectives from criterion-referenced data

SUMMARY

On the one hand, information from norm-referenced and criterion-referenced tests can be very useful in evaluating achievement and in considering instructional improvement. On the other hand, misuse of test results or lack of consideration of test errors and limitations can have a negative impact on instructional decisions affecting preschool and school-age children.

Despite ongoing concerns about their weaknesses, use of standardized tests is increasing and new instruments are being developed in response to pressures for accountability for the quality of education and minimum competency standards for students and teachers.

Teachers of preschool children should be especially aware of the misuse of screening and **readiness tests.** With the current trend toward retaining children in kindergarten or implementing an additional preschool year for many children after kindergarten, teachers and parents need to be knowledgeable about the functions and limitations of developmental screening tests and readiness tests. The use of readiness tests results to make placement decisions about young children is of major concern, particularly when the children are retained in a preschool program on the basis of readiness test results.

Increasingly, early childhood educators and specialists are urging the use of a variety of methods to evaluate or test children, particularly preschool children. Standardized tests have a role, but they are only one method that should be used to evaluate young children. Informal methods, such as teacher observation and teacher-designed tasks, can also be used to obtain a more accurate picture of what preschool and primary-age children have learned and achieved.

REVIEW QUESTIONS

1. How do norm-referenced and criterion-referenced tests report achievement differently?
2. Why are tests with dual referencing difficult to design?
3. Describe how test results can be used selectively.
4. How can achievement tests be used to evaluate a new instructional program?
5. Explain the purpose of a minimum-competency test.
6. What kinds of information are included on an individual test record of an achievement test?
7. What is a grade equivalent score?
8. How is a class report of an achievement test organized? What kinds of information are included?
9. Why do teachers report test results differently to different parents?
10. Explain why parents understand a stanine score more easily than a grade equivalent score.
11. Do parents find criterion-referenced scores more practical than norm-referenced scores? Why or why not?
12. Why do teachers need to understand how to interpret standardized test scores?
13. Explain the increase in the use of standardized testing.
14. Do you agree with the movement for the use of minimum-competency tests? Explain your position.
15. Explain the differences between developmental screening and readiness tests.

KEY TERMS

criterion-referenced test
developmental screening
diagnostic evaluation
individualized instruction
mastery testing

minimum-competency testing
norm-referenced test
readiness test
scaled score

SUGGESTED ACTIVITIES

1. Visit with an elementary school counselor to find out how standardized test results are used and reported, especially in the area of parental reporting.

2. Discuss with a teacher of children with special needs how standardized tests are used to identify and plan Individualized Educational Plans for children.

3. With a classmate, role-play a conference between a teacher and a parent to explain a child's results on a standardized test. The responsibility of the teacher is to explain the results of the standardized test; the role of the parent is to ask questions and contribute information about a hypothetical child.

REFERENCES

ALPERN, G. D., BOLL, T. J., & SHEARER, M. A. (1984). *Developmental Profile II manual.* Los Angeles: Western Psychological Services.

BOEHM, A. E. (1971). *Boehm Test of Basic Concepts.* New York: Psychological Corp.

BOEHM, A. E. (1985). Review of *Brigance K and 1 Screen for Kindergarten and First Grade.* In J. V. Mitchell (Ed.), *The ninth mental measurements yearbook* (Vol. 1, pp. 223–225). Lincoln, NE: Buros Institute of Mental Measurements.

BRIGANCE, A. H. (1982). *Brigance K and 1 Screen for Kindergarten and First Grade.* Billerica, MA: Curriculum Associates.

CALIFORNIA ACHIEVEMENT TESTS: TEST COORDINATOR'S HANDBOOK, FORMS C AND D. (1977). Monterey, CA: CTB/McGraw-Hill.

COMPREHENSIVE TESTS OF BASIC SKILLS (expanded ed.). (1974). Technical Bulletin No. 1. Monterey, CA: CTB/McGraw-Hill.

DUNN, L., & DUNN, L. (1981). *Manual Forms L and M, Peabody Picture Vocabulary Test—Revised.* Circle Pines, MN: American Guidance Service.

DURKIN, D. (1987). Testing in the kindergarten. *Reading Teacher, 40,* 766–780.

FRANKENBURG, W. K., DODDS, J. B., FANDAL, A. W., KAJUK, F., & COHR, M. (1975). *Denver Developmental Screening Test: Revised reference manual.* Denver, CO: LADOCA Foundation.

GNEZDA, M. T., & BOLIG, R. (1988). *A national survey of public school testing of prekindergarten and kindergarten children.* Washington, DC: National Academy of Sciences.

GOODLAD, J. I., KLEIN, M. R., & NOVOTNY, J. M. (1973). *Early schooling in the United States.* New York: McGraw-Hill.

GOODWIN, W. L., & DRISCOLL, L. A. (1980). *Handbook for measurement and evaluation in early childhood education.* San Francisco: Jossey-Bass.

GOODWIN, W. L., & GOODWIN, L. D. (1982). Measuring young children. In B. Spodek (Ed.), *Handbook of research in early childhood education* (pp. 523–563). New York: Free Press.

GOODWIN, W. L., & GOODWIN, L. D. (1993). Young children and measurement: Standardized and nonstandardized instruments in early childhood education. In B. Spodek (Ed.), *Handbook of research on the education of young children* (pp. 441–463). New York: Macmillan.

GRONLUND, N. E. (1990). *Measurement and evaluation in teaching* (6th ed.). New York: Macmillan.

KAMII, C., & KAMII, M. (1990). Why achievement testing should stop. In C. Kamii (Ed.), *Achievement testing in the early grades: The games grown-ups play* (pp. 15–38). Washington, DC: National Association for the Education of Young Children.

KARLSEN, B., & GARDNER, E. (1984). *Stanford Diagnostic Reading Test manual for administering and interpreting* (3rd ed.). Orlando, FL: Harcourt Brace Jovanovich.

KARLSEN, B., MADDEN, R., & GARDNER, E. F. (1976). *Stanford Diagnostic Reading Test manual for administering and interpreting.* Orlando, FL: Harcourt Brace Jovanovich.

KAUFMAN, A., & KAUFMAN, N. (1983). *Kaufman Assessment Battery for Children. Sampler manual.* Circle Pines, MN: American Guidance Service.

KUBISZYN, T., & BORICH, G. (1987). *Educational testing and measurement: Classroom application and practice.* Glenview, Il: Scott, Foresman.

LA CROSSE, E. R., Jr. (1970). Psychologist and teacher: Cooperation or conflict? *Young Children, 25,* 223–229.

LEINWAND, S. J. (1990). The dilemma for state department consultants. In C. Kamii (Ed.), *Achievement testing in the early grades: The games grown-ups play* (pp. 91–100). Washington, DC: National Association for the Education of Young Children.

MADDEN, R., & GARDNER, E. E (1969). *Stanford Early Achievement Test: Directions for administering levels I and II.* Orlando, FL: Harcourt Brace Jovanovich.

MADDEN, R., & GARDNER, E. E (1971). *Stanford Early Achievement Test: Directions for administering levels I and II.* Orlando, FL: Harcourt Brace Jovanovich.

MCCARTHY, D. (1972). *Manual for the McCarthy Scales of Children's Abilities.* New York: Psychological Corp.

MCCARTHY, D. (1978). *McCarthy Screening Test.* New York: Psychological Corp.

MEISELS, S. J. (1985). *Developmental screening in early childhood: A guide.* Washington, DC: National Association for the Education of Young Children.

MEISELS, S. J. (1987). Uses and abuses of developmental screening and school readiness testing. *Young Children, 42,* 4–6, 68–73.

MEISELS, S. J., & WISKE, M. S. (1983). *Early Screening Inventory.* New York: Teachers College Press.

NATIONAL ASSOCIATION FOR THE EDUCATION OF YOUNG CHILDREN (NAEYC). (1986). Position statement on developmentally appropriate practice in early childhood programs serving children from birth through age 8. *Young Children, 41,* 3–19.

PERRONE, V. (1990). How did we get here? In C. Kamii (Ed.), *Achievement testing in the early grades: The games grown-ups play* (pp. 1–13). Washington, DC: National Association for the Education of Young Children.

THE PSYCHOLOGICAL CORPORATION. (1980). *On telling parents about test results.* Test Service Notebook 154. New York: Author.

SANFORD, A. R. (1974). *A manual for use of the Learning Accomplishment Profile.* Winston-Salem, NC: Kaplan School Supply.

SHEPARD. L. A., & GRAUE, M. E. (1993). The morass of school readiness screening: Research on test use and test validity. In B. Spodek (Ed.), *Handbook of research on early childhood education* (pp. 293–305). New York: Macmillan.

WECHSLER, D. (1967). *Wechsler Preschool and Primary Scale of Intelligence: Manual.* New York: Psychological Corp.

WECHSLER, D. (1974). *Wechsler Intelligence Scale for Children—Revised: Manual.* New York: Psychological Corp.

WILSON, R. (1980). *Criterion-referenced testing.* Test Service Notebook 37. New York: Psychological Corp.

Chapter 5

Informal Measures: Observation

Chapter Objectives

As a result of reading this chapter you will be able to

1. understand the purposes for informal evaluation measures.
2. become familiar with a variety of informal evaluation measures.
3. conduct observations of physical, social, cognitive, and language development by using appropriate observation strategies.

In the three previous chapters, we discussed standardized tests—tests that have been tried and tested with a population of test takers to establish standards for analyzing and reporting the results. We covered how standardized tests are developed and used, their advantages and limitations, and some of the concerns of early childhood specialists concerning their use with young children.

In this chapter we discuss informal ways of assessing and evaluating young children. These include instruments and other strategies designed by teachers, other school staff members, early childhood specialists, curriculum textbook writers, and others to assess what children already know, what they have learned, and what they are prepared to learn.

TYPES OF INFORMAL EVALUATION MEASURES

Several types of informal evaluation measures are available for teachers of preschool and school-age children. These include observation, checklists and rating scales, and teacher-designed tests. In this chapter we discuss informal evaluation measures in general and observation strategies specifically. In the following chapters we examine checklists, rating scales, teacher-designed evaluations, and performance assessments.

Observation is a process whereby the teacher uses incidental or planned observation episodes to learn about young children. Although primary school teachers use observation techniques particularly as a part of daily instruction to evaluate their students, preschool teachers use observation as a primary method of understanding the cognitive, affective, and motor development of children throughout the school day in many instructional and play contexts.

Checklists and **rating scales** are teacher-developed or commercially designed lists of learning objectives for instruction in a checklist format. Checklists can be used for assessment, instructional planning, and record keeping, as well as for communicating the purposes and outcomes of the instructional program to parents and the community.

Teacher-designed evaluation measures may be written or oral tests but also may include activities that are developmentally appropriate for young children. All of these measures are for use by the teacher; their main purpose is to gain a better understanding of students. Regardless of the type of information acquired, the teacher's goal is to use the results to help children learn.

Teachers have other options for conducting informal evaluations. They can interview a child in the process of working with a concept to determine the child's understanding. In addition, games may be designed or assignments organized to assess the child's progress. Many teachers use simple contracts to document the child's interaction with learning opportunities and use successful completion of contract activities to document the child's progress or mastery.

Alternative methods of reporting the child's progress have been adopted to replace the traditional report card. In some schools report cards have been modified to reflect developmental progress, rather than mastery of skills. Portfolios are becoming more common to document performance-based or authentic types of informal assessment. Teachers and/or students collect work samples and results of informal assessments in a portfolio and use them to determine the child's progress. Narrative reports are another alternative to reporting through report cards. The teacher assesses the child's progress through informal strategies and summarizes and interprets the child's progress in a narrative that helps the parents and other interested parties understand how and why the child is or is not making progress in development and learning.

Informal approaches to evaluation have purposes beyond reporting to parents and others. In the following section some of these purposes are explained, particularly as tools to facilitate development and learning within the curriculum.

USES OF INFORMAL MEASURES

Standardized tests are used for two purposes: (1) to evaluate achievement compared with that of a sample group of children and (2) to measure the child's achievement on specific test objectives. The norm-referenced test measures achievement; the criterion-referenced test evaluates mastery of test objectives. Teachers can use criterion-referenced test results to determine an individual child's strengths and weaknesses in the content areas measured by the test. Test results provide a rough idea of the child's learning needs. However, because many objectives are measured on the standardized test, there are few test questions for each objective. Consequently, criterion-referenced test results cannot be considered a completely reliable picture of the individual child's progress and instructional needs. Informal evaluation measures allow the teacher to obtain more specific information about each student's knowledge and skills relative to the instructional objectives of the class. These informal measures can be used for placement, diagnostic evaluation and instructional planning, and formative and summative evaluation.

Placement Evaluation

At the beginning of the school year and periodically during the year, preschool and primary grade teachers must make decisions about how to place or group children. With preschool children, the teacher needs to know the skills and knowledge of each child. Because the backgrounds of the children can vary widely, the teacher will evaluate all students to determine how to plan for them in the instructional program. In preschool programs designed to prevent or deal with learning problems, the evaluation may be done to determine whether the child is eligible for the program.

For school-age children, informal testing may result in placement in a group for reading and mathematics. The teacher or teams of teachers give tests at the beginning of the school year to determine the child's mastery of content objectives; the purpose is to group together children with similar learning needs for instruction. This type of evaluation may be repeated whenever teachers believe that regrouping is needed to improve instructional services for the children.

Diagnostic Evaluation and Instructional Planning

Diagnostic evaluation is more specific than placement evaluation. When assessing for diagnostic purposes, the teacher investigates the child's ability in specific objectives. With preschool children, the teacher may assign tasks involving knowledge of colors to determine which children know the colors and which children need activities to learn them. With school-age children, the teacher may administer a paper-and-pencil test to determine which children have learned to add and which children need to be taught that skill.

Formative and Summative Evaluation

Formative and summative evaluation occur after instruction on a particular objective or a series of objectives. **Formative evaluation** is done to determine how students are progressing toward mastery of objectives. After students practice a skill or learn information, the teacher evaluates them to determine which ones have achieved mastery and which ones need additional work through different instructional methods or learning experiences.

Summative evaluation is a final assessment of what children have learned. It is conducted after diagnostic and formative evaluation. For some grade levels, summative evaluation is done for grading purposes: The child receives a grade for performance on the objectives tested. Whether or not grades are used, it is hoped that children who have not mastered the information or skills tested will have more opportunities to learn.

ADVANTAGES OF USING INFORMAL EVALUATION MEASURES

Informal measures have certain advantages over standardized tests. Although they have not been validated with large numbers of students before being used in the classroom, informal measures include measurement opportunities that standardized tests cannot provide.

The focus of informal evaluation measures is to encourage students to produce knowledge, rather than to reproduce knowledge. In keeping with Piaget's position that children construct knowledge, informal evaluation measures stress the child's active involvement in learning that is exhibited through performance of tasks or samples of work, rather than through assessments that are limited to mastery of discrete skills (Goodwin & Goodwin, 1993; Wiggins, 1989). The goal of informal evaluation is to measure long-term development that occurs slowly over a period of time, rather than short-term learning that is assessed without acknowledging interrelationships in development.

One advantage of informal measures is that they can be derived directly from the teacher's educational objectives and curriculum or from a commercial textbook curriculum. Standardized tests, by contrast, are developed to measure general objectives applicable to many children in different school districts and areas of the country. With informal measures, individual teachers or groups of teachers design both the curriculum and the measures to assess children's knowledge of the curriculum. Consequently, evaluation items can focus specifically on the teacher's instruction and assessment plans. Commercial publishers also can design informal means of assessment specifically for their instructional materials.

In chapter 3, we established that standardized tests may not measure the way children are being taught in the classroom. Because these tests are developed over a long period of time, the test items may reflect outdated learning objectives. As a result, teacher-designed evaluation strategies may measure learning more accurately than standardized tests.

Valencia and Pearson (1987) argue for teacher-designed evaluation measures because research in reading instruction suggests that young readers use available resources such as text, prior knowledge, and environmental clues to make sense of reading material, whereas standardized tests evaluate reading as a set of discrete skills. As a result, these authors state, teachers teach reading as discrete skills or teach so that students will do well on the standardized tests. Valencia and Pearson recommend that formal testing strategies be modified to better match reading research findings about effective instruction, but also that teachers use a combination of evaluation strategies that more accurately assess the reading process.

The developmental nature of emergent literacy is also used as a rationale for using informal evaluation measures. Literacy includes the development of language, listening, writing, and reading, which are interrelated and concurrent. The process of literacy begins at birth and continues throughout the early childhood years. The developmental progress of literacy is followed and evaluated by using the child's performance and examples of work collected over a period of time that reflect advances toward the ability to communicate through reading and writing. More specifically, assessment of literacy occurs through emergent writing samples, emergent reading of books, and oral discussions founded on the philosophy that the child's emerging skills reflect the child's ability to construct literacy through experiences with literacy over time (Goodwin & Goodwin, 1993; Sulzby, 1990; Teale, 1988). Likewise, stages of emergent literacy that are skills related, such as knowledge of letter-sound correspondence and encoding and decoding words, are assessed through learning activities and instructional events (Schickedanz, 1989).

Using outdated instructional methods so that children will perform well on standardized tests can affect mathematics as well as reading. Although current theory of mathematics instruction stresses that children construct concepts by becoming actively involved with concrete materials, tests still measure knowledge of numerals (Kamii, 1985a, 1985b). School systems teach to the test, rather than follow methods that are best for children (National Association for the Education of Young Children [NAEYC], 1988). Moreover, the tests stress lower-order thinking, rather than higher-order thinking, and improvement in test scores reflects improvement in computation, rather than in problem-solving (Dossey, Mullis, Lindquist, & Chambers, 1988; Kamii & Kamii, 1990). Alternative assessments such as interviews, projects, games, and observations are recommended by Kamii and Kamii to evaluate the constructivist nature of learning in mathematics.

In contrast to standardized tests, informal evaluation measures are current. Because standardized tests are developed over a period of time, there may be a lag of two or more years between test design and implementation. A test cannot be easily updated or modified. Teacher-designed evaluation measures, however, can be altered when necessary. If instructional materials are changed or learning objectives modified, the teacher can keep classroom measures current by redesigning assessment strategies to reflect the changes.

Another advantage of informal assessment measures is that they can be correlated with diagnostic needs. If the teacher wants certain types of information for placement, grouping, and individual instructional needs, the assessment measures can be easily adapted for these purposes. Although criterion-referenced standardized tests also serve diagnostic purposes, they are generally a starting point for effective teachers. The teacher must follow criterion-referenced results with informal strategies that provide additional diagnostic information. For preschool children, who have not been given standardized tests, teacher-designed strategies are a first step in evaluation. Criterion-referenced standardized tests can be administered later, when the child is better able to take them.

The flexibility of teacher-designed evaluation strategies is an important advantage. The objectives to be evaluated on a standardized test are established early in the test development process. Thereafter, objectives are not changed, and test items to measure them are evenly distributed and measure all general objectives equally. Individual teachers design both the curriculum and the measures to assess children's mastery of it; consequently, evaluation items can be tailored to the teacher's instruction and assessment plans.

DISADVANTAGES OF USING INFORMAL EVALUATION MEASURES

Although informal evaluation strategies have certain advantages, they also have limitations and weaknesses. Classroom teachers are more likely to use informal assessment measures than the results of standardized tests. Therefore, they must learn how to design and use informal measures appropriately if these measures are to be effective for evaluation and instructional planning. Improper development and implementation are the main disadvantages of informal measures—specifically, problems centered on their validity and reliability, their misapplication, and their inappropriate use.

Locally designed assessment and evaluation instruments are widely used in preschools and elementary schools. Since the 1970s, when informal measures such as instructional checklists first became popular, many school districts have developed their own checklists and other assessment measures. At the preschool level, teachers and administrators have devised screening tests to determine eligibility for preschool intervention programs. For example, in some states, only children who are at risk for academic failure are eligible for state-supported kindergarten programs. Local schools are expected to determine the eligibility of the five-year-old children in their district. The screening instruments vary greatly from one community to another.

In New York, Joiner (1977) found 151 different tests and other screening procedures being used. Only 16 of the tests were considered appropriate for screening preschool children. The Michigan Department of Education (1984) found 111 different tests being used for preschool, kindergarten, and pre-first-grade programs—and only 10 of them appropriately. Meisels (1987) states that many locally designed screening tests have never been assessed for reliability and validity or other established criteria.

Another disadvantage of informal measures is that teachers may misuse them. Checklists are frequently used as a framework for organizing or designing the curriculum, as well as a record of evaluation of student learning. Children are tested on the checklist's objectives, and the record of their progress follows them from grade to grade. Because teachers develop their own tasks or tests to assess checklist objectives, confusion over what constitutes mastery and what kind of assessment is appropriate can cause major problems within a school or throughout a school district. In an effort to arrive at a consensus on how to assess the objectives, the strategies used by individual teachers may be severely limited. In the primary grades, teachers must frequently place a workbook page or other pencil-and-paper documentation in the child's record as proof of successful performance. This requirement eliminates the use of other informal strategies such as teacher observation or developmentally appropriate tasks for evaluation.

Durkin (1987) also observed the inappropriate use of informal evaluation measures. In chapter 4, we discussed Durkin's reported misuse of standardized test scores for promotion and retention in preschool programs. Durkin also found that first-grade teachers used teacher-made tests and basal end-of-unit tests for grading purposes, but rarely used them to adapt instruction for students' individual learning needs.

Calfee (1987) expresses concern that curriculum, instruction, and assessment in response to external mandates are based on "a countless array of minuscule objectives" (p. 739). As a result, classroom assessment consists of curriculum-embedded multiple-choice tests of doubtful validity.

The current movement to incorporate authentic or performance-based assessments in early childhood programs offers additional options for evaluating young children. Interviews, directed assignments, narrative reports, and portfolios offer new techniques that permit teachers to develop assessments congruent with their teaching style and the constructivist approach to learning. However, there are serious concerns about the possible disadvantages to these new approaches to informal assessment. One disadvantage is that these measures must present evidence of validity, reliability, and freedom from bias. Another disadvantage is the extensive training needed by teachers to feel comfortable with the new techniques. Further, teachers have concerns about the issue of accountability with authentic assessments. The amount of time needed to conduct the newer measures and to keep records are a concern. Finally, there are concerns about acceptance by parents, the public in general, and policymakers (Goodwin & Goodwin, 1993; Smith, 1990; Teale, 1990).

The major disadvantage of informal measures seems to be that teachers are not prepared to develop and use them. They misuse or are unaware of the proper application of either standardized or informal measures. Some writers advocate the use of a variety of formal and informal strategies to assess young children. Teale, Hiebert, and Chittenden (1987), for example, believe that observation should be a primary tool for preschool teachers. The National Association for the Education of Young Children also strongly supports the use of observation for developmental evaluation. Its *Position Statement on Developmentally Appropriate Practice in Early Childhood Programs Serving Children from Birth Through Age 8* states the following about the developmental evaluation of children:

> Accurate testing can only be achieved with reliable, valid instruments and such instruments developed for use with young children are extremely rare. In the absence of valid instruments, testing is not valuable. Therefore, assessment of young children should rely heavily on the results of observation of their development and descriptive data. (NAEYC, 1986, p. 8)

Observation, like other informal strategies, requires an informed, well-prepared teacher who will use it effectively. In the rest of this chapter we discuss the purposes for observation and describe how observations are conducted and interpreted.

PURPOSES OF OBSERVATION

Observation is the most direct method of becoming familiar with the learning and development of the young child. Because it requires a focus on the child's behaviors, observation allows the teacher to get to know the child as a unique individual, rather than as a member of a group. Observation can be used for two major purposes: (1) to understand children's behavior and (2) to evaluate children's development.

To Understand Children's Behavior

Because young children have not yet mastered language and the ability to read and write, they are unable to express themselves as clearly as older children and adults. They cannot demonstrate how much they know or understand through formal or informal measures involving tasks and standardized tests. According to child development specialists, one of the most accurate ways to learn about children is to observe them in daily activities. Because children cannot explain themselves sufficiently through language, evidence of why they behave as they do is obtained through on-the-spot recording of their actions (Irwin & Bushnell, 1980).

Children communicate through their bodies. Their physical actions reveal as much about them as the things they say. Cohen, Stern, and Balaban (1983) describe how observation of children's behavior provides information or clues to their thoughts and feelings:

> Children communicate with us through their eyes, the quality of their voices, their body postures, their gestures, their mannerisms, their smiles, their jumping up and down, their listlessness. They show us, by the way they do things as well as by what they do, what is going on inside them. When we come to see children's behavior through the eyes of its meaning to them, from the inside out, we shall be well on our way to understanding them. Recording their ways of communicating helps us to see them as they are. (p. 5)

To Evaluate Children's Development

A second major purpose of observing children is to evaluate their development. When studying development, observation is specific. Rather than consider behavior in general, the observer's purpose is to determine the child's progress in physical, cognitive, social, or emotional development. Observation of development not only makes it easy to understand sequences of development but also helps teachers of young children be aware of individual growth and aids children who have delays in specific areas of development.

One purpose of observation is to evaluate a child's development.

Beaty (1993) describes observation of development as systematic. There are specific purposes for observing and particular methods for collecting and recording observation data. Beaty proposes eight reasons for systematically observing and recording the development of young children:

1. To make an initial assessment of the child's abilities
2. To determine a child's areas of strength and areas needing strengthening
3. To make individual plans based on observed needs
4. To conduct an ongoing check on the child's progress
5. To learn more about child development in particular areas
6. To resolve a particular problem involving the child
7. To use in reporting to parents or to specialists in health, speech, and mental health
8. To gather information for the child's folder, for use in guidance and placement (p. 5)

Because what is observed must be interpreted, the observer must know how to use observation to gather specific data. Background information on how children develop and learn is important if the observer is to convert the child's behaviors into information that can be used to understand the child's level of development and the need for experiences that will further that development.

Obviously the quality of the information gained from an observation depends on the skills of the observer. The sophisticated observer uses knowledge of developmental theories and of stages of development to identify the significant events of an observation and to interpret those events in a way that is useful in understanding the child. For example, a teacher may notice that a child is exploring or playing with a collection of buttons in making a pile of all the buttons with four holes. A knowledge of Piaget's cognitive developmental theory will enable the teacher to interpret this activity as the ability to classify objects.

Bentzen (1985) states that observation is not simply looking at something; it is a disciplined, scientific process of searching for a behavior in a particular way. The observer must know what to look for, how to record the desired information, and how to explain the behavior.

Young children develop rapidly, and their level of development changes continually. By observing frequently, teachers can track the child's development and respond to changes and advances in development with new opportunities and challenges.

TYPES OF OBSERVATION

What happens during an observation? What does the observer actually do? When conducting an observation, the student, teacher, or researcher visits a classroom or other place where a group of children may be observed as they engage in routine activities. The observer, having already determined the objectives or purpose of the observation, the time to be spent studying the child or children, and the form in which the observation will be conducted and recorded, sits at the side or in an observation booth and watches the children. The types of observation used include anecdotal records, running records, specimen records, time sampling, event sampling, and checklists and rating scales.

Anecdotal Record

An **anecdotal record** is a written description of a child's behavior. It is an objective account of an incident that tells what happened, when, and where. The record may be used to understand some aspect of behavior. A physician, parents, or teachers may use anecdotal records to track the development of an infant or a young child in order to explain unusual behavior. Although the narrative itself is objective, comments may be added as an explanation of or a reaction to the recorded incident.

The anecdotal record has five characteristics (Goodwin & Driscoll, 1980):

1. The anecdotal record is the result of direct observation.
2. The anecdotal record is a prompt, accurate, and specific account of an event.
3. The anecdotal record includes the context of the behavior.
4. Interpretations of the incident are recorded separately from the incident.
5. The anecdotal record focuses on behavior that is either typical or unusual for the child being observed.

Figure 5.1 is an example of the form and content of an anecdotal record.

Child Name(s): Robbie, Mary, Janie
Age: 4
Location: Sunnyside Preschool
Observer: Sue
Type of Development Observed: Social/Emotional

Incident	Social/Emotional Notes or Comments
Mary and Janie were in the Housekeeping Area pretending to fix a meal. Robbie came to the center and said he wanted to eat. The girls looked at him. Janie said, "You can't play here, we're busy." Ron stood watching the girls as they moved plastic fruit on the table. Robbie said, "I could be the Daddy and do the dishes." Mary thought for a minute, looked at Janie, and replied, "Oh, all right, you can play."	The girls play together frequently and tend to discourage others from entering their play. Robbie has learned how to enter a play group. He was careful not to upset the girls. They relented when he offered to be helpful. Robbie is usually successful in being accepted into play activities.

Figure 5.1
Example of an anecdotal record.

Running Record

The **running record** is another method of recording behavior. It is a more detailed narrative of a child's behavior that includes the sequence of events. The running record includes everything that occurred over a period of time—that is, all behavior observed—rather than particular incidents that are used for the anecdotal record. The description is objective. An effort is made to record everything that happened or was said during the observation period. Running records may be recorded over a period ranging from a few minutes to a few weeks or even months.

The observer comments on or analyzes the behaviors separately after studying the record. His or her task is to record the situation so that future readers can visualize what occurred (Cohen et al., 1983). Figure 5.2 is an example of a running record.

Running records are also used in connection with assessment of emergent literacy. When the teacher desires to acquire information about the child's current abilities and weaknesses in reading, the teacher may wish to listen to the child read and may record errors and corrections that are made as the child reads the passage. The teacher might mark on a copy of the material that the child is reading, using a systematic system of identifying errors such as reversals, substitutions, self-corrections, or omissions. As an alternative, the teacher might use a running record form separate from the passage being read. The intent is to conduct an informal assessment when the child is actually reading (Sulzby, 1993).

Specimen Record

The **specimen records** is very similar to a running record. It is even more detailed and precise. Beaty (1993) defines running records as informal methods used by teachers. Specimen records, in contrast, are used by researchers who are not part of classroom activities and who are removed from the children. Researchers may later code observation information to analyze the findings. For example, specimen records were used in a study of child care settings in Chicago. As part of the study, observation was used to determine caregiver behaviors. Researchers coded each utterance by a caregiver to a child, as well as every incident of playing, helping, teaching, touching, kissing, and hitting (Clark-Stewart, 1987).

Time Sampling

The purpose of **time sampling** is to record the frequency of a behavior for a designated period of time. The observer decides ahead of time what behaviors will be observed, what the time interval will be, and how the behaviors will be recorded. The observer observes these behaviors and records how many times they occur during preset, uniform time periods. Other behaviors that occur during the observation are ignored. After a number of samplings have been completed, the data are studied to determine when and perhaps why a behavior is occurring. The observer can use the information to help the child if a change in behavior is desired.

Child Name(s): <u>Christopher</u>
Age: <u>4</u>
Location: <u>KinderKare</u>
Date and Time: <u>June 21, 1994</u>   <u>8:40–9:10</u>
Observer: <u>Perlita</u>
Type of Development Observed: <u>Social and Cognitive</u>

Observation	Notes or Comments
Chris is playing with a toy. He says, "Kelly, can I keep it?" several times until he gets an answer. He moves on to a toy guitar and plays it while he supervises the other children by walking around the room. He tells everyone to sit down at the tables after the teacher says to.	Chris is polite to others. Chris is helping his classmates to follow the rules.
Chris sits by a friend and talks about eating granola bars. He watches and listens to the conversation on either side of him. He's still unaffected by the loud temper tantrum of another child. Then he notices her and watches. He tries to explain this behavior to the others by saying a plant was split.	Chris is interested in what others have to say. Chris tries to make sense of a child's behavior.
He follows teacher's directions. Then he decides he wants to be in on a secret. A boy shoves him away. Chris informs him that he *can* hear if he wants to. This has caused him to disobey the teacher. He has to sit out of the circle. He walks over to the chair, sits down, gets up immediately, comes back to the circle undetected by the teacher. He joins the circle.	Chris chooses appropriate ways to assert himself.

Figure 5.2
Example of a running record.

Time sampling may be used with young children because many of their behaviors are brief. By using time sampling, the observer can gain comprehensive information about the behavior. The length of the observation can be affected by the target behavior, the children's familiarity with the observer, the nature of the situ-

Observation	Notes or Comments
Chris tattles on a child hiding money. He is told to switch places and wants to know why. He gets up to push the chairs under the table without being asked directly. He wants to explain the temper tantrum to another child (it is still going on) who is curious.	Chris needs to know why he does some things.
Chris attends to the teacher's questions and the story that she is now reading. He begins to look around the circle and then back to the book. He plays with his socks and participates in the group answers to questions about the story (*Now One Foot, Now the Other Foot* by Tomie dePaola [he is in continuous motion with some part of his body during the story]). Now he becomes very still and attends to the story. He puts both hands over his ears when students remark about events in the story. He immediately makes his own remarks. He becomes very still again. The whole circle is quiet for the ending of the book.	Chris shows he has self-control. Chris responds to and sympathizes with the characters in the story.
As soon as the story is finished, Chris says, "I got a cut from a thorn bush." He sits very quietly but moves around. "How do we kill our plants over there?" he asks the teacher. (A plant was knocked off earlier.) "Not mine, not me!" he says.	

Figure 5.2 *(continued)*
Example of a running record.

ation, and the number of children to be observed (Webb, Campbell, Schwartz, & Sechrest, 1966).

Time sampling is frequently used by teachers or other school staff members when a child is behaving inappropriately at school—for example, one who behaves aggressively with other children and does not cooperate in classroom routines at certain times. It is used over a period of time during the hours of the daily schedule when the unwanted behavior occurs. After the time samples are studied, the teacher can determine what can be done to modify the behavior. Figure 5.3 is an example of time sampling as an observation method.

Event Sampling

Event sampling is used instead of time sampling when a behavior tends to occur in a particular setting rather than during a predictable time period. The behavior may occur at odd times or infrequently; event sampling is commonly used to discover its causes or results. The observer determines when the behavior is likely to occur and waits for it to take place. The drawback of this method is that if the event does not occur readily, the observer's time will be wasted.

Child Name(s): <u>Joanie</u>
Age: <u>5</u>
Location: <u>Rosewood School Kindergarten</u>
Date and Time: <u>May 17, 10:45–11:00</u>
Observer: <u>Susanna</u>
Type of Development Observed: <u>Joanie Has Difficulty Completing Tasks</u>

Event	Time	Notes or Comments
Art Center—leaves coloring activity on table unfinished	10:45	Some of Joanie's behaviors seem to be resulting from failure to follow procedures for use of materials.
Library—looks at book, returns it to shelf.	10:50	Behavior with the puzzles may come from frustration.
Manipulative Center—gets frustrated with puzzle, piles pieces in center—leaves on table. Pulls out Lego blocks, starts to play. When teacher signals to put toys away, Joanie leaves Lego blocks on table and joins other children.	10:55 11:00	Joanie may need help in putting away with verbal rewards for finishing a task and putting materials away. Encourage Joanie to get help with materials that are too hard.

Figure 5.3
Example of time sampling.

Because event sampling is a cause-and-effect type of observation, the observer is looking for clues that will assist in solving the child's problem. Bell and Low (1977) use *ABC analysis* with the observed incident to understand the cause of the behavior. *A* is the antecedent event, *B* is the target behavior, and *C* is the consequent event. Using ABC analysis with event sampling permits the observer to learn how to address the problem with the child. Figure 5.4 is an example of event sampling with ABC analysis to interpret the incident. Figure 5.5 is an observation form that is adaptable to various types of observations.

Checklists and Rating Scales

Although chapter 6 is devoted to checklists and rating scales, it is useful to include them in this discussion of observation techniques. A **checklist** is a list of sequential behaviors arranged in a system of categories. The observer can use the checklist to determine whether the child exhibits the behaviors or skills listed. The checklist is useful when many behaviors are to be observed. It can also be used fairly quickly and easily.

The **rating scale** provides a means to determine the degree to which the child exhibits a behavior or the quality of that behavior. Each trait is rated on a continuum, allowing the observer to decide where the child fits on the scale. Rating scales are helpful when the teacher needs to evaluate a wide range of behaviors at one time.

Child Name(s): Tamika
Age: 4
Location: May's Child Enrichment Center
Date and Time: 2/4   2:30–3:30
Observer: Marcy
Type of Development Observed: Social/Emotional
    Tamika uses frequent hitting behavior

Time	Antecedent Event	Behavior	Consequent Event
2:41	Tamika and Rosie are eating a snack. Rosie takes part of Tamika's cracker.	Tamika hits Rosie.	Rosie calls to the teacher.
3:20	John is looking at a book in the Library Center. Tamika asks for the book. John refuses.	Tamika grabs the book and hits John.	John hits back and takes back the book. Tamika gets another book and sits down.

Figure 5.4
Example of event sampling.

Name _____

Date _____

Time _____

Location _____

Child(ren) Observed _____

_____

Age _____

Type of Development Observed: _____

Type of Observation Used: _____

Purposes of Observation:

1.

2.

3.

Questions Answered:

1.

2.

3.

Description of Observation (Anecdotal, Time Sampling, Running Record, Event Sampling):

Summary of Important Behaviors Recorded and Comments:

Figure 5.5

Sample observation form.

OBSERVING DEVELOPMENT

Young children develop rapidly. At this time we need to consider the meaning of development in more detail. Development is continuous, sequential, and involves change over time.

Development can be defined, in part, as the process of change in an individual over time. As the individual ages, certain changes take place. Development is thus affected by the child's chronological age, rate of maturation, and individual experiences. Children of the same chronological age are not necessarily in the same stage or level of development, possibly because they mature at different rates and have different experiences and opportunities. The child who has many opportunities to climb, run, and jump in outdoor play may demonstrate advanced motor development skills, compared with the child who spends most play periods indoors.

Developmental change can be both quantitative and qualitative. Physical growth is quantitative and cumulative. New physical skills are added to those already present. Developmental change can also be qualitative. When changes in psychological characteristics such as speech, emotions, or intelligence occur, development is reorganized at a higher level.

Development is characterized as continuous. The individual is constantly changing. In quantitative change, the individual is continually adding new skills or abilities. In qualitative change, the individual is incorporating new development with existing characteristics to create more sophisticated psychological traits.

Finally, development is sequential. Each individual develops at a different rate; however, the sequence or pattern of development is the same. All children move through stages of development in the same sequence, whose characteristics are described by Bentzen (1985) as follows:

1. Stages or steps in development do not vary. Children do not skip a stage of development.
2. Children progress through the stages in the same order.
3. All children, regardless of cultural or social differences, progress through the stages in the same order. The stages are universal. (p. 21)

Physical Development

Preschool children are in the most important period of physical and motor development. Beginning with babies, who are in the initial stages of learning to control their bodies, physical development is rapid and continues into the primary school years.

Observations of physical development focus on both types of motor development: gross and fine. *Gross motor skills* refer to the movements and abilities of the large muscles of the body in physical activities such as walking, running, climbing, swinging, jumping, and throwing. Preschool children are in a period of mastering large motor skills. At play, they use play equipment and other activities to practice motor skills

Fine motor skills involve the body's small muscles—specifically, the hands and the fingers. These skills are used for eating, dressing, writing, using small construction toys, and performing many other tasks. They evolve after gross motor skills have been mastered.

Purposes for Observing Physical Development

Physical development is observed for the following reasons:

1. To learn how children develop gross and fine motor skills
2. To become familiar with the kinds of physical activities young children engage in as they practice the use of gross and fine motor skills
3. To become familiar with individual differences in physical development

Questions Answered by Observation of Physical Development

Physical development is observed to answer the following questions:

1. What are the child's physical characteristics? How do these characteristics affect the child's motor abilities?
2. What types of large motor activities does the child enjoy? What kinds of activities does the child use to exercise and develop gross motor skills?
3. What types of small motor activities does the child enjoy? What kinds of activities does the child use to develop and exercise fine motor skills?

Observation of children's movement activities can be useful in assessing physical development.

Social and Emotional Development

Social and emotional development are significant areas of development during the preschool years. In this period, the child moves from egocentricity to social interaction with others. When a child is able to use social behaviors, he or she influences others and is influenced by them. As children interact in various contexts, they develop and expand their repertoire of social skills.

Emotional development parallels and affects social development. The preschool child refines behaviors as he or she experiences such emotions as happiness, anger, joy, jealousy, and fear. According to Bentzen (1985), the most common emotions in preschool children are aggression, dependency, and fear. *Aggression* is a behavior intended to hurt another person or property. *Dependency* causes such behaviors as clinging, seeking approval, assistance, reassurance, and demands for attention. *Fear* includes behaviors such as crying and avoiding the feared situation.

Purposes for Observing Social and Emotional Development

Social and emotional development is observed for the following reasons:

1. To learn how children develop social skills
2. To become familiar with how children learn about social interactions
3. To understand how children differ in social skill development
4. To become familiar with the ways preschool children handle their emotions
5. To be aware of differences in children's emotional behaviors and responses

Questions Answered by Observations of Social and Emotional Development

Social and emotional development is observed to answer the following questions:

1. How do children demonstrate social awareness and prosocial skills?
2. How do children develop leadership skills? What behaviors make it easier to assume a leadership role?
3. How do children use different prosocial styles? How do they develop successful prosocial skills?
4. How does the child resolve conflicts? How is the behavior representative of the child's social and emotional development?
5. How does the child use and handle aggressive behaviors?
6. What kinds of events trigger dependence or fear?
7. What kinds of behaviors demonstrate the interdependence of social and emotional development?

Cognitive Development

Cognitive development, which stems from mental functioning, is concerned with how the child learns about and understands the world. Cognitive abilities develop as the child interacts with the environment. Our descriptions of cognitive development are derived largely from Piaget's theory of development.

Piaget described cognitive development in terms of stages. The quality of the child's thinking progresses as the child moves through the stages. The infant is in the sensorimotor stage, which lasts until about 18 months of age. During this stage, intellectual growth occurs through the senses and innate reflexive actions. In the latter part of the sensorimotor stage, symbolic thought develops that is characterized by improved memory.

Between the ages of 2 and 6 years, the child moves through the preoperations stage. In this stage, the ability to use language is developed. The child is egocentric, unable to view another person's perspective. Thinking is bounded by perception. Later, when the child reaches the stage of concrete operations, he or she is able to move beyond perceptual thinking. Cognitive abilities become qualitatively different. The child is now able to grasp concepts such as classification, seriation, one-to-one correspondence, and causality because he or she has attained conservation (Morrison, 1988).

The child's use of mental processes to understand knowledge develops gradually, and cognitive abilities evolve over a long period of time. Piaget attributed cognitive development to maturity, experiences, and social transmission. Therefore, the child's family, environment, and opportunities for experiences affect the development of cognitive abilities. Knowledge is reconstructed as the child organizes and restructures experiences to refine and expand his or her own understanding.

Purposes for Observing Cognitive Development

Cognitive development is observed for the following reasons:

1. To understand how children use their cognitive abilities to learn
2. To understand the differences in children's cognitive styles
3. To become familiar with how children develop the ability to use classification, seriation, and one-to-one correspondence
4. To understand how the child uses play and interaction with materials to extend his or her cognitive abilities
5. To become familiar with how children think and what they are capable of learning
6. To evaluate what children have learned

Questions Answered by Observation of Cognitive Development

Cognitive development is observed to answer the following questions:

1. How is the child's learning affected by his or her cognitive abilities?
2. How does the child use emerging cognitive abilities (conservation, one-to-one correspondence, seriation) naturally in classroom experiences?
3. How do children differ in cognitive development and cognitive characteristics?

4. How do classroom experiences affect the opportunities for cognitive development?
5. How is the child's cognitive knowledge demonstrated nonverbally?
6. What behaviors does the child exhibit to indicate that learning has occurred following classroom experiences and instruction?

Language Development

The acquisition of language is one of the major accomplishments of children during the preschool and primary grade years. During the first 8 years of life, the child rapidly acquires vocabulary, grammar, and syntax. As in other types of development, the child's use of language changes, increases, and is refined over a period of time.

Whereas babies begin using speech as single utterances, toddlers and preschoolers expand their repertoire into two words, three words, and increasingly complex statements. As the child's ability to use language expands to include questions and other grammatical elements, the child uses trial and error to approximate more closely the syntax and grammar of adult speech.

Language development is also related to cognitive development. When the child's thinking is egocentric, his or her language reflects this pattern. The egocentric child talks to him- or herself and does not use language to communicate with other children. The child who is shedding egocentric thinking uses socialized speech to communicate with others. He or she not only shares conversations with peers and adults but also listens and responds to what others are saying.

Purposes for Observing Language Development

Language development is observed for the following reasons:

1. To become aware of the child's ability to use language to communicate
2. To understand the difference between egocentric and socialized speech
3. To learn how the child uses syntax, grammar, and vocabulary in the process of expanding and refining his or her language
4. To become aware of differences in language development among individual children

Questions Answered by Observation of Language Development

Language development is observed to answer the following questions:

1. How does the child use language to practice using speech?
2. When do children tend to use egocentric speech? Socialized speech?
3. How does the extent of vocabulary vary among children?
4. What can be observed about the child's use of sentence structure?
5. How can errors in the use of language reveal the child's progress in refining language?

ADVANTAGES AND DISADVANTAGES OF USING OBSERVATION FOR EVALUATION

Observation is a valuable evaluation tool. Teachers may use it to gather the kind of information that may not be available from structured methods of measurement.

When observed, children are engaged in daily activities that are a natural part of the classroom routine. The observer is able to see the typical ways children respond to learning tasks, play activities, and individual and group lessons. The observer can notice the child's behaviors and the background factors that influence the behaviors.

Learning can also be evaluated by observation. The teacher can observe the child's responses in a group during a lesson or while the child engages in exploration with construction materials. Areas of development such as gross motor skills can be observed on the playground; language skills can be noted by listening to the language of two children in the art center.

An advantage of observation is that the observer can focus on the behavior or information that is needed. If a child is exhibiting aggression, the observer can focus on aggressive incidents to help the child use more appropriate behaviors in interactions with other children. If a child is beginning to use prosocial skills more effectively, the teacher can observe group interactions and encourage the child to continue to improve.

Although observation allows one to concentrate specific behaviors, it can also cause difficulties. The observer can miss details that make a significant difference in the quality of the data gathered. Because many incidents and behaviors may occur during the observation, the danger is that the observer may focus on the wrong behaviors. Or the observer may become less attentive during the observation period, resulting in variations in the information obtained (Webb et al., 1966).

Observer bias is another disadvantage. If the observer has preconceived notions about how the child behaves or performs, these ideas can affect the observer's interpretation of the information obtained from watching the child.

Observations can be misleading when the incident observed is taken out of context. Although an observed behavior is often brief, it must be understood in context. A frequent mistake of inexperienced observers is to interpret a single incident as a common occurrence. For example, the observer who witnesses a teacher losing patience with a child may interpret the incident as that teacher's normal behavior. In reality, however, this behavior may be rare. The presence of the observer can also affect children's behavior. Because children are aware that they are being watched, their behaviors may not be typical. As a result, the validity of the observation may be doubtful (Webb et al., 1966).

OBSERVATION GUIDELINES

For college students and others who have not previously conducted observations, certain guidelines are now presented. The observer seeking a site for observation needs to know how to go about finding a school or early childhood center and how to observe effectively once it has been selected.

Determining the Observation Site

The observation site depends on the type of observation to be done. First, the observer must determine the purpose of the observation. He or she will want to know that children at the school or early childhood center engage in the activities of interest to the observer. For example, if the observer wishes to see activities typical of a Montessori classroom, it would be wise to find out whether these activities will be taking place during the observation period. Once the purpose of the observation has been determined, the observer must decide on an optimum location. If the objective is to learn about creativity in the young child, it is frustrating to spend time in a program in which art experiences are limited or infrequent. Likewise, if the purpose is to observe behaviors in a child-centered environment, it would be inappropriate to visit a structured program directed by the teacher.

Once the center or school has been selected, the observer should contact it ahead of time. Although many settings welcome observers on a walk-in basis, most early childhood programs request or require advance notification. Some settings do not allow observers or schedule them in ways designed to protect children from interruptions. Some schools allow observations on certain days. Others wish to be contacted well in advance because many people wish to observe their program. Many child care centers schedule field trips frequently and wish to avoid inconveniencing their observers. Whatever the reason, it is best to contact the observation site before scheduling the observation.

Observer Behaviors during the Observation Visit

The observer is a guest of the center or school. Although the opportunity to study the children is important, it is also important to avoid disrupting activities in progress. The observer may want to share the purpose of the observation with staff members or the teacher in the classroom being visited. In addition, the observer should conduct the observation in a manner that is compatible with the teacher's style of leadership in the type of program being observed. For example, Montessori schools frequently restrict visitors to certain areas of the classroom and may discourage any interaction with the children. Another school or program may encourage the observer to talk to the children or to take part in their activities.

In most cases the observer should be unobtrusive. Because children are sensitive to the presence of visitors and may alter their behaviors when a stranger is in the room, observers can minimize such changes by drawing as little attention to their presence as possible. Observers may seat themselves in a position that does not draw the children's attention. Sometimes it is helpful to avoid looking at the children for a few minutes, until they become acclimated. Postponing the writing of observation notes for a few minutes may also help prevent disruption.

Dress can make a difference. Observers dressed in simple clothing of one color rather than bright garments with bold patterns are less likely to draw undue attention to their presence. Dress should also be appropriate. Clothing that is too casual may be offensive to the adults in the early childhood center. Observers should err on the side of being dressed too formally, rather than in an unprofessional manner (Irwin & Bushnell, 1980).

Ethics during the Observation Visit

Observers must be alert to the proper way to use the information gathered during an observation. The privacy of the children, the children's families, and school staff members must be considered. When individual children are observed, only the child's first name should be used. Information from any observation should be considered confidential and safeguarded from casual perusal by others. The child should not be discussed in an unprofessional manner with other observers, school staff members, or outsiders.

Avoiding Personal Bias

Personal bias can affect the observer's reaction to and report of an observation. If observers are aware of how their background and previous experiences can influence their report, they can avoid using personal opinion when analyzing the data collected during an observation.

One cause of observer bias is differences in value systems. It is easy to apply one's own value system when observing in a school. For example, a middle-class observer may misunderstand the nature of aggression exhibited by young children in an inner-city school. It is also possible to impose personal values on the language of a child from a home where cursing is a common form of communication. The observer needs to be aware of such possible biases and avoid them when interpreting observational information.

The observer's reaction to the site can also distort his or her use of observational data. Each observer has a perception of the characteristics of a "good" school or center. When observing an early childhood program that does not fit this definition, the observer may impose a negative interpretation on the information gathered. The reaction to the setting affects how the observer perceives the behaviors observed.

An observation can also be biased by the time of the observation or by the briefness of the visit. Observers frequently react to a teacher's behavior and conclude that the teacher always engages in practices that the observer considers inappropriate. Observers need to understand that what they see during a short visit may give them an incomplete, distorted perception of the teacher or setting. The observer would have to make many visits during different times of the day over a long period of time before being able to draw conclusions about the quality of teaching or the environment. One or two brief observations provide only a small glimpse of the nature of the teacher and the classroom visited.

SUMMARY

Although standardized tests are used to evaluate children's learning, informal strategies are also essential, particularly for use by classroom teachers. They provide a variety of evaluation methods by which teachers can acquire comprehensive information about their students' development and learning.

Informal evaluation methods include checklists and rating scales, teacher-designed activities and written tests, and observation. Each type of evaluation gives the teacher flexibility and variability in acquiring information needed to assess children's learning and development and to plan instruction to meet the needs of each student.

Observation is used to assess learning and to gather information regarding children's development. Because young children cannot demonstrate knowledge in a written test, teachers of preschool children use observation to learn about children's development, as well as about the knowledge the children have acquired.

Observations are of several types, each with a specific purpose. Observers can use anecdotal records, running records, time sampling, event sampling, and checklists and rating scales to gather information about young children.

REVIEW QUESTIONS

1. Why is it important to use informal evaluation methods, particularly with preschool and primary school children?
2. Explain how different types of informal evaluation provide unique kinds of information about young children.
3. How do the purposes of informal evaluation differ from the purposes of standardized testing?
4. Describe some ways that teachers can use informal evaluation measures for instructional planning.
5. What is diagnostic evaluation?
6. What are the differences between formative and summative evaluation?
7. Why do informal evaluation measures produce immediate results, compared with standardized test results?
8. How may informal measures be misused in elementary schools?
9. How may teachers be unaware of the proper use of formal and informal evaluation measures?

10. Describe some purposes of using observation techniques with preschool and school-age children.
11. Why is observation of development systematic and specific?
12. Explain the purposes of the different types of observation: (a) anecdotal records, (b) running records, (c) specimen records, (d) time sampling, (e) event sampling, and (f) checklists and rating scales. What is unique about specimen records?
13. How are other types of development related to the child's cognitive development?
14. How does egocentrism affect cognitive, social, and language development?
15. How can an observer's experience and skills affect the quality of the information gained from observing young children?

KEY TERMS

anecdotal record
checklist
event sampling
formative evaluation
rating scale

running record
specimen record
summative evaluation
time sampling

SUGGESTED ACTIVITY

Conduct three observations of development. Use a different category of development for each observation. Use a different type of observation for each, selected from anecdotal records, running records, time sampling, and event sampling. Use an adaptation of the sample observation form in Figure 5.5 for each of the three observations.

REFERENCES

BEATY, J. J. (1993). *Observing development of the young child.* New York: Merrill/Macmillan.

BELL, D., & LOW, R. M. (1977). *Observing and recording children's behavior.* Richland, WA: Performance Associates.

BENTZEN, W. R. (1985). *Seeing young children: A guide to observing and recording behavior.* Albany, NY: Delmar.

CALFEE, R. C. (1987). The school as a context for assessment of literacy. *The Reading Teacher, 40,* 738–743.

CLARK-STEWART, A. (1987). Predicting child development from child care forms and features: The Chicago study. In D. A. Phillips (Ed.), *Quality in child care: What does research tell us?* (pp. 21–41). Washington, DC: National Association for the Education of Young Children.

COHEN, D. H., STERN, V., & BALABAN, N. (1983). *Observing and recording the behavior of young children.* New York: Teachers College Press.

DOSSEY, J. A., MULLIS, I.V.S., LINDQUIST, M. M., & CHAMBERS. D. L. (1988). *The mathematics report card: Are we measuring up?* Princeton, NJ: Educational Testing Service.

DURKIN, D. (1987). Testing in the kindergarten. *The Reading Teacher, 40,* 766–770.

GOODWIN, W. R., & DRISCOLL, L. A. (1980). *Handbook for measurement and evaluation in early childhood education.* San Francisco: Jossey-Bass.

GOODWIN, W. R., & GOODWIN, L. D. (1993). Young children and measurement: Standardized and nonstandardized instruments in early education. In B. Spodek (Ed.), *Handbook of research on the education of young children* (pp. 441–463). New York: Macmillan.

IRWIN, D. M., & BUSHNELL, M. M. (1980). *Observational strategies for child study.* New York: Holt, Rinehart & Winston.

JOINER, L. M. (1977). *A technical analysis of the variation in screening instruments and programs in New York State.* ERIC: ED 154596.

KAMII, C. (1985a). Leading primary education toward excellence: Beyond worksheets and drill. *Young Children, 40,* 3–9.

KAMII, C. (1985b). *Young children reinvent arithmetic.* New York: Teachers College Press.

KAMII, C., & KAMII, M. (1990). Negative effects of achievement testing in mathematics. In C. Kamii (Ed.), *Achievement testing in the early grades: The games grown-ups play* (pp. 135–145). Washington, DC: National Association for the Education of Young Children.

MEISELS, S. J. (1987). Uses and abuses of developmental screening and school readiness testing. *Young Children, 42,* 4–6, 68–73.

MICHIGAN DEPARTMENT OF EDUCATION. (1984). *Superintendent's study group on early childhood education.* Lansing: Author.

MORRISON, G. (1988). *Education and development of infants, toddlers, and preschoolers.* Glenview, IL: Scott, Foresman.

NATIONAL ASSOCIATION FOR THE EDUCATION OF YOUNG CHILDREN (NAEYC). (1986). Position statement on developmentally appropriate practice in early childhood programs serving children from birth through age 8. *Young Children, 41,* 3–19.

NATIONAL ASSOCIATION FOR THE EDUCATION OF YOUNG CHILDREN (NAEYC). (1988). Position statement on standardized testing of young children 3 through 8 years of age. *Young Children, 43,* 42–47.

SCHICKEDANZ, J. A. (1989). The place of specific skills in preschool and kindergarten. In D. S. Strickland & L. M. Morrow (Eds.), *Emerging literacy: Young children learn to read and write* (pp. 96–106). Newark, DE: International Reading Association.

SMITH, J. K. (1990). Measurement issues in early literacy assessment. In L. M. Morrow & J. K. Smith (Eds.), *Assessment for instruction in early literacy* (pp. 62–74). Englewood Cliffs, NJ: Prentice-Hall.

SULZBY, E. (1990). Assessment of writing and children's language while writing. In L. M. Morrow & J. K. Smith (Eds.), *Assessment for instruction in early literacy* (pp. 83–109). Englewood Cliffs, NJ: Prentice-Hall.

SULZBY, E. (1993). *Teacher's guide to evaluation: Assessment handbook.* Glenview, IL: Scott, Foresman.

TEALE, W. H. (1988). Developmentally appropriate assessment of reading and writing in the early childhood classroom. *Elementary School Journal, 89,* 173–183.

TEALE, W. H. (1990). The promise and challenge of informal assessment in early literacy. In L. M. Morrow & J. K. Smith (Eds.), *Assessment for instruction in early literacy* (pp. 45–61). Englewood Cliffs, NJ: Prentice-Hall.

TEALE, W. H., HIEBERT, E. H., & CHITTENDEN, E. A. (1987). Assessing young children's literacy development. *The Reading Teacher, 40,* 772–777.

VALENCIA, S., & PEARSON, P. D. (1987). Reading assessment: Time for a change. *The Reading Teacher, 40,* 726–732.

WEBB, E. J., CAMPBELL, D. T., SCHWARTZ, R. D., & SECHREST, L. (1966). *Unobtrusive measures.* Chicago: Rand McNally.

WIGGINS, G. (1989). Teaching to the (authentic) test. *Educational Leadership, 46,* 41–47.

Chapter 6

Informal Measures: Checklists and Rating Scales

Chapter Objectives

As a result of reading this chapter you will be able to

1. describe purposes for using checklists for informal evaluation.
2. explain how developmental checklists are used with preschool children.
3. explain differences between the uses of checklists with preschool and primary grade children.
4. identify the four basic steps in checklist design.
5. discuss advantages and disadvantages of using checklists for informal evaluation.
6. describe purposes for using rating scales for informal evaluation.
7. discuss advantages and disadvantages for using rating scales.

In chapter 5 we considered the topic of informal measurement instruments and strategies. The purposes of informal measures were discussed, as well as their strengths and weaknesses. One informal evaluation strategy—observation—was described in detail. In this chapter we discuss another type of evaluation strategy that involves the use of teacher-designed instruments: *checklists* and *rating scales*. Because checklists are used more extensively than rating scales by early childhood and primary school teachers, we discuss them first. A description of rating scales follows so that the reader can understand how they are designed and used and how they differ from checklists.

CHECKLISTS

Purposes of Checklists

Checklists are made from a collection of learning objectives or indicators of development. The lists of items are arranged to give the user an overview of their sequence and of how they relate to each other. The lists of items are then organized into a checklist format so that the teacher can use them for various purposes in the instructional program. Because the checklists are representative of the curriculum for the grade level, they become a framework for assessment and evaluation, instructional planning, record keeping, and communicating with parents about what is being taught and how their child is progressing.

Using Checklists with Preschool Children

Children in the years from birth to age eight move rapidly through different stages of development. Doctors, psychologists, parents, and developmental specialists want to understand and monitor the development of individual children and groups of children. The developmental indicators for children at different stages and ages have been established; lists and checklists of these indicators can be used to monitor development. When evaluating a child's development, many types of professionals use a **developmental checklist** format to evaluate development and record the results.

Developmental checklists usually are organized into categories of development: physical, cognitive, and social. Physical development is frequently organized into fine and gross motor skills. Cognitive, or intellectual, development might include language development. Some checklists have language development as a separate category. Social development checklists can also be organized to include emotional development and development of social skills.

Preschool teachers use checklists to evaluate and record preschoolers' developmental progress. The individual child's developmental progress provides important clues to the kinds of experiences he or she needs and can enjoy. For instance, the teacher keeps track of the child's use of fine motor skills. After the child is able to use the fingers to grasp small objects, cutting activities may be introduced. In language development the teacher can evaluate the child's speaking vocabulary and use of syntax and thus choose the best stories to read to the child.

Teachers often use checklists to screen children who enter preschool programs or to select them for programs. Developmental or cognitive tasks are used to identify children with special needs. Because these checklists include behaviors that are characteristic of a stage of development, children who do not exhibit these behaviors can be referred for additional screening and testing (Morrison, 1988).

Checklists are also used to design learning experiences at the preschool level. The teacher surveys the list of learning objectives appropriate for that age group of children and uses the list to plan learning activities in the classroom. These checklists can be used to assess the child's progress in learning the objectives and to keep records of progress and further instructional needs. When talking to parents about the instructional program, the teacher can discuss what is being taught and how their child is benefiting from the learning experiences.

Using Checklists with School-Age Children

The use of checklists for primary school children is very similar to their use with preschool children. In fact, curriculum checklists can be a continuation of those used in the preschool grades. However, there are two differences. First, fewer developmental characteristics are recorded, and cognitive or academic objectives become more important. Second, school-age checklists become more differentiated in areas of learning. Whereas teachers are concerned with motor development, language development, social and emotional development, and cognitive development at the preschool level, at the primary level, curriculum content areas become more important. Thus, with primary grade checklists, objectives are more likely to be organized in terms of mathematics, language arts, science, social studies, and physical education.

Diagnosis of learning strengths and weaknesses in curriculum objectives becomes more important in the primary grades, and assessment of progress in learning may become more precise and segmented. Checklist objectives may appear on report cards as the format for reporting achievement to parents. Likewise, the checklist items may be representative of achievement test objectives, state-mandated objectives, textbook objectives, and locally selected objectives.

HOW CHECKLISTS ARE DESIGNED AND USED

Checklists of developmental and instructional objectives have been used in education for several decades. When educators and early childhood specialists worked with Head Start and other programs aimed at improving education for special populations of students, they developed outlines of educational objectives to describe the framework of learning that children should experience. Since that time, checklists have been further developed and used at all levels of education. Reading series designed for elementary grades include a scope and sequence of skills, and many school districts have a list of objectives for every course or grade level. Figure 6.1 is a typical checklist developed by a school district for mathematics at the elementary level.

The Texas Education Agency has developed a sequence of objectives for all school districts in the state to follow called *Essential Elements*. The Essential Elements range from preschool programs for four-year-olds to all content areas at the secondary level (Texas Education Agency, 1985). The prekindergarten and kindergarten Essential Elements Revision in 1991 describes the elements for intellectual development in kindergarten to include knowledge of communication and knowledge of integrated content. The Essential Elements for knowledge of integrated content are described as follows:

(2) Knowledge of integrated content. Integrated content acquired through processes of identifying, comparing and contrasting, classifying, sequencing and ordering, predicting cause/effect relationships, and exploring. The student shall be provided opportunities to:
   A. identify:
       i. match objects in one-to-one correspondence:
       ii. become familiar with a variety of geometric shapes in the environment:
       iii. use the senses to gain information about objects from the environment emphasizing color, texture, taste, odor, sound, size, shape, direction, motion, heat/cold and sink/float:
       iv. celebrate special events (e.g., birthdays, holidays) including those that are culturally related:
       v. identify ways people can help and learn from each other:
       vi. count objects orally through the highest number conceptualized:
       vii. recognize and describe changes in objects, organisms, and events:
       viii. recognize traffic and danger symbols critical to the safety of children: and
       ix. identify how basic human needs (e.g., food, clothing, shelter) are met by different people:

```
                            CHECKLIST
                            LEVEL 1

Name _____     Date _____

Age  _____    Math Teacher _____    Unit _____

                                                    Advisor _____

Dates
┌───┬───┐
│ I │ M │      NUMERATION
├───┴───┤      0. Knows vocabulary:
│       │         ___ same    ___ different    ___ more    ___ less    ___ before    ___ after
├───────┤      1. Rote Counts:
│       │         ___ 1  ___ 2  ___ 3  ___ 4  ___ 5  ___ 6  ___ 7  ___ 8  ___ 9  ___ 10
├───────┤      2. Counts Objects:
│       │         ___ 1  ___ 2  ___ 3  ___ 4  ___ 5  ___ 6  ___ 7  ___ 8  ___ 9  ___ 10
├───────┤      3. Matches equivalent sets with concrete objects.
├───────┤      4. Reproduces equivalent sets with concrete objects.
├───────┤      5. Matches like pairs
├───────┤      6. Matches unlike pairs
├───────┤      7. Compares nonequivalent sets with concrete objects
├───────┤      8. Reproduces nonequivalent sets with concrete objects
├───────┤      9. Sorts objects using more than one classifying characteristic
├───────┤      10. Matches numerals:
│       │          ___ 1  ___ 2  ___ 3  ___ 4  ___ 5  ___ 6  ___ 7  ___ 8  ___ 9  ___ 10
├───────┤      11. Identifies numerals:
│       │          ___ 1  ___ 2  ___ 3  ___ 4  ___ 5  ___ 6  ___ 7  ___ 8  ___ 9  ___ 10
├───────┤      12. Constructs sets for numerals:
│       │          ___ 1  ___ 2  ___ 3  ___ 4  ___ 5
├───────┤      13. Names numerals:
│       │          ___ 1  ___ 2  ___ 3  ___ 4  ___ 5
│       │
│       │      MEASUREMENT
│       │      A.  Linear
│       │          1. Matches objects
├───────┤             ___ size  ___ length  ___ width  ___ height
│       │          2. Compares objects
├───────┤             ___ size  ___ length  ___ width  ___ height
│       │          3. Seriates objects
├───────┤             ___ size  ___ length  ___ width  ___ height
│       │      B.  Weight
│       │          1. Classifies objects according to weight
├───────┤             ___ heavy  ___ light
│       │          2. Compares objects according to weight
├───────┤             ___ heavy  ___ light
├───────┤          3. Demonstrates use of balance
├───────┤          4. Identifies instruments for measuring weight
└───┴───┘
```

Figure 6.1
Mathematics checklist: level 1.

    B. compare and contrast:
       i. recognize that there are different types of families, homes, and communities:
      ii. compare sets using concepts such as more than, as many as, and less than to solve relevant problems:
     iii. recognize part and whole relationships with manipulative materials:
     iv. compare two concrete objects as to length, height, capacity, and size:
    C. classify:
       i. form groups by sorting and matching objects using more than one attribute: and
      ii. classify a variety of objects from the environment as being living or nonliving:
    D. sequence and order:
       i. copy, extend, and record linear patterns made up of concrete objects (e.g., beads, blocks): and
      ii. describe sequences in basic family and school routines:
    E. predict cause/effect relationships:
       i. observe changes in nature and daily events:
      ii. draw conclusions and predict outcomes based on experience: and
     iii. assist in setting class rules including rules of safety:
    F. explore:
       i. demonstrate creative thinking through fluency, flexibility, elaboration, creation of new ideas, spontaneity:
      ii. construct structures using blocks and other manipulative materials of different sizes and shapes:
     iii. explore basic concepts of weight, mass, and volume through water play, sand play, and cooking:
     iv. explore positional relationships such as under, over, above, below, in front of, far away from, inside, outside, between:
      v. interpret simple visuals (e.g., photographs, pictures, rebus charts): and
     vi. use sensory information to explore and recognize attributes, patterns, and relationships using concrete objects.

Preschool developmental checklists and curriculum checklists in the elementary grades are used in the same manner for the same purposes; however, developmental checklists add the developmental dimension to curriculum objectives (Wortham, 1984). Because the young child's developmental level is an important factor in determining the kinds of experiences the teacher will use, our discussion of the purposes of checklists includes the implications of child development during the early childhood years. Those purposes are as follows:

1. To understand development
2. To serve as a framework for curriculum development
3. To assess and evaluate development and learning

Checklists As a Guide to Understand Development

All developmental checklists are organized to describe different areas of growth, including social, motor, and cognitive development. The checklist items in each area for each age or developmental level indicate how the child is progressing through maturation and experiences. When teachers, caregivers, and parents look at the checklists, they can trace the sequence of development and also be realistic in their expectations for children. See, for example, the *Frost Wortham Developmental Checklist* (Wortham, 1984) in Figure 6.2. The *Social Play and Socializing Checklist* for preschool children is divided into three levels. Level III roughly corresponds to children at age three and describes characteristics of social development for children at that developmental level. Levels IV and V describe social development as children move through more advanced levels of development.

Checklists As a Guide to Develop Curriculum

Because developmental checklists describe all facets of development, they can serve as a guide in planning learning experiences for young children. Curriculum is not necessarily described as content areas such as science, art, or social studies, as these are commonly organized in elementary school; rather, it follows the experiences and opportunities that young children should have in the early childhood years. Thus teachers and caregivers who study the objectives on the checklists have guides for learning activities that will be appropriate for their children.

Because checklists are organized by developmental level or age, they also serve as a guide for sequencing learning. Teachers can match the experiences they wish to use with the checklist to determine whether they are using the correct level of complexity or difficulty. They can determine what came before in learning or development and what should come next. The Program Framework for the Houghton Mifflin reading program, *Houghton Mifflin Reading: The Literature Experience* (Houghton Mifflin, 1993), shown in Figure 6.3, includes objectives and skills for reading, literature, and writing. By studying the range of concepts to be taught, the teacher can plan to teach those concepts within his or her instructional program by using both the materials supplied with the Houghton Mifflin program and the experiences he or she has designed for the children. Moreover, because the framework includes all grades from kindergarten through eighth grade, teachers can see whether the program addresses each item in the framework at different grade levels.

Developmental checklists help teachers and caregivers plan for a balance of activities. With the current emphasis on academic subjects even in preschool programs, teachers feel compelled to develop an instructional program that is limited to readiness for reading, writing, and mathematics. Preschool teachers are caught between the emphasis on "basics" and developmentally appropriate instruction that recognizes that young children learn through active learning based on interaction with concrete materials. Developmental checklists help the preschool teacher maintain a perspective between developmentally appropriate instruction and pressures to prepare children for first grade. Inclusion of developmental experiences helps the teacher ensure a balanced curriculum that is best for the children's level of development.

In planning the curriculum and instruction in early childhood or preschool programs, teachers must incorporate the use of learning centers in classroom

FROST WORTHAM DEVELOPMENTAL CHECKLIST

SOCIAL PLAY AND SOCIALIZING — PRESCHOOL

Color code: Green	Introduced	Progress	Mastery
LEVEL III			
1. Engages in independent play			
2. Engages in parallel play			
3. Plays briefly with peers			
4. Recognizes the needs of others			
5. Shows sympathy for others			
6. Attends to an activity for ten to fifteen minutes			
7. Sings simple songs			
LEVEL IV			
1. Leaves the mother readily			
2. Converses with other children			
3. Converses with adults			
4. Plays with peers			
5. Cooperates in classroom routines			
6. Takes turns and shares			
7. Replaces materials after use			
8. Takes care of personal belongings			
9. Respects the property of others			
10. Attends to an activity for fifteen to twenty minutes			
11. Engages in group activities			
12. Sings with a group			
13. Is sensitive to praise and criticism			
LEVEL V			
1. Completes most self-initiated projects			
2. Works and plays with limited supervision			
3. Engages in cooperative play			
4. Listens while peers speak			
5. Follows multiple and delayed directions			
6. Carries out special responsibilities (for example, feeding animals)			
7. Listens and follows the suggestions of adults			
8. Enjoys talking with adults			
9. Can sustain an attention span for a variety of duties			
10. Evaluates his or her work and suggests improvements			

Figure 6.2
Frost Wortham Developmental Checklist.
Source: Wortham, 1984. Developed by Joe Frost and Sue Wortham. Used by permission of Joe L. Frost.

Houghton Mifflin Reading
The Literature Experience
Program Framework

COMPREHENDING	K	1	2	3	4	5	6	7	8
Comprehension Skills									
Categorizing/Clarifying	✓	✓	✓	✓	✓	✓	✓	✓	✓
Cause-Effect	✓	✓	✓	✓	✓	✓	✓	✓	✓
Compare/Contrast	✓	✓	✓	✓	✓	✓	✓	✓	✓
Draws conclusions	✓	✓	✓	✓	✓	✓	✓	✓	✓
Fact/Opinion			✓	✓	✓	✓	✓	✓	✓
Fantasy/Realism	✓	✓	✓	✓	✓	✓	✓	✓	✓
Follows directions	✓	✓	✓	✓	✓	✓	✓	✓	✓
Inferencing	✓	✓	✓	✓	✓	✓	✓	✓	✓
Main Idea/Topic		✓	✓	✓	✓	✓	✓	✓	✓
Noting details	✓	✓	✓	✓	✓	✓	✓	✓	✓
Predicting outcomes	✓	✓	✓	✓	✓	✓	✓	✓	✓
Sequence	✓	✓	✓	✓	✓	✓	✓	✓	✓
Summarizing	✓	✓	✓	✓	✓	✓	✓	✓	✓
Story organization	✓	✓	✓	✓	✓	✓	✓	✓	✓
Text organization		✓	✓	✓	✓	✓	✓	✓	✓
Comprehension Strategies									
Reading new words	✓	✓	✓	✓	✓	✓	✓	✓	✓
Preview and Predict	✓	✓	✓	✓	✓	✓	✓	✓	✓
Story map prediction			✓	✓	✓	✓			
Preview and Self-Question		✓	✓	✓	✓	✓	✓	✓	✓
Stop and Think		✓	✓	✓	✓	✓	✓	✓	✓
Reread		✓	✓	✓	✓	✓	✓	✓	✓
Read ahead		✓	✓	✓	✓	✓	✓	✓	✓
Adjusts reading rate		✓	✓	✓	✓	✓	✓	✓	✓
Skims, scans				✓	✓	✓	✓	✓	✓
Summarizing stories		✓	✓	✓	✓	✓	✓	✓	✓
Summarizing information		✓	✓	✓	✓	✓	✓	✓	✓
K-W-L, SQ3R, SQP3R				✓	✓	✓	✓	✓	✓
Critical Reading/Thinking	✓	✓	✓	✓	✓	✓	✓	✓	✓
Responding to Literature									
Generates questions	✓	✓	✓	✓	✓	✓	✓	✓	✓
Discusses	✓	✓	✓	✓	✓	✓	✓	✓	✓
Dramatizes	✓	✓	✓	✓	✓	✓	✓	✓	✓
Draws or paints	✓	✓	✓	✓	✓	✓	✓	✓	✓
Retells stories	✓	✓	✓	✓	✓	✓	✓	✓	✓
Writes a response	✓	✓	✓	✓	✓	✓	✓	✓	✓
Shares ideas and reactions	✓	✓	✓	✓	✓	✓	✓	✓	✓
Answers questions	✓	✓	✓	✓	✓	✓	✓	✓	✓

COMPREHENDING (Cont.)	K	1	2	3	4	5	6	7	8
Evaluating/Critical Thinking									
Fantasy/Realism	✓	✓	✓	✓	✓	✓	✓	✓	✓
Fiction/Nonfiction		✓	✓	✓	✓	✓	✓	✓	✓
Fact/Opinion			✓	✓	✓	✓	✓	✓	
Compare/Contrast	✓	✓	✓	✓	✓	✓	✓	✓	✓
Important details	✓	✓	✓	✓	✓	✓	✓	✓	✓
Point of view			✓	✓	✓	✓	✓	✓	✓
Author qualifications					✓	✓	✓	✓	✓
Bias/Assumption							✓	✓	✓
Writes a response/critique	✓	✓	✓	✓	✓	✓	✓	✓	✓
Problem solving	✓	✓	✓	✓	✓	✓	✓	✓	✓
Critical Reading/Thinking	✓	✓	✓	✓	✓	✓	✓	✓	✓

PHONICS/DECODING/WORD MEANING

Context	K	1	2	3	4	5	6	7	8
Oral language	✓	✓	✓	✓	✓	✓	✓	✓	✓
Picture clues	✓	✓	✓	✓	✓	✓			
Printed language	✓	✓	✓	✓	✓	✓	✓	✓	✓
Context plus phonics	✓	✓	✓	✓	✓	✓	✓	✓	✓
Flexible combination of context, phonics, structural analysis, and analogy		✓	✓	✓	✓	✓	✓	✓	✓
Phonics/Decoding									
Consonants (Initial)	✓	✓	✓	✓	✓	✓	✓	✓	✓
Consonants (Final)		✓	✓	✓	✓	✓	✓	✓	✓
Phonograms	✓	✓	✓	✓	✓	✓	✓	✓	✓
Short vowels	✓	✓	✓	✓	✓	✓	✓	✓	✓
Long vowels		✓	✓	✓	✓	✓	✓	✓	✓
Consonant clusters		✓	✓	✓	✓	✓	✓	✓	✓
Consonant digraphs		✓	✓	✓	✓	✓	✓	✓	✓
Vowel pairs		✓	✓	✓	✓	✓	✓	✓	✓
Decoding/Structural Analysis									
Basic words		✓	✓	✓	✓	✓	✓	✓	✓
Inflected forms		✓	✓	✓	✓	✓	✓	✓	✓
Contractions		✓	✓	✓	✓	✓	✓	✓	
Compound words		✓	✓	✓	✓	✓	✓	✓	✓
Syllabication		✓	✓	✓	✓	✓	✓	✓	✓
Prefixes/Suffixes		✓	✓	✓	✓	✓	✓	✓	✓
Greek word parts					✓	✓	✓	✓	✓
Latin roots					✓	✓	✓	✓	✓

Figure 6.3
Houghton Mifflin Program Framework.

PHONICS/DECODING WORD MEANING (Cont.)

	K	1	2	3	4	5	6	7	8
Vocabulary/Word Meaning									
Categorizes	✓	✓	✓	✓	✓	✓	✓	✓	✓
Classifies	✓	✓	✓	✓	✓	✓	✓	✓	✓
Synonyms/Antonyms		✓	✓	✓	✓	✓	✓	✓	✓
Multiple meanings, Homographs		✓	✓	✓	✓	✓	✓	✓	✓
Homonyms, Homophones		✓	✓	✓	✓	✓	✓	✓	✓
Connotation, Denotation							✓	✓	✓
Developing selection vocabulary		✓	✓	✓	✓	✓	✓	✓	✓
Vocabulary expansion	✓	✓	✓	✓	✓	✓	✓	✓	✓

STUDY SKILLS

	K	1	2	3	4	5	6	7	8
Locating Information									
Alphabetical order		✓	✓	✓	✓	✓	✓	✓	✓
Glossary/Dictionary		✓	✓	✓	✓	✓	✓	✓	✓
Encyclopedia			✓	✓	✓	✓	✓	✓	✓
Graphic aids		✓	✓	✓	✓	✓	✓	✓	✓
Parts of book			✓	✓	✓	✓	✓	✓	✓
Special reference sources (globe, almanac, atlas, thesaurus)			✓	✓	✓	✓	✓	✓	✓
Library Skills		✓	✓	✓	✓	✓	✓	✓	✓
Organizing/Remembering Information									
Follows directions	✓	✓	✓	✓	✓	✓	✓	✓	✓
Categorizing/Classifying		✓	✓	✓	✓	✓	✓	✓	✓
Text organization		✓	✓	✓	✓	✓	✓	✓	✓
Rate of reading		✓	✓	✓	✓	✓	✓	✓	✓
Graphic aids		✓	✓	✓	✓	✓	✓	✓	✓
Note taking			✓	✓	✓	✓	✓	✓	✓
Outlines					✓	✓	✓	✓	✓
Synthesizing					✓	✓	✓	✓	✓
Report Writing			✓	✓	✓	✓	✓	✓	✓
Summarizing		✓	✓	✓	✓	✓	✓	✓	✓
Study strategies			✓	✓	✓	✓	✓	✓	✓
Test-taking strategies		✓	✓	✓	✓	✓	✓	✓	✓

COMPOSING/WRITING

	K	1	2	3	4	5	6	7	8
Writing Process									
Prewriting	✓	✓	✓	✓	✓	✓	✓	✓	✓
Drafting	✓	✓	✓	✓	✓	✓	✓	✓	✓
Revising		✓	✓	✓	✓	✓	✓	✓	✓
Proofreading		✓	✓	✓	✓	✓	✓	✓	✓
Publishing	✓	✓	✓	✓	✓	✓	✓	✓	✓
Modes of Writing									
Informative/Descriptive		✓	✓	✓	✓	✓	✓	✓	✓
Informative/Narrative		✓	✓	✓	✓	✓	✓	✓	✓
Expressive/Narrative		✓	✓	✓	✓	✓	✓	✓	
Informative/Classificatory		✓	✓	✓	✓	✓	✓	✓	
Persuasive/Descriptive		✓	✓	✓	✓	✓	✓	✓	✓
Persuasive/Classificatory							✓	✓	✓

LITERATURE

	K	1	2	3	4	5	6	7	8
Types of Literature									
Fantasy	✓	✓	✓	✓	✓	✓	✓	✓	✓
Realistic fiction	✓	✓	✓	✓	✓	✓	✓	✓	✓
Nonfiction	✓	✓	✓	✓	✓	✓	✓	✓	✓
Poetry	✓	✓	✓	✓	✓	✓	✓	✓	✓
Folklore (Folktale, Fable, Fairy Tale, Myth, Legend, Tall Tale)	✓	✓	✓	✓	✓	✓	✓	✓	✓
Biography/Autobiography			✓	✓	✓	✓	✓	✓	✓
Historical Fiction					✓	✓		✓	
Content area reading	✓	✓	✓	✓	✓	✓	✓	✓	
Author's Craft									
Repetition, Rhythm, Rhyme	✓	✓	✓	✓	✓	✓	✓	✓	✓
Dialogue	✓	✓	✓	✓	✓	✓	✓	✓	✓
Exaggeration/Humor	✓	✓	✓	✓	✓	✓	✓	✓	✓
Figurative language (Similes, Metaphors, Personification)		✓	✓	✓	✓	✓	✓	✓	✓
Alliteration		✓	✓	✓	✓	✓	✓	✓	✓
Onomatopoeia		✓	✓	✓	✓	✓	✓	✓	✓
Idioms		✓	✓	✓	✓	✓	✓	✓	✓
Imagery	✓	✓	✓	✓	✓	✓	✓	✓	✓
Flashback						✓	✓	✓	✓
Foreshadowing						✓	✓	✓	✓
Formal/Informal language						✓	✓	✓	✓
Denotation/Connotation							✓	✓	✓

Figure 6.3 (continued)
Houghton Mifflin Program Framework.

Source: From WITH A CRASH AND A BANG! Teacher's Book from HOUGHTON MIFFLIN READING by Pikulski, et al. Copyright © 1993 by Houghton Mifflin Company. Reprinted by permission of Houghton Mifflin Company. All rights reserved.

experiences. Developmental checklists with a sequence of objectives provide guidelines for selecting the materials to place in centers to support curriculum and instruction. For example, for five-year-olds the sequence on a checklist for fine motor development might be similar to the following:

Cuts and pastes creative designs

Creates recognizable objects with clay

Ties shoes

Puts together a twenty-piece puzzle

Creates or copies a pegboard design

Copies letters

Can copy numerals (Wortham, 1984, p. 33)

By studying the sequence, the teacher can determine that activities for cutting and pasting should be part of center activities earlier in the year. Later, when fine motor skills are better developed, opportunities to copy letters and numerals should be included in centers to complement instructional activities in writing. Thus developmental checklists help teachers decide what to select for learning centers as the year progresses. Early in the year the teacher may introduce simple toys, puzzles, and construction materials in centers. Later, more complex, challenging activities and materials are more appropriate. As the year progresses, the materials available in the centers should be compatible with developmental growth.

Because the rate of development varies from child to child, the sequence of development reflected in the checklists allows the teacher to vary materials for individual children. Certain games, activities, and materials can be placed in the centers and designated for a particular child's needs or interests. Materials for experiences placed in centers provide a means of individualizing learning, with checklists serving as the guide for a sequence from simple to complex. The more complex concepts or objectives lead to the selection of materials for the child whose development is more advanced.

Checklists As a Guide to Evaluate Learning and Development

Having information on how children are growing and learning is one of the important requirements of an early childhood program. Teachers must know how children's development and learning are progressing and must be able to discuss it with parents, other teachers, and staff members of other schools that later may teach the child. Figure 6.2, the *Social Play and Socializing Checklist,* is an example of a checklist that may be used to evaluate a child's social development (Wortham, 1984).

Because the checklists cover all kinds of development, they allow teachers to keep track of individual children and groups of children. When teachers keep consistent records on individual children, they can give parents information about the child's progress. Parents then have a clear idea of what is happening in school and what their child is accomplishing.

Teachers who use developmental checklists to assess, evaluate, and record children's progress may eventually realize that they have a better understanding of each child in the class than they had before. If a teacher uses a checklist for gross motor skills to keep track of large muscle development in his or her students, systematic observation of students engaged in physical activities will make the teacher more aware of how each child is progressing and reveal individual differences in development. When reporting to one child's parent, for example, the teacher may discuss the improvement in throwing and catching a ball. In another case, the teacher may focus on the child's ability to ride a bicycle or to jump rope.

EVALUATING AND ASSESSING WITH CHECKLISTS

If a checklist is used as a framework for curriculum development and instruction, it can also be used for evaluation and assessment. The curriculum objectives used to plan instructional experiences can also be used to evaluate the children's performance on the same objectives. After a series of activities is used to provide opportunities to work with new concepts or skills, the children are assessed to determine how successful they were in learning the new skill or information. Evaluation can be accomplished through observation, during ongoing learning activities, and through specific assessment tasks.

Evaluating Checklist Objectives by Observation

Observing young children is the most valuable method of understanding them. Because children in early childhood programs are active learners, their progress is best assessed by watching their behaviors, rather than by using a test. If you look at the items on developmental checklists, you will see that some objectives or indicators of development can be evaluated only by observing the child. For example, in the area of language development, if a teacher wants to know whether a child is using complete sentences, he or she observes the child in a play activity and listens for examples of language. Likewise, if the teacher is interested in evaluating social development, he or she will observe the children playing outdoors to determine whether they engage mostly in solitary or parallel play or whether individual children play cooperatively as part of a group.

Observation can be incidental or planned. The teacher may decide to evaluate during center time and decide which items on a checklist can be evaluated by observing children in the art center or the manipulative center. The teacher then places materials in those centers that are needed to observe specific behaviors and records which children are able to use the materials in the desired manner. For example, the ability to cut with scissors can be assessed by having a cutting activity in the art center. As an alternative, the teacher might use a cutting activity with an entire group and observe how each child is performing during the activity.

Teachers frequently use observation to assess checklist objectives.

Evaluating Checklist Objectives with Learning Activities

Some objectives cannot be assessed through observation alone. Objectives in a cognitive area such as mathematics may require a specific learning activity for evaluation. However, instead of having a separate assessment task, the teacher can have children demonstrate their performance on a particular skill as a part of the lesson being conducted. The teacher notes which children demonstrate understanding of the concept or mastery of the skill during the lesson. If a mathematics objective to be assessed involves understanding numbers through five, the teacher might instruct a small group of children to make groups of objects ranging from one to five and note which children are successful.

Evaluating Checklist Objectives with Specific Tasks

Sometimes, at the beginning or end of a school year or grading period, the teacher will want to conduct a systematic assessment. He or she will assess a series of objectives at one time. In this situation, the teacher determines a number of objectives that can be evaluated at one time and devises tasks or activities to conduct with a child or a small group of children. The activities are presented in the same fashion as in a lesson, but the teacher has the additional purpose of updating and recording progress. Assessment tasks are organized on the basis of children's previous progress and will vary among groups of children. Some children will perform one group of activities; others will have a completely different set of activities related to a different set of objectives.

There is a time and place for each type of evaluation. The more experience a teacher has in including assessment in the instructional program, the easier it becomes. It is important to use the easiest and least time-consuming strategy whenever possible.

STEPS IN CHECKLIST DESIGN

A checklist is an outline or framework of development and curriculum. When designing a checklist, the developer first determines the major categories that will be included. Thereafter, development follows four basic steps:

1. Identification of the skills to be included
2. Separate listing of target behaviors
3. Sequential organization of the checklist
4. Record keeping

Identification of the Skills to Be Included

The teacher studies each checklist category and determines the specific objectives or skills that will be included. Using established developmental norms or learning objectives, the teacher decides how to adapt them for his or her needs. For example, on a checklist for language development and reading under the category of Language and Vocabulary, the following objectives might be included:

Listens to and follows verbal directions

Identifies the concept of word

Identifies the concept of letter

Invents a story for a picture book

Separate Listing of Target Behaviors

If a series of behaviors or items is included in an objective, the target behaviors should be listed separately so that they can be recorded separately (Irwin & Bushnell, 1980). For the objective of identifying coins, the best way to write the item would be as follows:

Identifies:
  penny
  nickel
  dime
  quarter

When the teacher is assessing the child's knowledge of coins, he or she may find that the child knows some of the coins but not others. Information can be recorded on the mastery status of each coin.

CONFLICTS ABOUT INFORMAL ASSESSMENT RESULTS

Mary Howell and Francesca Carrillo are having a heated argument in the teacher's lounge. Mary teaches first grade, and Francesca teaches second grade. At issue is the checklist from the first grade that is placed in students' folders at the end of the year, before they are promoted to second grade. Francesca's complaint is that the first-grade teachers' assessments are inaccurate. They have indicated that students accomplished first-grade objectives, but these objectives have to be retaught in the second grade because the students either never know them or forget them over the summer.

Mary clearly is offended that her professionalism has been questioned. She defends the process by which first-grade teachers determine whether the children have learned the objectives. Josie, another teacher sitting nearby, says nothing. Under her breath, she mutters, "It's all a waste of time. I wait until the end of the year and then mark them all off, anyway."

After Mary and Francesca have left, the conversation about the merits of using checklists for assessment and record keeping continues. Gunther Sachs, a third-grade teacher, supports the use of checklists for evaluating the students. He observes that he uses the checklist record when having conferences with parents. He believes that the parents gain a better understanding of what their child is learning in school when he can tell them how the child is progressing on curriculum objectives listed on the checklist. Lily Wong, another third-grade teacher, strongly disagrees. Her experience with the checklists leads her to believe that record keeping takes a great deal of time that she would rather use to plan lessons and design more interesting and challenging learning activities for her students.

Sequential Organization of the Checklist

The checklist should be organized in a sequential manner. Checklist items should be arranged in order of difficulty or complexity. If the checklist is sequenced correctly, the order of difficulty should be obvious. For example, the ability to count on a mathematics checklist might be listed as "Counts by rote from 1 to 10." At the next higher level, the checklist item would be "Counts by rote from 1 to 50."

Record Keeping

A system of record keeping must be devised. Because a checklist indicates the objectives for curriculum development or developmental characteristics, it must have a method of recording the status of the items. Although many record-keeping strategies have been used, commonly two columns indicate that the child either has or has not mastered the skill or behavior. Two types of indicators frequently used are a simple *Yes/No* or *Mastery/Nonmastery*. Another approach is to record the date when the concept was introduced and the date when it was mastered. In this instance the columns would be headed *Introduced/Mastery* or could indicate an intermediate step in evaluation with three columns headed *Introduced/Progress/Mastery*. Figure 6.4 is a checklist with two columns for record keeping in motor development. In this example the columns indicate when the assess-

MARKING N = Needs improvement S = Satisfactory		Task 1		Task 2		Task 3		Task 4		Task 5		Task 6		Task 7	
		Identify body parts		Walking board		Hopping		Jump and land		Obstacle course		Ball catch		Optional	
NAME		Fall	Spr.	Fall	Spr.	Fall	Spr.	Fall	Spr.	Fall	Spr.	Fall	Spr.	Fall	Spr.
1															
2															
3															
4															
5															
6															
7															
8															
9															
10															
11															
12															
13															
14															
15															
16															
17															
18															
19															
20															
21															
22															
23															
24															
25															
26															
27															
28															
29															
30															

Photocopy this page to make your own record sheet.

Figure 6.4
Perceptual Motor Evaluation Scale: record sheet.
Source: Capon, 1975

ment was conducted. The codes *N = Needs Improvement* and *S = Satisfactory* are used to indicate the child's progress in mastery (Capon, 1975).

The teacher can use a checklist to record individual or group progress. Whether the teacher uses observation, lesson activities, or tasks for assessment, the checklist is used to keep a record of the child's progress. Checklist information can be shared periodically with parents to keep them informed about what their child is learning or is able to do.

Checklists can also be used to keep a record of all of the children in the class or group. The group record lists all of the children's names, as well as the checklist objectives. By transferring information about individual children to a master or group record, the teacher can plan instruction for groups of children as the group record indicates their common needs. Figure 6.5 is a checklist record for a group of students in language development.

ADVANTAGES AND DISADVANTAGES OF USING CHECKLISTS

Using checklists for assessment and evaluation has definite advantages and disadvantages or problems. Teachers must weigh both sides before deciding how extensively they will use checklists for measurement and record-keeping purposes.

Advantages of Using Checklists

Checklists are easy to use. Because they require little instruction or training, teachers can quickly learn to use them. Unlike standardized tests, they are available whenever evaluation is needed.

Checklists are flexible and can be used with a variety of assessment strategies. The teacher can evaluate in the most convenient manner and obtain the needed information. Because of this flexibility, the teacher can combine assessment strategies when more than one assessment is indicated.

Behaviors can be recorded frequently; checklists are always at hand. Whenever the teacher has new information, he or she can update records. Unlike paper-and-pencil tests or formal tests, the teacher does not have to wait for a testing opportunity to determine whether the child has mastered an objective.

Disadvantages of Using Checklists

Checklists can be time-consuming to use. Particularly when teachers are just beginning to use checklists, they report that keeping records current on checklists reduces the time spent with children. Teachers have to become proficient in using checklists without impinging on teaching time.

Teachers may find it difficult to get started. When they are accustomed to teaching without the use of checklists, teachers often find it difficult to adapt their teaching and evaluation behaviors to include checklists. In addition, teachers can have too many checklists. They become frustrated by multiple checklists that overwhelm them with assessment and record keeping.

NAME	LANGUAGE ABILITY													FOLLOWING DIRECTIONS			
	1. Shares personal experiences	2. Voluntarily participates	3. Voluntarily answers	4. Tells observed activity	5. Answers factual questions	6. Answers probing questions	7. Answers higher order questions	8. Answers divergent questions	9. Problem solving	10. Asks factual questions	11. Interprets story picture	12. Comprehension	13. Attention span	14. Follows simple directions	15. Carries messages	16. Two or more directions	17. Makes simple object with specified materials

Figure 6.5
Language arts: class record sheet.

Some teachers may not consider assessment strategies used with checklists as valid measures of development and learning. For some teachers, particularly those in the primary grades, who are accustomed to conducting a test for evaluation, the observation and activity strategies used to measure progress may seem inconclusive. They may feel the need for more concrete evidence of mastery of learning objectives for accountability.

Checklists do not indicate how well a child performs. Unlike a paper-and-pencil test that can be used to record levels of mastery, checklists indicate only whether the child can perform adequately. For teachers who are required to give grades at the elementary level, checklists can be an incomplete strategy for assessment (Irwin & Bushnell, 1980).

Checklists themselves are not an assessment instrument. They are a format for organizing learning objectives or developmental indicators. The teacher's implementation of evaluation strategies by using a checklist makes it a tool for evaluation. In addition, recording the presence or absence of a behavior is not the main purpose of the checklist. The significant factor is what the teacher does with the assessment information recorded. If the information gained from evaluating the objectives is not used for instructional planning and implementation followed by further ongoing evaluation, the checklist does not improve learning and development.

RATING SCALES

Rating scales are similar to checklists; however, there are important differences. Whereas checklists are used to indicate whether a behavior is present or absent, rating scales require the rater to make a qualitative judgment about the extent to which a behavior is present. A rating scale consists of a set of characteristics or qualities to be judged by using a systematic procedure. Rating scales are of many forms; **numerical** and **graphic rating scales** seem to be used most frequently.

Types of Rating Scales

Numerical Rating Scales

Numerical rating scales are among the easiest rating scales to use. The rater marks a number to indicate the degree to which a characteristic is present. A sequence of numbers is assigned to descriptive categories. The rater's judgment is required to rate the characteristic. One common numerical system is as follows:

1-unsatisfactory

2-below average

3-average

4-above average

5-outstanding

The numerical rating system might be used to evaluate classroom behaviors in elementary students as follows:

1. To what extent does the student complete assigned work?
   1 2 3 4 5
2. To what extent does the student cooperate with group activities?
   1 2 3 4 5

Numerical scales become difficult to use when there is little agreement on what the numbers represent. The interpretation of the scale may vary.

Numerical rating scales are useful in recording progress in emerging progress in reading. In Figure 6.6 four categories of reading characteristics are assessed by using the numerical categories of limited, below expectation, average, above average, and outstanding (Farr, 1993). A summary assessment uses three descriptors to rate progress.

Graphic Rating Scales

Graphic rating scales function as continuums. A set of categories is described at certain points along the line, but the rater can mark his or her judgment at any location on the line. Commonly used descriptors for graphic rating scales are as follows:

never

seldom

occasionally

frequently

always

The classroom behaviors described earlier would be evaluated on a graphic rating scale as follows:

1. To what extent does the student complete assigned work?
   never   seldom   occasionally   frequently   always
2. To what extent does the student cooperate with group activities?
   never   seldom   occasionally   frequently   always

The behavioral descriptions on graphic rating scales are used more easily than numerical descriptors. Because the descriptors are more specific, raters can be more objective and accurate when judging student behaviors; nevertheless, graphic rating scales are subject to bias because of disagreement about the meaning of the descriptors.

Uses of Rating Scales

One of the most familiar uses of rating scales is report cards. Schools often use them to report characteristics of personal and social development on a report

Review of Portfolio Reading Materials
Primary Level

Student's Name _____

Teacher's Name _____

Date _____   Grade _____   School _____

1 = Limited   2 = Below expectation   3 = Average   4 = Above expectation   5 = Outstanding

Assessment	1	2	3	4	5	Teacher Comments
Emergent reading skills						
Recognizes speech/print relationship						
Understands concepts of letters/words						
Handles books appropriately						
Attitudes toward reading						
Chooses reading during free time						
Reads many books/stories						
Listens attentively to stories						
Reading interests						
Has favorite books/stories						
Discusses favorite books/stories						
Participates in discussions about books/stories						
Reading skills/strategies						
Constructs meaning when reading						
Relates stories to background						
Shows confidence as a reader						

Summary Assessment

Assessment	For This Review			Since Last Review		
	Outstanding	Average	Limited	Improving	About The Same	Seems Poorer
Amount of reading						
Attitudes toward reading						
Reading/skills strategies						

Figure 6.6

Review of portfolio reading materials.

Source: From the Integrated Assessment System - Language Arts. Copyright © 1990 by The Psychological Corporation. Reproduced by permission. All rights reserved.

Item	Inadequate 1 2	Minimal 3 4	Good 5 6	Excellent 7	SAMPLE SCORING STRIP
24. Sand/water	No provision for sand or water play.	Some provision for sand or water play outdoors *or* indoors.	Provision for sand and water play outdoors *or* indoors including toys (Ex. cups, spoons, funnels, shovels, pots and pans, trucks, etc.). Used at least weekly.	Provisions for sand and water play outdoors *and* indoors with appropriate toys.	24. Sand/water 1 2 3 4 5 6 7
25. Dramatic play	No special provisions made for dress-up or dramatic play.	Dramatic play props focused on housekeeping roles. Little or no provisions for dramatic play involving transportation, work, or adventure.	Variety of dramatic play props including transportation, work, adventure, fantasy. Space provided in the room and outside the room permitting more active play (either outdoors or in a multipurpose room or gym).	Everything in 5 plus pictures, stories, trips, used to enrich dramatic play.	25. Dramatic play 1 2 3 4 5 6 7
26. Schedule	Routine care (eating, sleeping, toileting, etc.) takes up most of the day. Little planning for interesting activities either indoors or outdoors.	Schedule is *either* too rigid leaving no time for individual interests *or* too flexible (chaotic) with activities disrupting routines.	Schedule provides balance of structure and flexibility. Several activity periods, some indoors and some outdoors, are planned each day in addition to routine care.	Balance of structure and flexibility, with smooth transitions between activities (Ex. materials ready for next activity before current activity ends). Plans included to meet individual needs (Ex. alternative activity for children whose needs differ from group).	26. Schedule (creative) 1 2 3 4 5 6 7

Figure 6.7

Examples from the *Early Childhood Environment Rating Scale.*

Source: Reprinted by permission of the publisher from Harms, Thelma, & Clifford, Richard M., EARLY CHILDHOOD ENVIRONMENT RATING SCALE. (New York: Teachers College Press, © 1980 by Thelma Harms & Richard M. Clifford. All rights reserved), p. 29.

card. Such attributes as work habits, classroom conduct, neatness, and citizenship commonly appear on elementary school report cards. Students and parents often believe that such ratings are particularly subject to teacher bias and feelings about the student.

An example of a rating scale is given in Figure 6.7. Taken from the *Early Childhood Environment Rating Scale* (Harms & Clifford, 1980), the page pictured shows a numerical scale for rating how the early childhood teacher provides for sand/water play and dramatic play, as well as the quality of the daily schedule.

An observation form (Kamii & Rosenblum, 1990) used for recording progress in numerical reasoning is another example of a rating scale that is used to evaluate concept development in young children. The form (Figure 6.8) was developed to record the child's progress in understanding the ability to make ten with two numbers through games with cards. The graphic indicators—counts-all, counts-on, counts-on from larger, and selects without counting—indicate the steps the child takes in being able to make combinations that equal ten. Each category describes a more complex or advanced process used by the child from counting

Figure 6.8
Observation form for tens
with playing cards.

		OBSERVATIONAL FORM FOR TENS WITH PLAYING CARDS		
Name _____ Date _____				
	Counts-all	Counts-on	Counts-on from larger	Selects without counting (looks for)
5 + 5				
9 + 1				
8 + 2				
7 + 3				
6 + 4				
Combos ≠ 10				

Source: Kamii, C., & Rosenblum, V. (1990). An approach to assessment in mathematics. In C. Kamii (Ed.), *Achievement testing in the early grades: The games grown-ups play* (pp. 146–162). Washington, DC: National Association for the Education of Young Children. (p. 151)

all of the symbols at the lowest level to selecting two appropriate cards without counting at the most advanced level.

ADVANTAGES AND DISADVANTAGES OF RATING SCALES

Rating scales are a unique form of evaluation. They serve a function not provided by other measurement strategies. Although some of the limitations of rating scales have already been discussed, it is useful to review their strengths and weaknesses.

Advantages of Using Rating Scales

Rating scales can be used for behaviors not easily measured by other means. In the area of social development, for example, a scale might have indicators of cooperative behavior. When the teacher is trying to determine the child's ability to work with children and adults in the classroom, the scale of indicators is more usable than a yes/no response category on a checklist. Unlike an observation, which might be completely open-ended, the rating scale indicators have clues to behaviors that describe the child's level of cooperation.

Rating scales are quick and easy to complete. Because the rater is provided with the descriptors of the child's behavior, it is possible to complete the scale with a minimum of effort. The descriptors also make it possible to complete the scale some time after an observation. The user can apply knowledge about the child after an observation or as a result of working with the child on a daily basis and will not always need a separate time period to acquire the needed information.

A minimum of training is required to use rating scales. The successful rating scale is easy to understand and use (Southeastern Day Care Project, 1973). Often paraprofessionals in schools can complete some rating scales. The scale's indicators offer the information needed to complete the scale.

Rating scales are easy to develop and use. Because descriptors remain consistent on some rating scales, teachers find them easy to design. When using rating indicators such as "always," "sometimes," "rarely," or "never," the teacher can add the statements for rating without having to think of rating categories for each one. Figure 6.9 is a sample of cognitive behaviors for three-year-olds measured on the rating scale *Evaluating Children's Progress: A Rating Scale for Children in Day Care* (Southeastern Day Care Project, 1973).

Finally, rating scales are a useful strategy for assessing progress in the child's journey into understanding the world or in reconstructing knowledge. A rating scale permits the teacher to describe the child's steps toward understanding or mastery, instead of whether the child has achieved a predetermined level or not as is the case in the use of checklists.

Disadvantages of Using Rating Scales

Rating scales are highly subjective; therefore, rater error and bias are common problems. Teachers and other raters may rate a child on the basis of their previous interactions or on an emotional rather than an objective basis. The subsequent rating will reflect the teacher's attitude toward the child (Guilford, 1954).

Ambiguous terms cause rating scales to be unreliable sources of information. Raters disagree on the descriptors of characteristics. Therefore, raters are likely to mark characteristics by using different interpretations. For example, it is easy to have different interpretations of the indicator "sometimes or rarely."

Rating scales tell little about the causes of behavior. Like the checklists that indicate whether the behavior is present or absent, rating scales provide no additional information to clarify the circumstances in which the behavior occurred. Unlike observations that result in more comprehensive information about the context surrounding behaviors, rating scales provide a different type of information from checklists, but include no causal clues for the observer unless notes are taken beyond the rating scale itself.

SUMMARY

Informal evaluation measures are useful for teachers who need specific information about their students to use when planning instruction. Checklists and rating scales are informal instruments that can be designed and used by teachers to obtain specific diagnostic and assessment data that will assist them in developing learning experiences for their children.

THREE-YEAR-OLDS RATING FORM (From Age Three to Age Four)
   (Rate at six-month intervals)

Cognitive

1.   Compares size   Extends "matching" concept to size,
                      as "big" or "little." Comparisons
                      may be easy, but should be verbalized.
                      Child chooses between two items--
                      "Show me the little block" (spoon,
                      doll, etc.), "the big block."

2.   Counts three   Extends concept of counting to three.
                      Understands process of counting beyond
                      two. May rote count beyond this.
                      Ask child to "hand me three pieces
                      of candy from the bowl" (or three
                      blocks from the pile).

3.   Dramatizes   Acts out, singly or with others, simple
                      stories, Mother Goose rhymes and charac-
                      ters and scenes. Acts out role playing.
                      May make up from book or story that
                      group has been reading.

4.   Uses plurals

                      Take into account that the 's' may sound
                      different if the child comes from a
                      different cultural or language background.

5.   Converses   In short sentences, answers questions,
                      gives information, repeats, uses language
                      to convey simple ideas.

6.   Sings   Sings short snatches of songs
                      Songs such as "Happy Birthday" or
                      "Jingle Bells" pass. At least one
                      chorus or verse.

Figure 6.9

Sample of the *Southeastern Day Care Project Rating Scale.*

Source: Southeastern Day Care Project, 1973.

Checklists are used for more than assessment or evaluation. They are a form of curriculum outline or a framework of curriculum objectives. With checklists, teachers can plan instruction, develop learning center activities, and evaluate children's progress and achievement on specific objectives.

Rating scales allow teachers to evaluate behaviors qualitatively. Raters can indicate the extent to which the child exhibits certain behaviors.

Checklists and rating scales are practical and easy to use. Teachers can develop them to fit the curriculum and administer them at their convenience. Unlike standardized tests, checklists and rating scales are current and provide the teacher with immediate feedback on student progress.

Using checklists and rating scales also has disadvantages. Because they are not standardized, they are subject to error and teacher bias. Checklists do not include the level or quality of performance on the objectives measured. Rating scales in particular are subject to rater bias. Rating scale descriptors are ambiguous in definition. Differing interpretations of descriptors by raters lead to different responses and interpretations of children's behaviors.

REVIEW QUESTIONS

1. Describe the different functions of checklists. How can checklists be used by teachers for purposes other than evaluation or assessment?
2. Why is it important to use developmental checklists in early childhood programs?
3. How do developmental checklists serve as a guide for the sequence of development and curriculum?
4. Explain the different strategies that teachers can use to measure progress with checklist objectives.
5. How does the design of a checklist affect its use as an evaluation instrument?
6. What is sequenced organization in checklist design?
7. What methods can be used to record assessment results on checklists? Which form is best?
8. Why do some teachers have difficulty in using checklists? Do you see any solution to their problems?
9. How do rating scales differ from checklists?
10. Why are rating scales vulnerable to rater error and bias?
11. Is it better to use numerical rating scales or graphic rating scales? Why?

KEY TERMS

developmental checklist
graphic rating scale
numerical rating scales

SUGGESTED ACTIVITIES

1. Collect samples of checklists used in preschool and primary classrooms. Compare the checklists in terms of objectives, evaluation strategies, and record keeping.

2. Develop a checklist for the first six weeks of school for behavior you wish to see demonstrated in the classroom or a learning center.

3. Ask a reading specialist, speech therapist, or other special programs teacher for examples of checklists and how they are used. Write a brief report on the importance and need for the checklists that are collected.

REFERENCES

CAPON, J. J. (1975). *Perceptual motor development: Basic movement activities.* Belmont, CA: Pitman Learning.

FARR, R. C. (1993). *Portfolio assessment teacher's guide grades k–8.* Orlando, FL: Harcourt Brace Jovanovich.

GUILFORD, J. P. (1954). *Psychometric methods* (2nd ed.). New York: McGraw-Hill.

HARMS, T., & CLIFFORD, R. M. (1980). *Early Childhood Environment Rating Scale.* New York: Teachers College Press.

HOUGHTON MIFFLIN. (1993). *Houghton Mifflin Reading: The Literature Experience.* Boston: Author.

IRWIN, D. M., & BUSHNELL, M. M. (1980). *Observational strategies for child study.* New York: Holt, Rinehart & Winston.

KAMII, C., & ROSENBLUM, V. (1990). An approach to assessment in mathematics. In C. Kamii (Ed.), *Achievement testing in the early grades: The games grown-ups play* (pp. 146–152). Washington, DC: National Association for the Education of Young Children.

MORRISON, G. S. (1988). *Education and development of infants, toddlers, and preschoolers.* Glenview, IL: Scott, Foresman.

SOUTHEASTERN DAY CARE PROJECT. (1973). *Evaluating children's progress: A rating scale for children in day care.* Mt. Rainier, MD: Gryphon House.

TEXAS EDUCATION AGENCY. (1985). *State Board of Education rules for curriculum: Principles, standards, and procedures for accreditation of school districts.* Austin: Author.

WORTHAM, S. C. (1984). *Organizing instruction in early childhood.* Boston: Allyn & Bacon.

Chapter 7

Informal Measures: Classroom and Teacher-Designed Tests and Assessments

Chapter Objectives

As a result of reading this chapter you will be able to

1. describe why teacher-designed assessments and tests are used.
2. understand the relationship between teacher-designed assessments and curriculum and instruction.
3. design assessments for preschool and primary grade students.
4. understand the process of mastery learning.
5. write an instructional or behavioral objective.
6. develop formative and summative tests and learning, enrichment, and corrective activities for learning objectives.

Another type of informal evaluation to be discussed is teacher-designed assessments. In assessing and evaluating children from birth through the primary grades, measures other than paper-and-pencil tests are generally more appropriate. As children progress through the primary grades, however, they develop skills in reading and writing that will make it possible for them to demonstrate learning on a written test. In this chapter we discuss how teachers design their own assessments of classroom instruction and use commercially designed classroom tests.

PURPOSES OF TEACHER-DESIGNED ASSESSMENTS AND TESTS

Although all types of evaluation, both formal and informal, are used to measure and evaluate children's behavior and learning, there are circumstances under which teacher-designed assessments or written classroom tests are especially useful for the teacher. Paper-and-pencil tests, when given to students who are able to use them, can supplement other types of evaluation and provide teachers with information that the other types lack. These purposes include providing objective data on student learning and accountability and providing additional information for making instructional decisions.

Teacher-designed assessments supplement other evaluation measures, enabling the teacher to make more accurate decisions for the instruction of individual students. The teacher uses observation, tasks during group instruction, and manipulative activities to determine a child's progress in learning. A written test used with older children can reinforce or support the teacher's evaluation with an objective assessment. Objective testing complements the teacher's more subjective, personal evaluation, which can be subject to individual impressions or biases.

Classroom assessments can also support teachers' decisions that may be questioned by parents or school staff members. The teacher may understand, from ongoing work with a child, that the child needs to be instructed at a different level or requires extended experiences with a concept that other children have mastered. Although the teacher is confident in making the decision, a task or paper-and-pencil assessment can support it and, at the same time, help the parents understand the nature of the problem. The teacher-designed assessment thus can increase the teacher's accountability for decisions that affect students' learning.

Teachers must make instructional decisions, both immediate and long-term. As they teach, they must decide how long to spend on a particular science unit or math concept. In addition to using informal evaluation strategies such as individual tasks and ongoing observations of class progress, they can use written tests to provide more information that will help them decide whether to include more experiences, use review activities, skip planned activities, or conclude the current topic and move on to a new one.

Unfortunately, at present, the increased emphasis is on grading young children. Although kindergarten children may be exempt, primary grade students are being given letter or numerical grades in many schools, and the practice expanded with the recent emphasis on higher instructional and grading standards. Teachers find it difficult to assign letter grades to primary school children. Whether the practice should continue is debatable; nevertheless, testing can help the teacher make decisions about student achievement. To use only written evaluations for grading would be inappropriate for all of the reasons discussed throughout this book; however, when combined with other developmentally appropriate evaluation strategies, paper-and-pencil tests add supporting information on which grades can be based.

In the same fashion, tests can be used to support diagnostic decisions about student needs. The classroom teacher can supplement information from standardized tests and informal evaluations to determine student strengths and weaknesses in content areas. Assessments can be designed that correspond to local instructional objectives and that provide specific information on student accomplishment and instructional needs. Once diagnostic information has been analyzed, the teacher can place students more accurately into instructional groups and regroup periodically as students move through the program at different rates.

Finally, teacher-made assessments allow evaluation of the local instructional program. Unlike standardized tests, which reflect general objectives suitable for a broad range of school programs at a state, regional, or national level, the teacher-designed test assesses specific or local learning objectives. These objective-based tests evaluate more closely the effectiveness of the local educational program. Without evaluation measures designed for the classroom, there is no ready method to assess local curriculum objectives.

TYPES OF TESTS USED WITH PRESCHOOL AND PRIMARY GRADE CHILDREN

Teacher-designed assessments for preschool children must match the way these children learn—through active interaction with concrete materials. Children who do not yet read cannot demonstrate their learning effectively with a paper-and-pencil test. The teacher constructs assessment activities that allow the child to manipulate materials, explain understanding orally, or point to the correct response if expressive language is limited.

Teacher assessments using tasks or oral responses can be conducted during a teaching activity, as part of a learning center experience, or as a separate assessment or series of assessments (Wortham, 1984). For example, for the objective of recognizing uppercase and lowercase letters, the teacher may present a set of cards with five letters and ask the child to match the uppercase and lowercase letters. Figure 7.1 pictures an array of cards that can be used for this purpose.

To demonstrate an understanding of counting, the preschool child is given objects to count. The teacher can conduct the assessment in two ways. He or she may either select five objects and ask the child to count them or ask the child to group five of the objects.

Pictures also may be used for assessment tasks with nonreaders. To assess knowledge of shapes, a pictured array of basic shapes could be used. If the objective is to identify shapes, the teacher can ask the child to find a given shape by saying, "Show me a triangle." The teacher can also point to the shape and ask the child to name it if the objective is to be able to name shapes. Figure 7.2 shows an array of shapes that can be used to identify circles, squares, triangles, and rectangles (Wortham, 1984).

For some preschool assessments, an oral response may be most appropriate. For example, a common preschool objective is for the child to know his or her first and last name. The teacher would ask the child to give this information.

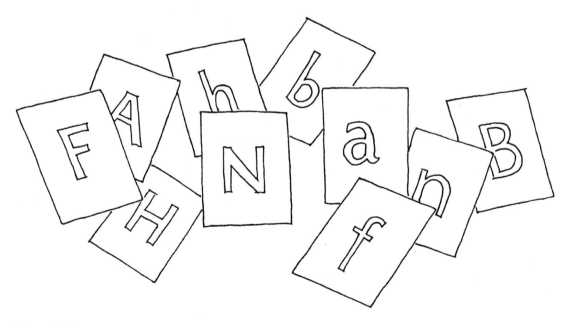

Figure 7.1
Uppercase and lowercase letters.

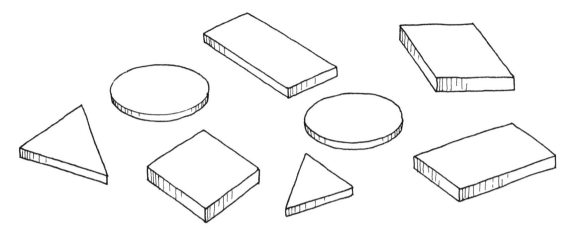

Figure 7.2
Array of basic shapes.

For the objective of sequencing events in a story, the teacher shows the child a set of three to five pictures that have a logical sequence and asks the child to put them in order. The child then is asked to tell the story. Figure 7.3 shows a series of pictures that can be used for sequencing the cards and providing a verbal description.

As children learn to read, the teacher's assessments begin to include printed test activities with pictures and some written words. Instead of a physical response using concrete materials or an oral response, the child uses a pencil with a printed test. These written assessments may be commercially produced materials designed for classroom use with basal textbooks or as supplementary resources. The teacher must also be able to design his or her own tests to evaluate his or her own or individual learning objectives most effectively.

Paper-and-pencil tests must be adapted to the child's limited reading and writing skills. Therefore, tests designed for children in the primary grades use a format that provides pictorial or visual clues to assist the student in selecting or writing the correct response. To prepare beginning readers and writers for written tests, the teacher introduces key words such as *circle* or *draw* that are commonly used in paper-and-pencil assessments. More words are taught until the child is able to read written instructions. Throughout the primary grades, the teacher will introduce the assessment page with the children before asking them to complete the page independently.

Once the students can successfully complete a written assessment, the teacher may use a commercially prepared activity or design one. Regardless of which type is chosen, certain tasks are used to accommodate the child's limited reading and writing abilities. The most common tasks include marking or circling a response, drawing a line to a response, and writing simple numeral or word answers. Although both commercial and teacher-designed tests use these responses, the following examples are from commercial sources. Later in the

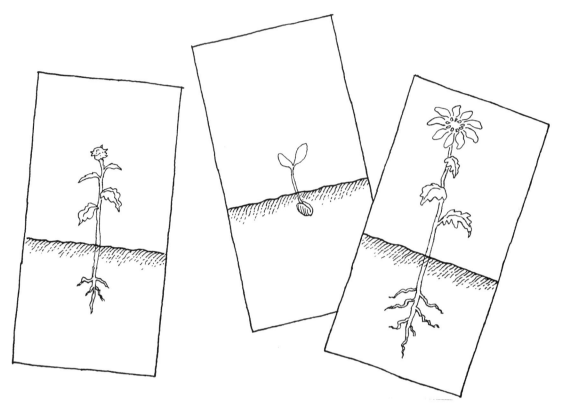

Figure 7.3
Sequencing pictures.

chapter the process of preparing teacher-designed assessments and tests is described.

Children can circle pictures in response to questions before they have learned to read and write. This type of response is continued in the grades where beginning reading skills are acquired. Figure 7.4 presents a page from a commercially designed test in which the child is asked to circle the correct responses. In this figure the child is asked to circle the shapes that correspond with a given shape in a mathematics evaluation. The example is from a second-grade text.

A similar type of response can be made by marking a test question with an X or bubbling in an answer. Figure 7.5 (p. 156) uses a multiple-choice format. The child must mark the correct box with an X.

Matching by drawing a line from one figure to another can be used in the early grades in various content areas. Figure 7.6 (p. 157) shows the use of this test in a science unit on weather.

The child may be expected to write a correct response. In the examples given, the words are provided as clues to be used when selecting and writing the cor-

Figure 7.4
Circling the correct answer.

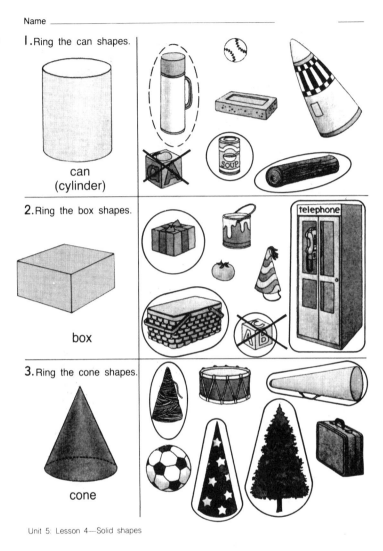

Source: From *Harper & Row Mathematics, Teacher's Edition, Grade 2* by J. N. Payne et al. New York, Macmillan, 1985.

rect word. In Figure 7.7 (p. 158), a science test, the child looks below the blank in a sentence and selects the correct word to write in the blank. To respond, the child must be able to read the sentence and determine which word fits the context of the statement.

Although each of the examples given has been taken from a commercially designed test, teacher-designed tests follow the same or similar formats. Not only

Figure 7.5
Putting an X on the correct answer.

CHAPTER 6
Matter

Chapter Test 79
Page 1

Name ____________________

Choose the best word to finish the sentence.

1. All things on earth that take up space

and have weight are ______________.
solids matter

Is it a solid, liquid, or gas?
Put an *X* in the box.

		Solid	Liquid	Gas
2.	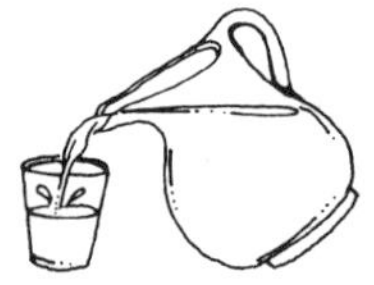 milk			
3.	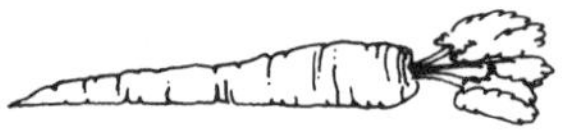 carrot			
4.	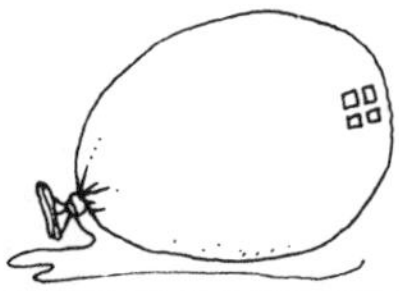 air inside balloon			
5.	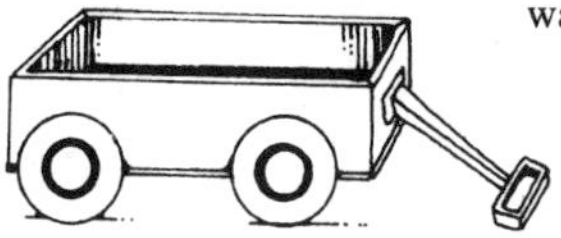 wagon			

79 Level 2 • Chapter 6 • Use at the end of Chapter 6.

Source: Addison-Wesley Science Teacher's Resource Book by V. N. Rockcastle, B. McKnight, F. Solomon, and V. Schmidt, 1984, p. 79. Copyright 1984 by Addison-Wesley Publishing Company, Inc. Used by permission.

must the child have visual clues to be able to respond, but an example also is usually given to help the child understand the task. Also, although there are written instructions for the child to read, in reality the teacher may need to read and discuss the instructions with the students to ensure that they understand what is required. In the following section we discuss the design of teacher-constructed assessments and tests.

Figure 7.6
Drawing a line to the correct answer.

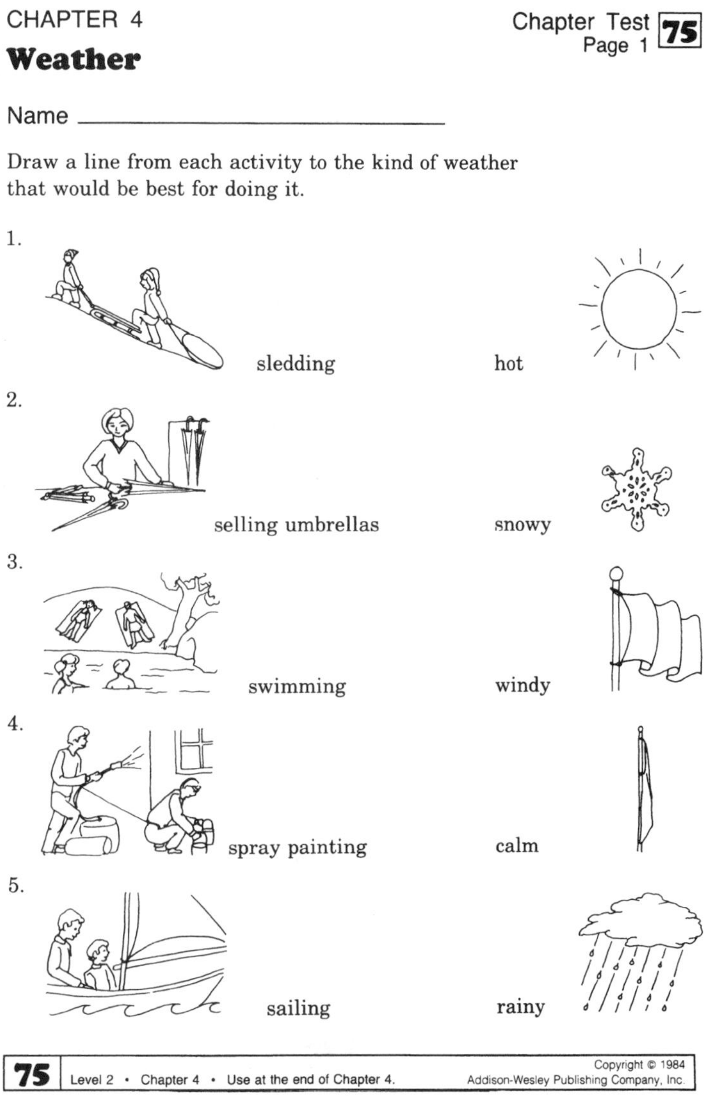

CHAPTER 4
Weather

Chapter Test 75
Page 1

Name ______________________

Draw a line from each activity to the kind of weather that would be best for doing it.

1. sledding — hot
2. selling umbrellas — snowy
3. swimming — windy
4. spray painting — calm
5. sailing — rainy

75 | Level 2 • Chapter 4 • Use at the end of Chapter 4. | Copyright © 1984 Addison-Wesley Publishing Company, Inc.

Source: Addison-Wesley Science Teacher's Resource Book by V. N. Rockcastle, B. McKnight, F. Solomon, and V. Schmidt, 1984, p. 75. Copyright 1984 by Addison-Wesley Publishing Company, Inc. Used by permission.

HOW TESTS ARE DESIGNED AND USED

Classroom tests are closely matched to curriculum objectives and content. Whether designed by the teacher or obtained from a textbook or other commercial source, they are used to measure the student's ability to benefit from classroom instruction.

Figure 7.7
Writing a word for a response.

CHAPTER 2

Living Things in Fall and Winter

Chapter Test **72**
Page 2

Name _____

Write the answer on each blank.

1. Winter is the _____ time of year.
     coldest   warmest

2. Some plants die in winter.

   New plants of this kind grow from _____.
                                        seeds   leaves

3. Some plants do not lose all their leaves in winter.

   They are called _____.
                    winter greens   evergreens

4. Some animals _____ before winter.
                 hatch babies   lay eggs

5. Some animals store food for _____.
                                summer   winter

6. Beavers store _____ under water.
                  nuts   sticks

7. In winter, some animals _____.
                            move away   make fires

8. Some animals rest all _____.
                          winter   summer

72 | Level 2 · Chapter 2 · Use at the end of Chapter 2.   Copyright © 1984
Addison-Wesley Publishing Company, Inc.

Source: Addison-Wesley Science Teacher's Resource Book by V. N. Rockcastle, B. McKnight, F. Solomon, and V. Schmidt, 1984, p. 72. Copyright 1984 by Addison-Wesley Publishing Company, Inc. Used by permission.

Unlike standardized tests that provide general information about student achievement, classroom tests measure student accomplishment and learning needs in relation to specific classroom objectives. Classroom tests can be used for placement and diagnosis, formative testing, and summative testing (Gronlund, 1990).

Placement and diagnostic testing have a similar function. In placement testing, the student is assessed to determine the instructional group into which he or she should be placed. Tests are given to determine what the student already knows and is ready to learn. Diagnostic testing is used to determine student weaknesses that need to be corrected. The same tests can be used for both purposes unless learning difficulties are persistent and need more extensive diagnosis by the school diagnostician or psychologist. Placement and diagnostic testing in the classroom are similar to criterion-referenced testing using standardized tests; however, the tests may assess selected learning objectives, rather than objectives for an entire grade level.

Formative and summative tests are related to mastery learning (Bloom, Madaus, & Hastings, 1981). **Formative tests** are given periodically while teaching specific objectives to monitor student progress. These tests measure a limited number of objectives at a time so that the teacher can identify which objectives have been mastered and which call for additional work or activities. They provide feedback and are not used for grading purposes.

The **summative test,** in contrast, is the final test given on completion of a unit of work. The unit of work may be organized for a single objective or for a small group of objectives. The summative test is given after instruction and formative testing reveal that the material has been mastered. It is administered as the final step to verify the student's achievement on the material covered in the unit or by a group of objectives.

The information gained from diagnostic, placement, formative, and summative testing provides the teacher with current, relevant information for instructional planning. It allows the teacher not only to group students for instruction effectively but also to determine how long the class needs to continue working on objectives and whether alternative types of experiences are needed to correct learning weaknesses in particular students. Unlike standardized tests that are administered once a year, classroom tests provide ongoing, criterion-related information about student progress on objectives being covered in a particular classroom. To use classroom testing effectively, the teacher must know how to design appropriate tasks that match the students' ability to use paper-and-pencil tests. The teacher must also know what kinds of tests will accurately measure the students' progress or mastery of each learning objective.

STEPS IN TEST DESIGN

Teacher-designed classroom evaluations, although less rigorously constructed than standardized tests, must accurately measure objectives for classroom instruction. Whether the teacher is organizing assessment strategies for preschool or primary school students, tests are carefully designed to fit the learning objectives. Although in this section of the chapter we discuss teacher assessment in terms of test design, we refer to evaluation strategies for preschool students who are nonreaders, as well as for students in the primary grades who are beginning to read and write.

Several steps in test design must be followed if a test is to measure student learning accurately. Based on Bloom's model of mastery learning (Block, 1971), the process includes the following:

1. Determination of instructional objectives
2. Construction of a table of specifications
3. Design of formative and summative evaluations
4. Design of learning experiences
5. Design of correctives and enrichment activities

Determining Instructional Objectives

In chapter 5 we discussed objectives relative to skills continuums and checklists. The same types of sources are used to develop instructional objectives that will be used to design classroom tests. School districts have various sources to draw from when determining curriculum objectives for each grade level.

One common source of curriculum objectives is basal textbook series used in the classroom. Most textbooks in reading, mathematics, social studies, and science are based on learning objectives appropriate for that grade level in school districts in many states. A commonly accepted pool of learning objectives can be found in the content areas for each grade level; however, objectives can vary markedly among different basal series. Textbooks are organized around these objectives, and teachers' editions of the textbooks contain activities to implement instruction for the objectives and tests to evaluate student learning on the objectives.

School districts, particularly large, urban ones, establish their own learning objectives in various content areas for each grade level. These objectives may draw on commercial resources, which are supplemented with other objectives that are deemed important in the school district.

The state's department of education may produce learning objectives for each grade level in each content area. The state-mandated curriculum objectives are followed by each school district. These objectives may be the minimum required by the state. If this is so, local districts may have the freedom to supplement state learning objectives with commercial and local sources for additional objectives.

The *Addison-Wesley Mathematics Teacher's Edition* for first grade (Eicholz et al., 1985) includes sets of skills divided into fourteen chapters or units. Chapter 2 of the text covers "Sums to 5." The objectives for the unit are as follows:

2.1 Recall addition facts through sums to 5.
2.2 Solve problems using cumulative computational skills.

The teacher using this textbook can use these objectives, plus others, to determine the learning objectives for mathematics in the first-grade classroom. The objectives will be followed in designing instructional experiences and testing procedures to evaluate achievement.

Writing Behavioral Objectives

Behavioral or **instructional objectives** provide the framework for curriculum and instruction and the measurement of the effectiveness of instruction and learning. According to Kubiszyn and Borich (1987, p. 45), instructional objectives should have the following characteristics:

> An instructional objective should be a clear and concise statement of the skill or skills that your students will be expected to perform after a unit of instruction. It should include the level of proficiency to be demonstrated and the special conditions under which the skill must be demonstrated. Furthermore, an instructional objective should be stated in observable, behavioral terms, in order for two or more individuals to agree that a student has or has not displayed the learning outcome in question. In short, a complete instructional objective includes:
>
> > an observable behavior (action verb specifying the learning outcome)
> > any special conditions under which the behavior must be displayed, and
> > a performance level considered sufficient to demonstrate mastery.

For example, a common objective for preschool children is to be able to sort objects into two groups by using some type of criterion. An instructional or behavioral objective could be written as follows:

> Given an array of nuts, the student will be able to sort the nuts correctly into two groups of nuts with smooth shells and nuts with rough shells.

An analysis of the objective would identify the components of an instructional objective as follows:

> Given an array of nuts (condition), the student will be able to sort nuts correctly (100% performance standard implied) into groups of nuts with smooth shells and nuts with rough shells (behavior).

An objective for physical development might include the ability to catch a ball with both hands. Stated behaviorally, the objective might be worded as follows:

> Following a series of activities throwing and catching large rubber balls, the child will be able to catch the ball with both hands in four out of six tries.

To analyze the parts of this objective, it would be described as follows:

> Following a series of activities throwing and catching large rubber balls (condition), the child will be able to catch the ball with both hands (behavior) in four out of six tries (standard of performance or performance level).

Before a learning objective or outcome can be measured, then, it must be stated clearly in terms of its content and the desired behavior. The *content* refers to the knowledge or skill to be learned. The *behavior* is what the student does to demonstrate that the knowledge or skill has been attained (Gronlund, 1990). In the objectives described for the *Addison-Wesley Mathematics Teacher's Edition* for first grade, the content is clearly stated but the required behavior is missing. Objective 2.1, "Recall addition facts through sums to 5," describes the required skill but does not specify how the student will demonstrate it or the performance standard. If the statement is changed to read, "The student will recall addition facts through sums to 5 by correctly adding sums in ten problems," the desired behavior and performance standard have been described.

Analyzing Objectives to Determine Prerequisite Skills

The teacher must not only develop the learning objective but also determine what must be taught for the student to master it. Part of the planning for instruction involves studying the learning objective to decide what prior knowledge or skill the student must have to be able to learn the new information. In Objective 2.1, "Recall addition facts through sums to 5," the teacher will plan instruction to help students learn to combine all possible groups of numbers that equal five. In addition, the teacher determines what the student must already know to understand and use addition skills. Prior skills to be considered include the following:

1. Knowledge of numbers through 5
2. Identification of numerals through 5
3. Understanding that small groups can be combined to make a larger group

The teacher must decide whether the students have the prerequisite skills to be able to master the targeted learning objective. If not, the prior skills will have to be taught, or retaught if necessary, before the new objective is introduced. A pretest or a diagnostic test may be used to determine student readiness for the learning objective.

Setting a Standard for Mastery

The final step in determining the instructional objectives is to set the level of mastery that will be expected for the student to learn the objective. In the section on writing behavioral objectives, information was included on how to include the performance level for the objective. In this context the process for determining the level of performance desired or required is discussed. The level of accomplishment may be set by the teacher, the school district, or the state department of education. This is the minimum standard required to pass the objective. The learning objective can reflect the established standard for mastery. If 80 percent is established as the minimum standard for mastery, the learning objective can be stated to reflect the standard. Objective 2.1, the mathematics objective for first grade, can be rewritten to include the standard of mastery as follows: "The student will be able to recall addition facts through sums to 5 by correctly completing eight of ten addition problems." If each objective does not include the written standard of mastery, the standard can be set separately for all of the learning objectives.

Constructing a Table of Specifications

After the learning objectives for a unit of study or the content of an entire course have been described behaviorally, the teacher or curriculum developer is ready to outline the course content. Before a test can be organized to measure the curriculum objectives, it is necessary to understand more accurately what concepts or skills are to be measured and to what extent the student will be expected to perform to demonstrate mastery of the objective. Will the student be expected to remember information, use the information to solve problems, or evaluate the information? The test items will reflect the level of understanding that is required to master the objective.

Analysis of objectives to determine the level of understanding is commonly done by constructing a **table of specifications** (Gronlund, 1990). Here learning objectives are charted by using Bloom's *Taxonomy of Educational Objectives* (Bloom, 1956). This work describes levels of understanding in the cognitive domain ranging from the ability to recall information (the knowledge level) to the highest level of understanding (evaluation). Figure 7.8 (p. 164) is an explanation of the levels of Bloom's taxonomy, with examples of terms that characterize each level. In Figure 7.9 (p. 165), an adaptation of the taxonomy is used to make a table of specifications for the mathematics unit covering addition sums to five. The two objectives for the unit are listed to the left of the figure. The columns to the right describe how the objectives are charted on the taxonomy. The first objective requires that the student be able to recall addition facts and problems, understand the facts and problems, and apply that understanding. The second objective also requires that the student be able to analyze or solve problems. When designing test or assessment items, the teacher must know the type and level of understanding that test items will reflect and must organize the test so that the described levels of understanding are adequately sampled. Figure 7.10 (p. 166) is a table of specifications for a unit on classification at the kindergarten level.

Designing Formative and Summative Evaluations

After the teacher has determined what is to be measured by designing a table of specifications for the learning objectives to be taught, it is time to design the formative and summative evaluations. Both types of evaluation are derived from the table of specifications. Assessment items will be designed to measure the student's achievement at the levels on Bloom's taxonomy, as described on the table of specifications. The assessment items on the two forms are equivalent, but the evaluation purposes differ. The formative evaluation is not a test; it is a checkup or progress report on the student. The teacher uses the formative evaluation to decide whether the student needs further work with the objective.

Level of Understanding	Descriptive Terms	
Knowledge Recognition and recall The ability to remember or recognize information	Tell List Name	Define Identify Locate
Comprehension The ability to translate information in your own words Show that you understand	Restate Discuss Explain Review	Describe Summarize Interpret
Application The ability to use information or apply learning to new situations and real-life circumstances	Demonstrate Construct Imply	Dramatize Practice Illustrate
Analysis The ability to break down information into parts To identify parts of information and its relationship to the whole	Organize Differentiate Compare Distinguish	Solve Experiment Relate

Synthesize
The ability to assemble separate parts into a new
   whole
The ability to take information from various sources
   and present it in a created form
	Design
	Plan
	Develop
		Compile
		Create
		Compose

Evaluation The ability to make judgments about information To be able to evaluate based on criteria or standards	Decide Conclude Appraise Choose	Judge Assess Select

Figure 7.8
Explanation of Bloom's taxonomy.
Source: Bloom, 1956.

If the student needs additional experiences, more activities, known as **correctives,** are implemented. Correctives are learning resources designed to approach the objective differently from the original instruction. The intent is to provide various kinds of activities to meet individual students' needs.

If the student's responses indicate mastery on the formative evaluation, the teacher provides **enrichment activities.** The student engages in activities that are

Sums to 5	Know	Comprehend	Apply	Analyze	Synthesize	Evaluate
2.1 Recall addition facts through sums to five	X	X	X			
2.2 Solve problems using cumulative computational skills	X	X	X	X		

Figure 7.9
Table of specifications for a unit on sums to 5.

at a higher level on Bloom's taxonomy than are required for mastery. Thus, if the mastery level on the table of specifications is at the application level, students who master the information after an initial period of instruction may benefit from activities at the analysis, synthesis, or evaluation levels (Bloom et al., 1981).

The summative evaluation is the final assessment or test of what the student has learned or accomplished. It is given after all instruction has been concluded. Although formative and summative evaluations are interchangeable in content, only the summative form is used as a test. The decisions to be made about both assessments include the format, selection of assessment items, determination of length, and assembly of the assessment.

Test Format

Earlier in the chapter, we talked about test formats for use with children in the primary grades. When the teacher is ready to design classroom tests, the appropriate format will have to be determined. Most preschool children respond best to concrete tasks and oral questions. With first graders, the teacher must limit student responses to tasks that require little or no reading and writing, such as circling pictures, marking the correct response, and drawing lines to correct responses. Later in the year, and for children in second and third grades, more writing and reading can be incorporated into the test format. If several different tasks are to be used, more than one format may be used for a test. Figure 7.11, (p. 167) designed for an assessment of a second-grade unit on money, shows the format used. The student must draw a line from the coin to its name and write the numerical value below the coin.

Assessment Items

In addition to determining the format or formats to be used in the assessment, the teacher must develop the items that reflect the table of specifications describing the objectives to be tested. Figures 7.12 (p. 169) and 7.13 (p. 170) are examples of an assessment that fulfills a cell of the table of specifications developed for the unit on coins. In Figure 7.12, Objective 5 requires the student to count collections

Behavioral Objectives	Knowledge	Comprehension	Application	Analysis	Synthesis	Evaluation
A. Classifying 1. The student will describe the object by naming one of its attributes	X	X				
2. The student will construct a set from various objects by classifying together those with common attributes	X	X	X			
B. Noting Differences 1. From a set of four objects, the student will remove the one object that is different from the others.	X	X	X	X		
C. Classifying by Name 1. The student will classify a group of pictures into two categories, using class names	X	X	X			
D. Classifying by Design 1. The student will classify objects into sets according to design, such as stripes, dots, etc.	X	X	X			

Figure 7.10
Unit objective: classifying objects by common attributes in a table of specifications.

of coins up to ninety-nine cents. In Figure 7.13 the directions require the student to count the value of the coins and to record the total on the line provided with each of the six collections of coins.

At the preschool level, Figure 7.10 shows a table of specifications for a unit on classification. Objective B specifies that the student will be able to remove the object that is different from a set of four objects. Figure 7.14 (p. 171) pictures a group of objects that may be used to evaluate the child's performance on the objective. The child chooses or points to the object that does not belong in the group.

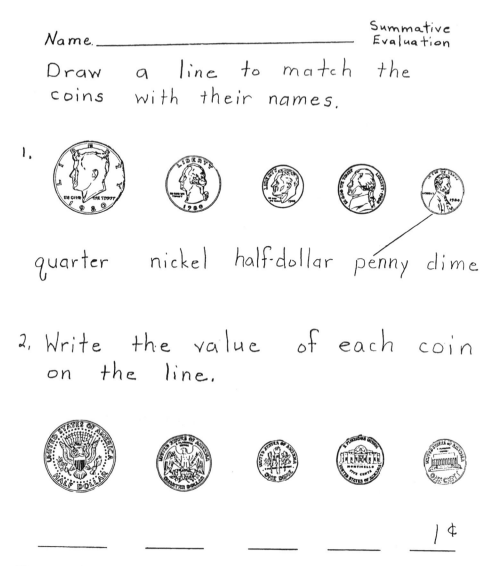

Name._____ Summative Evaluation

Draw a line to match the coins with their names.

1.

quarter nickel half-dollar penny dime

2. Write the value of each coin on the line.

|¢

Figure 7.11
Teacher-designed test on coins.

Test Length

After determining the format and developing a pool of items to provide the levels of understanding expected from the table of specifications, the test developer must determine how many test items or tasks will be included in the test. For young children, a balance is reached between the number of items needed to demonstrate the child's responses to determine understanding and a reasonable length that will not overtax the child's ability to attend to the task. For preschool

Teacher-designed assessments used with preschool children should be conducted orally and/or use concrete materials.

and primary grades, the test length should not exceed the time normally needed to complete classroom activities and assignments. A maximum of 20 to 30 minutes is reasonable in testing primary school students. Commercial tests designed to evaluate these students commonly are one page long.

Assembly

The final step in test design is to assemble test items into both a formative and a summative form. The teacher should construct enough items so that both forms of the test can be put together at the same time. The formative evaluation, conducted after the students have had some work with the objective, will enable the teacher to assess how well the students are learning the information. After the formative assessment has been examined, the teacher can reteach, provide different types of experiences or practice for some students, or move on to the summative test if the students show adequate progress. The teacher should have enough items to obtain the feedback needed to monitor student learning and mastery. The formative and summative assessments should be equivalent in terms of the level of understanding required and the types of items used.

When assembling the tests, the teacher must decide how instructions will be given to the students. If written instructions requiring reading skills will be used, they must be simply stated to match the students' reading ability. Pictures used must be clear and easily interpreted. Poorly drawn or inappropriate pictures will hamper the child's ability to respond correctly and distort the child's perfor-

OBJECTIVES	KNOWLEDGE	COMPREHENSION	APPLICATION	ANALYSIS	SYNTHESIS	EVALUATION
1. The student will be able to identify the five coins (half-dollar, quarter, dime, nickel, penny) by sight with 100% accuracy.	X					
2. The student will be able to match the five coins with their letter names with 100% accuracy.	X					
3. The student will be able to match the five coins to their number value using a cent sign (¢) with 100% accuracy.	X	X				
4. The student will be able to classify like coins by counting: pennies by ones, nickels by fives, dimes by tens, and quarters by twenty-fives, with 80% accuracy.	X	X	X	X		
5. The student will be able to differentiate like/unlike coins by switch counting from twenty-fives to tens to fives to ones in necessary order to count collections of coins up to 99¢ with 80% accuracy.	X	X	X	X		
6. The student will be able to analyze and solve story problems by counting coins with 80% accuracy.	X	X	X	X		

Figure 7.12
Unit on coins: table of specifications.

mance on the test. If the teacher is unable to draw simple pictures, he or she should obtain them from another source or ask a colleague for help.

Designing Learning Experiences

After the table of specifications and the formative and summative evaluations have been constructed, the teacher collects and prepares the activities and instruction that will enable the student to learn the information designed in the objective. Instruction also matches the level on the table of specifications. Instruction to introduce and work with the objectives includes teacher instruction and

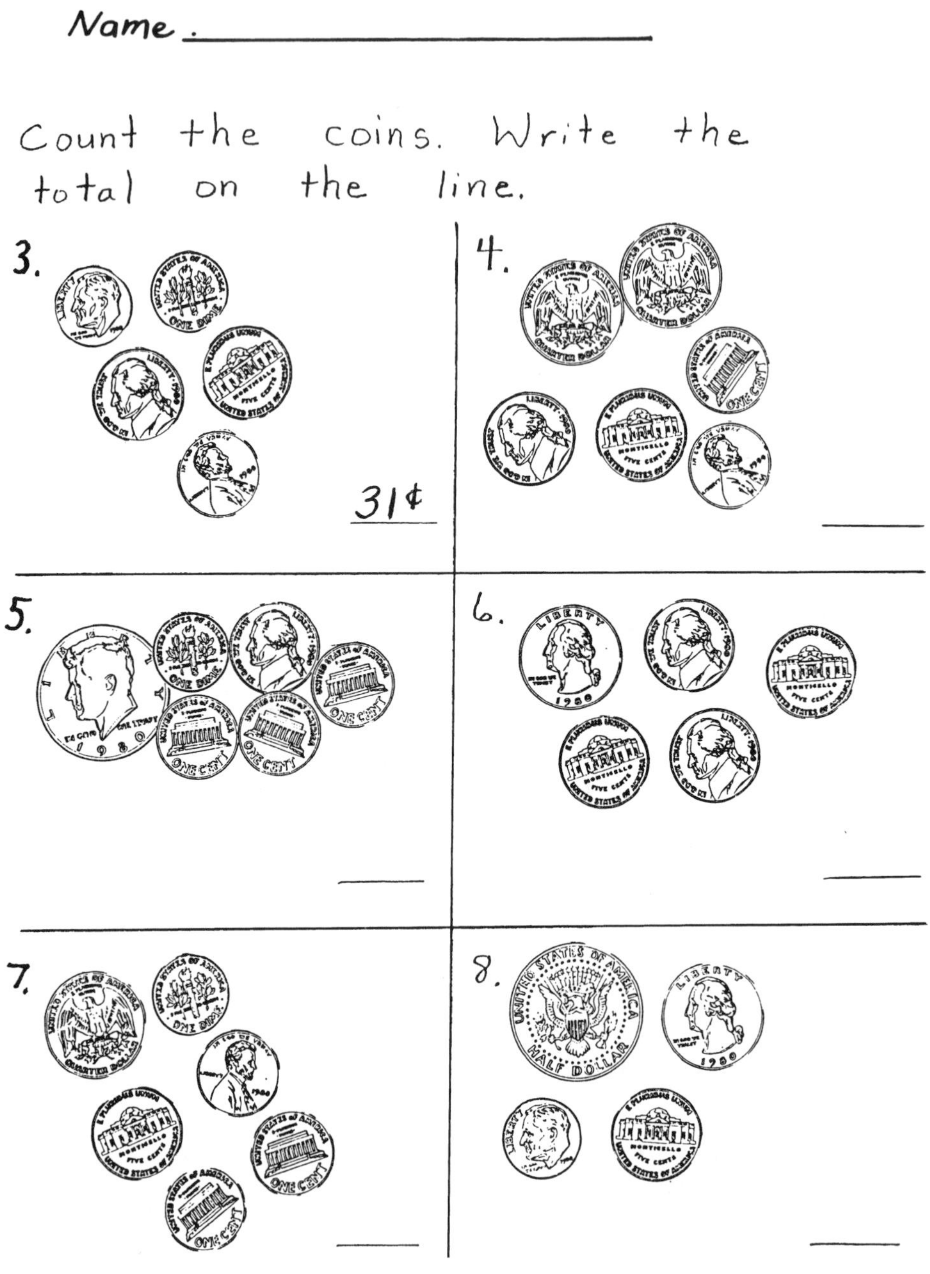

Name _____

Count the coins. Write the
total on the line.

3.

31¢

4.

_____

5.

_____

6.

_____

7.

_____

8.

_____

Figure 7.13
Test on coins.

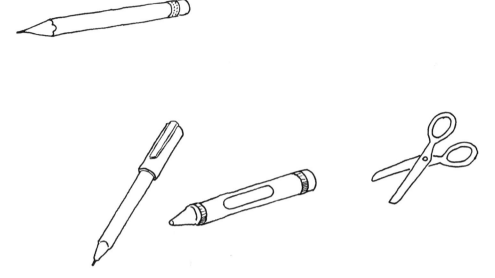

Figure 7.14
Unit on classification: array of objects.

other resources normally used by the teacher to help children practice and master new concepts and skills.

The instructional objective contains the structure for the learning experiences that will be provided for the students to interact with and master concepts. The teacher-directed lessons and child-centered activities enable the child to work with information and skills. When planning the activities, the teacher will want to establish some type of format to describe each activity and how it will be used. The activity description will include the objective, the materials needed, and any other relevant information.

For example, one of the objectives used for the unit on classifying objects discussed earlier could be used to describe appropriate activities. Figure 7.10 had the objective under "B. Noting Differences" as follows: From a set of four objects, the student will remove the one object that is different from the others. Figure 7.14 shows an assessment task that uses an array of objects to permit the child to demonstrate understanding the objective. Figure 7.15 describes an activity that can be used for young children to experience the same concepts.

Designing Correctives and Enrichment Activities

Corrective activities for students who need additional work after initial instruction and formative evaluation provide learning alternatives. These include audiovisual resources, games, workbooks, peer tutoring, student-teacher discussions, and other opportunities that are different from the original instruction and activi-

Objective
From a set of four objects, the student will remove the one object that is different from the others.

Materials Needed
A group of 2-inch blocks, 5 of one color, 1 of a different color
Several socks of different types and sizes, 1 shoe
An array of leaves of one type, 1 leaf of a different shape and size

Type of Activity
Teacher-directed, to be placed later in the math-science center. Small group.

Activity Description
The teacher will introduce the concept by using the group of blocks. The words *alike* and *different* will be modeled to describe the blocks.

Next, the socks and the shoe will be explored, with children encouraged to identify the one that is different. The leaves will then be used for the same activity.

As a final step, the teacher will ask each child to find examples in the classroom that are alike and different and to make a group similar to the examples that have been used: three things that are identical and one that is different. Each child is encouraged to describe his or her collection.

Figure 7.15
Example of a learning activity.

ties. The purpose is to provide different or alternative ways for the student to learn the information in the learning objective.

Examples of corrective activities and enrichment activities may use the objective cited above: From a set of four objects, the student will remove the one object that is different from the others. A child who needs additional activities to internalize the concept would benefit from opportunities to practice, but with alternative types of experiences. If the teacher-directed activities have focused on concrete objects, a corrective activity might consist of a card game of several sets of four cards that could be played by two children. Another corrective might use a flannel board and have the child remove the item that is different from an array of four items.

Enrichment activities provide opportunities for higher level thinking. If additional complexity is desired, the number of items might be increased to five, with two items that are different, rather than one. Another way to increase complexity is to make the difference in the item more difficult to identify. Only a slight difference is evident between the three identical items and the one that is different. For example, if the four pictured items are gift-wrapped boxes, the ribbon on one of the boxes is different or part of the ribbon is missing.

Enrichment activities also allow students who easily mastered the objective initially to engage in challenging and more creative activities. The students can work on individual projects that allow them to problem-solve and apply their own ideas in various types of activities that emerge from their own efforts (Block, 1977). Students might engage in developing pictures of items that are alike and different or write a story in which each page has a different category of items with one that is different.

ADVANTAGES AND DISADVANTAGES OF USING TEACHER-DESIGNED EVALUATIONS

Teacher-designed assessments in the classroom have several advantages over commercially produced tests developed for the same purpose. The advantages are related to the flexibility of the tests constructed for the teacher's own classroom.

When a teacher plans an assessment activity or test, the objective or objectives to be tested may be selected to suit individual class needs. Unlike commercial tests, which may be programmed to fit student progress in a grade level textbook, the teacher-designed test can vary from the structure or plan of the book. A teacher may be concerned about an objective outside of the textbook sequence and feel compelled to conduct an evaluation. Because he or she is developing tests to fit classroom needs, the targeted objective can be tested within the teacher's assessment plans whenever needed.

In addition, teacher-constructed assessments can be designed for a particular class. If the children are nonreaders but have advanced concepts that normally are introduced to children who have reading skills, the teacher can write the test to accommodate their abilities. If the students are advanced readers, the test can be designed to take advantage of their reading skills. The most common difficulty with commercial classroom tests is that they are set for a certain reading level or penalize the child for being unable to perform well because pencil-and-paper skills are required. The teacher can modify test tasks to include manipulative activities, oral responses, and assessment within instructional periods if the child understands concepts but cannot yet respond on a written test.

Teacher-designed assessments can be improved whenever needed. Each time the teacher administers a test, student responses provide feedback on its effectiveness. The test can be changed and improved whenever students' responses indicate problems with the format or test items.

Teacher-designed tests also have disadvantages; potential weaknesses generally focus on the teacher's skill in designing classroom assessments. Because teachers do not generally have extensive experience in developing their own tests, the evaluations they design may not be effective in evaluating student learning.

Because of the abundance of commercially designed tests that accompany curriculum texts and kits, teachers are not always required to construct their own tests. Teachers become dependent on commercial tests and do not consider the necessity of designing their own. As a result, the teacher may not clearly understand the purpose of the tests or the levels of knowledge that are tested.

Teachers may lack the training in test design that affects both the understanding of the purpose of the commercial tests and the skills needed to construct tests. For example, teachers may not have learned how to use a table of specifications

ASSESSMENTS FOR INSTRUCTIONAL OBJECTIVES: HOW USEFUL ARE THEY?

Norris teaches kindergarten. He and the other kindergarten teachers have been sent to a training session on designing assessments for instructional objectives using mastery learning. In the session, the teachers have reviewed how to write behavioral objectives and how to construct a table of specifications based on Bloom's taxonomy of educational objectives. Working with the table of specifications prepared them to design assessment strategies for the objectives.

On the way home after the training session, Norris and the other teachers voice skepticism. How can this kind of testing be used with kindergarten children? Norris comments, "I can see how some areas, such as math, can be organized and assessed by behavioral objectives, but how do you decide what 80 percent accuracy is on learning the Pledge of Allegiance, or what they learn from art or using concepts in science?" Jane, another kindergarten teacher in the group, agrees in principle with the strategies they have learned. She remarks, "I can see why they want us to learn the process. It forces us to be more specific in our understanding of what the objectives are meant to accomplish. My problem is that I'm afraid we are going to end up teaching to objectives and fragmenting the curriculum with the children."

Norris finally decides that it is a matter of common sense. The teacher can apply the strategies with some parts of the curriculum in kindergarten, but not others. The question is whether the school's principal and the kindergarten coordinator will share his perspective. He and the other kindergarten teachers decide to talk to teachers at other grade levels to determine how they are implementing the assessment strategies. Afterward they want to study their curriculum and decide where they can use assessments based on a table of specifications. They want to meet with the principal and the coordinator to discuss where the process will work and which parts of the curriculum do not lend themselves to that type of assessment.

When Norris and the other teachers meet with the principal and the kindergarten coordinator, they present tables of specifications and assessments for mathematics and units in science. After they explain their reluctance to use the process with their reading program and other curriculum components, the kindergarten coordinator supports their position. The principal is more reluctant, but decides to let the coordinator work with the teachers to determine how and where the assessment strategies will be implemented at the kindergarten level.

for curriculum objectives. When they design tests, they are not aware of the levels of knowledge in the curriculum that need to be part of the evaluation process. This lack of awareness may be more true of early childhood teachers than of teachers in intermediate grades and secondary school. Teachers of preschool and primary grade children need to be aware of the various levels of cognitive understanding, as well as alternative methods of evaluation that are developmentally suited to young students.

Finally, the process of developing good classroom tests, especially for younger students, is time-consuming. Because test items must be developed to accommodate emerging reading and writing skills, each item must be carefully considered both for content and for method or format. This consideration takes more time than developing items for students who have good reading and writing skills. The method of presentation is as important as the concepts and skills being tested.

A discussion of the weaknesses of teacher-designed assessments must include mention of the issues surrounding the use of mastery learning in early childhood education. Because mastery learning requires that the teacher analyze learning objectives and determine the level of mastery to be achieved, it would seem to be in conflict with the philosophy that early childhood educators should provide developmentally appropriate classroom experiences; that is, the teacher is encouraged to provide learning experiences that are consistent with the child's level of development, rather than to ask the child to fit into a predetermined style of learning that requires specific types of responses to achieve mastery.

The interest in providing developmentally appropriate practices also extends to the use of behavioral or instructional objectives specifically. One criticism of the objectives is the division of learning into small, skill-based objectives, rather than more global constructivist learning. The performance standard or level of mastery seems limiting when compared to the emphasis on child-centered learning that emerges from the child's interests and previous experiences.

Certain components of the preschool classroom curriculum lend themselves to the mastery learning approach. Concept development, particularly in mathematics, has sequential objectives that can be taught within the mastery learning format. Nevertheless, many early childhood educators object to attempts to limit early childhood programs to this approach. The need for exploratory and inquiry-based experiences, originating from the child's opportunity to initiate activities both indoors and outdoors and using self-directed learning, is essential in early childhood classrooms. In fact, these experiences are essential for both preschool and primary grade levels.

Teachers must ultimately be able to understand and use their own assessments appropriately to match the curriculum and their students' development. Mastery learning must also be used appropriately in early childhood programs.

Despite their weaknesses, teacher-designed evaluations have an important place in early childhood classrooms. An answer to the difficulties in using these assessments may be to help teachers understand the process of test design and to support their efforts to develop tests.

SUMMARY

Although written tests are the least commonly used method of evaluating the learning of young students, there is a place for these tests once children have mastered some reading and writing skills. Teachers and parents can use written tests as sources of objective information of student progress.

Like standardized tests, teacher-designed and commercially produced classroom assessments are developed through the use of procedures that ensure they are correct in content and method of evaluation. Test design begins with careful analysis and description of learning objectives for the curriculum. The objectives are examined for the prerequisite skills that must be mastered prior to their use and for how the content and skills must be taught. In addition to determining the level of mastery for the learning objectives, the test developer must use a developmentally appropriate test format that will maximize the performance of students who are learning to read and write.

Before test items are constructed, the test designer must describe the level at which the student must demonstrate the new knowledge. A table of specifications organized for the learning objectives is used for this purpose. While constructing the formative and summative evaluations, the teacher must consider length, equivalent items for both evaluations, and what types of test instructions are most appropriate.

Because paper-and-pencil tests may not be the most effective way to evaluate or assess children through the primary grades, teachers must understand when and how such tests are appropriate. The teacher must have acquired the skills to develop such tests if they are to measure learning accurately and appropriately. Teachers of young students must also understand the limitations of written tests and become skilled in combining them with alternative evaluation methods to ensure that each student is tested with procedures that are most appropriate for his or her own level of development and ability to respond.

REVIEW QUESTIONS

1. How do written tests serve a purpose different from other types of tests and evaluation methods?

2. Why should teachers be careful when using written tests with students in the primary grades?

3. How do written tests provide records of student learning that facilitate teaching accountability?

4. Why is the description of content and student behavior important in using learning objectives for assessment design?

5. How does the standard of mastery affect both the learning objective and the test developed to measure achievement of the objective?

6. What is a table of specifications? How is it used with learning objectives?

7. Why do teachers need to understand the levels of knowledge used to chart objectives on a table of specifications?

8. Describe different formats used in written tests developed for beginning readers.

9. What kinds of guidelines should the teacher consider when determining the length of a test for primary grade children?

10. Can more than one format be used in an assessment?

11. How are formative and summative tests alike? Different?

12. Why are written tests for primary grade children difficult to design?

13. Why do classroom teachers tend not to develop their own tests?

14. How can teacher-designed tests be more effective than commercially designed tests that evaluate the same objectives?

15. When should teachers use written tests? When should they not use written tests?

KEY TERMS

behavioral objective
correctives
enrichment activities
formative test

instructional objective
summative test
table of specifications

SUGGESTED ACTIVITIES

1. Write behavioral objectives for the following: (a) The child will be able to match upper- and lowercase letters; (b) The child will be able to sort objects by color; (c) The child will be able to match sets of objects with the correct numeral.

2. Develop a teacher-designed assessment for a learning center.

3. Develop a mastery learning unit based on three objectives. The unit should include a table of specifications, two learning activities for each objective, two correctives for each objective, and two enrichment activities for each objective.

REFERENCES

BLOCK, J. H. (1971). Introduction to mastery learning: Theory and practice. In J. H. Block (Ed.), *Mastery learning: Theory and practice* (pp. 2–12). New York: Holt, Rinehart & Winston.

BLOCK, J. H. (1977). Individualized instruction: A mastery learning perspective. *Educational Leadership, 34,* 337–341.

BLOOM, B. S. (Ed.). (1956). *Taxonomy of educational objectives: The classification of educational goals. Handbook I: Cognitive domain.* New York: McKay.

BLOOM, B. S., MADAUS, G. E., & HASTINGS, J. T. (1981). *Evaluation to improve learning.* New York: McGraw-Hill.

EICHOLZ, P. E., O'DAFFER, P., FLUXOR, C., CHARLES, R., YOUNG, S., & BARNETT, C. (1985). *Addison-Wesley mathematics teacher's edition. Book I.* Menlo Park, CA: Addison-Wesley.

GRONLUND, N. E. (1990). *Measurement and evaluation in teaching* (6th ed.). New York: Macmillan.

KUBISZYN, T., & BORICH, G. (1987). *Educational testing and measurement: Classroom application and practice* (2nd ed.). Glenview, IL: Scott, Foresman.

PAYNE, J. N., BEARDSLEY, L., BUNCH, B., CARTER, B., COBURN, T., EDMONDS, G., PAYNE, R., RATHMELL, E., & TRAFTON, P. (1985). *Mathematics teacher's edition: Grade 2.* New York: Harper & Row.

ROCKCASTLE, V. N., MCKNIGHT, B., SOLOMON, F., & SCHMIDT, V. (1984). *Addison-Wesley science teacher's resource book. Level 2.* Menlo Park, CA: Addison-Wesley.

WORTHAM, S. C. (1984). *Organizing instruction in early childhood.* Boston: Allyn & Bacon.

Chapter 8

Informal Measures: Performance-Based Evaluation

Chapter Objectives

As a result of reading this chapter you will be able to

1. understand the definition of and purposes for performance-based evaluation.
2. describe several types of performance-based assessments and how they are used.
3. understand the advantages and disadvantages of using performance-based evaluation tools.

In chapters 5, 6, and 7 we discussed types of informal evaluations such as observation, checklists and rating scales, and teacher-designed assessments. In this chapter we discuss how those informal evaluations contribute to a broader strategy—**performance-based evaluation.** Each of the informal assessments discussed in previous chapters contributes to the collection of assessment information that is part of performance-based evaluation. The strategies used to conduct those assessments permit the teacher to measure a child's performance.

Before proceeding further, I should explain what is meant by performance-based evaluation and how it is seen as a positive alternative to the use of standardized tests to measure children's development and learning.

Traditional, formal methods of measuring learning have focused on assessing what the child knows. Achievement tests are accurately labeled in that they measure what the child has achieved. Performance assessments require more in that they measure what the child can do or apply in addition to knowing (Pierson & Beck, 1993). Moreover, performance assessment includes completion of a task in a realistic context. Another term frequently used for this type of assessment is **authentic assessment** or **authentic performance assessment.** Bergen (1994) proposes that a good authentic performance assessment must have some connection to the real world and be an application of learning. Further, it possesses the following qualities (p. 99):

> 1) it is integrative, measuring many facets simultaneously; 2) it is applied, having the complexity of real world roles; 3) it may be individual, but is often group-based and the performance of every group member is essential for success as both individual and group performance effectiveness is evaluated.

Performance-based evaluation is considered to be particularly useful with young children because it measures progress as well as achievement. Children in the early childhood years are proceeding through rapid changes in development that are described as complex because of the interaction between maturation, experience, and learning (Hills, 1993). Performance assessments provide a vehicle for measuring developmental progress in addition to progress in learning new concepts. Performance assessments permit teachers to understand the processes children use to learn and how they actively construct meaning through analysis, synthesis, and evaluation (Brown, 1989; Meisels, 1993).

PURPOSES FOR PERFORMANCE-BASED EVALUATION

What, then, are the purposes for using performance-based evaluation with young children? First, the importance of measuring young children appropriately has been an ongoing theme in this text. Contrary to many of the standardized tests and more formal strategies that have been criticized as inappropriate to the young child's development, performance assessments can be good tools for evaluating progress in development. Because they are designed to measure a child's performance of a real or designed task or activity relevant to the desired learning, performance observations are directly related to the child's development and achievement.

Second, performance assessments are integrally related to instruction. The performance activity is a natural outcome of ongoing curriculum and instruction and not a separate, unrelated type of experience that is unfamiliar to the child. Krechevsky (1991, p. 45) characterizes the close relationship as "blurring the line between curriculum and assessment." When using performance-based evaluation, the classroom teacher needs to know how to design appropriate, related assessment tools, how to interpret assessment results to understand the child's progress and plan for further instruction, and how to interpret performance assessment results to parents and administrators (Hills, 1993).

Finally, performance assessments are used to evaluate whether preschool programs are meeting the needs of the young students. Good performance assessment tools help clarify the goals of preschool programs to provide developmental curriculum. Progress assessment reflects both individual developmental progress and accomplishment of developmental program goals (Schweinhart, 1993). The teacher then has the responsibility to report program accomplishments in a meaningful way to administrators (Hills, 1993).

In the next sections we discuss types of evaluation strategies that use performance assessments. Although most of the tools are selected or created by the teacher, others use examples of the child's work. Some are planned by both teacher and child, while others are spontaneous and not preplanned when the teacher takes advantage of an ongoing activity or event to conduct an assessment.

TYPES OF PERFORMANCE-BASED EVALUATION

Many strategies can be used to conduct performance-based evaluation. Like checklists and observations, performance-based evaluation has been used for many decades; however, in this context, it may have a broadened purpose or a more comprehensive role as part of a system of evaluation. The assessment strategies appropriate for use with young children are **interviews, directed assignments, contracts, games, work samples,** and **portfolios.**

Interviews

Teachers use interviews to find out what children understand about concepts. Interviews are especially appropriate for young children who are just beginning to develop literacy skills and cannot yet express themselves with a paper-and-pencil activity. The strategies followed in interviews complement the techniques used by Piaget to understand children's thinking. By questioning and asking more questions based on children's responses, Piaget was able to determine not only what the child understood but the thinking processes used to organize responses to the questions (Seefeldt, 1993).

Interviews can be described as informal, structured, or diagnostic. An *informal interview* can occur when children are playing, working in centers, or otherwise engaged in classroom activities. The teacher becomes aware that it is an opportune time to engage the child in an interview and takes a few minutes to question the child.

Structured interviews are preplanned by the teacher and conducted to acquire specific understandings about the child. For example, the teacher might want to ascertain the beginning reader's understanding of a story. After a reading of the story, the teacher asks probing questions to elicit the child's thoughts about the meaning of the story (Engel, 1990). Likewise, concepts in mathematics can be assessed through a structured interview when the teacher asks oral questions about a concept or process and explores the child's responses with further questions. Kamii and Rosenblum (1990) describe an activity to determine the kinder-

During structured interviews, teachers ask students questions planned to evaluate their understanding of concepts.

A STRUCTURED INTERVIEW TO ASSESS CLASSIFICATION SKILLS

Nykesha Hillmon's kindergarten class has been studying classification skills. Over a period of weeks, Nykesha has conducted lessons on sorting objects into two groups by using physical characteristics the objects have in common. The children have worked with the classification of nuts, rocks, and classroom plants. Today Nykesha has placed an assortment of beans in the science center. She is interviewing Tyrone, who has been asked to make two groups of beans. As Tyrone is in the process of forming the groups, Nykesha begins the interview with questions she has planned earlier:

Nykesha: Tyrone, can you explain how you decided to make the two groups of beans?

Tyrone: Well, one group of beans is round. They are all round.

Nykesha: And the other group?

Tyrone: They are all the same as this one (lima bean). I don't know what to call them.

Nykesha: Good. You have one group of beans that are round and another group of beans that have the same shape. You have made your groups by using their shape. Can you think of another way you could make two groups?

Tyrone: (After some hesitation) I could make groups of big ones and little ones.

Nykesha: Could you think of another way?

Tyrone: I don't think so.

Nykesha: How about using their color?

Tyrone: Oh, yes. I could put the ones that have brown together, and the rest that don't have brown together.

garten child's understanding of small addends by dropping beads into two glasses. The child was interviewed about the sum of the two groups of beads to assess the child's progress in mental arithmetic.

Diagnostic interviews serve an additional purpose: to determine the child's instructional needs. The interview may be informal or structured. The teacher's questioning is directed more at understanding what kind of help the child needs through responses to questions. If the teacher notices the child is confused or making errors, the diagnostic interview can reveal the difficulty the child is experiencing in thinking about the concept or skill.

Teachers can use several techniques to enhance the effectiveness of interviewing for assessment. In addition to taking notes when conducting an interview, teachers can make an audiotape of the child's responses for later review. Seefeldt (1993) suggests that when interviewing children about a social studies concept, responses need not be limited to talking. The child could act out a concept, find an example of the concept in pictures, or draw the things he or she knows about the concept. These possibilities would be helpful for children who are first speakers of another language or otherwise have difficulty expressing themselves verbally.

Interviews with young children should be short. Engel (1990) suggests that 10 minutes is an appropriate length of time. Other tips are to (1) continue questions after the child's initial responses to find out more than whether the child's response is correct or not and (2) give the child plenty of time to think about and respond to the teacher's questions. The child needs to feel comfortable with the process if pertinent responses are to be elicited.

Directed Assignments

Directed assignments are an extension of teacher-designed assessments, discussed in chapter 7. They are also similar to interviews, except that a specific task is involved in acquiring the child's understanding, rather than an interview. Children who are beginning to read independently might be asked to read a story and discuss it. Preschool children might be asked to use concrete objects to solve a problem in mathematical thinking. The important point is that the teacher makes a specific assignment or task for the purposes of assessment. Discussion and questioning may be a part of the process, but the child's ability to carry out the assignment is the focus of the assessment process (Hills, 1992).

Contracts

Contracts serve a dual purpose. They provide a plan between the teacher and the child and a record of the child's progress. Contracts of activities the child will engage in are designed for a period during a day, for the whole day, or for several days. Preschool children will need pictures or other visual representations of activities that are to be completed. Primary grade children can follow simple written instructions. After the child has completed an activity, some type of check-off system can be used to record the accomplishment.

Contracts can also be used to keep a record of accomplishment of skills and concepts. The teacher and the child can use the contract as a guide for conferences and interviews or as a recording system for the teacher to indicate when the child has completed an objective or needs more opportunities to interact with a concept. Over a period of time, completed contracts can provide information on progress and accomplishments.

Games

Games can be used to understand children's progress with a skill or a concept. Although more than one child will be playing the game at one time, the teacher can use observation to assess the child's abilities and thinking. Kamii and Rosenblum (1990) suggest that the teacher use games for systematic observation of an entire class. Two children or a slightly larger group play the game until all of the children have been assessed. The ability to make ten with two numbers is one example of a skill that can be assessed through the child's performance in a game. Cards from one to nine are arranged in groups of nine at one time. The child shows all of the pairs that can be combined to make ten. In addition to determining whether the child has mastered the skill, the teacher can observe the process the child uses to solve the problem. If the child arranges combinations quickly, a higher level of progress of mental addition has been achieved than that of a child who must count

USING CONTRACTS TO ASSESS PERFORMANCE

Graciela, a second-grade student, is discussing her mathematics contract with her teacher, Luis Garza. Luis plans contracts with the students on Monday of each week and conducts conferences with the students throughout the week to monitor their progress. Graciela has worked on her contract for two days. Her contract on Monday and Tuesday included the following:

Monday:
1. Small group lesson on subtraction
2. Center activity solving subtraction problems
3. Worksheet of subtraction problems

Tuesday:
1. Game with a partner solving subtraction problems

2. Subtraction worksheet
3. Conference with Mr. Garza

Luis discusses Graciela's work to date. They review her work, which includes the worksheets and problems solved in the math center. Luis notices that Graciela has made several subtraction errors. He questions Graciela and then gives her blocks to help her work out the subtraction problem. After she has described how she arrived at her answer, he tells her to work out the problem with the blocks again. After the conference, Luis makes a note to observe Graciela the following day to determine whether she needs further help with the subtraction process.

up from the first card to get the sum with the second card. Figure 6.8 in chapter 6 shows a form for recording levels of understanding for this concept.

Games may be used for concepts and skills in other content areas. Over many decades, many games have been developed for reading skills. Card games to identify letter knowledge are one ready example. Board games can be adapted or developed for language arts, mathematics, and social studies. A game similar to Trivial Pursuit, in which children must respond to an oral or a written question related to a topic being studied, is an example of how games can be used to test the child's ability to perform a task or solve a problem as an assessment activity.

Work Samples

Teachers and students are equal participants in the use of work samples for performance assessment. Work samples are examples of all types of children's work that can demonstrate the child's developmental progress or accomplishments. For preschool children, work samples may be clay models of animals that reflect the child's understanding of concepts in a thematic study related to animals. Other work samples include paintings, emergent writing, and dictated interpretations of wordless books. Primary grade children might have samples of book reports, creative writing that has been illustrated, and work pages of computation problems. Grace and Shores (1991) suggest using other visual media such as photographs, videotapes, and tape recordings or audiotapes.

ASSESSING PROGRESS WITH GAMES

Joan Harrison, a first-grade teacher, is using a board game to assess reading words. Each student has an individual bank of words from books they have read. Kim Soo and Martha are playing the game. The children take turns drawing a word card. If they name the word correctly, they can advance one square on the board. The first child to reach the end wins the game. Words that are missed are put in a separate pile, and Joan notes them in her notebook so that she can work the words into small group activities.

Work samples are often included in discussions about portfolios because portfolios become the means through which work samples and other types of information related to performance assessment are stored. A system for selecting and organizing work samples is important if the collection is to serve appropriately for performance assessment (Meisels, 1993).

Portfolios

The portfolio is one of the most popular methods of authentic assessments in the 1990s. In looking for alternatives to standardized tests, drill worksheets, and other assessment measures that reflect skills development rather than developmental progress evolving from the student's own demonstrations of performance, school districts across the United States have implemented portfolios as a preferred type of performance-based evaluation.

Portfolios are a process or method whereby student performance information can be stored and interpreted. Portfolios may be a folder very similar to collections of student work that many teachers have used for decades for reporting to parents. They may contain examples of papers that students have completed, as well as checklists, anecdotal records, summary reports for a grading period, and any other materials that students and teachers think are relevant to demonstrate the student's performance.

Portfolios may also be the vehicle used for assessing and reporting the student's progress and accomplishments to parents and administrators. This role of portfolios is discussed in chapter 9.

UNDERSTANDING THE INTERRELATED NATURE OF TYPES OF PERFORMANCE ASSESSMENTS

Different types of informal and performance-based assessments have been discussed both in this chapter and in earlier chapters. At this point it is important to describe how these assessments are used in an interrelated manner to understand characteristics of a child's performance. For example, observation is the basis for assessing a child's performance on a directed assignment, whereas a

Teachers and children can share in selection of work samples that will be included in individual portfolios.

checklist might be used to record the child's progress on the same assignment. In the following sections we explore characteristics of performance assessments and how they are used by the teacher to evaluate the development and achievement of the whole child.

The Role of the Teacher

The teacher has the primary role in selecting the types of performance assessments to be used and how they will be used. Because teachers assess and use the assessment information, they also have the responsibility to decide which strategies will be the most effective for their purposes.

Performance assessment occurs continually in the early childhood classroom. Information is collected throughout the day when children are working in centers, playing outdoors, participating in small group instruction, and during whole group activities. The teacher is observing and participating in these activities to acquire information about each child's progress and the child's own thinking about what and how he or she is learning.

Collecting information is only part of the teacher's role. Interpreting and using the data is another responsibility. First, the teacher must obtain enough information to know the child's abilities and needs so that appropriate planning can further growth and development. Second, the teacher must collect comprehensive information about each child so that all areas of development and learning are addressed. The teacher's goal is to design and implement a program that is appropriate for the child's physical, intellectual, and social development. Likewise, the program should be developmentally appropriate for all of the children. In summary, Hills (1992, p. 46) describes the teacher's role and responsibilities for assessment:

1. To integrate instruction and assessment fully in planning and carrying out the program
2. To use knowledge of young children to choose or design assessment processes
3. To analyze the results to find their meaning for the program and the children
4. To apply what has been learned to planning next steps and improving the program
5. To communicate with parents and involve them in an exchange of information about their child's learning and development

Classification and Organization of Performance Assessments

Although all performance assessments are considered to be informal measures, they can be categorized as structured or unstructured and direct and indirect. These organizational patterns are similar to structured and unstructured interviews but are more comprehensive in the types of assessments that are included.

One approach to categorizing assessments is by the type of activity used for assessment. Lee (1992) describes **unstructured** or **nonstructured performance assessments** as those that are part of regular classroom learning activities such as writing samples, projects, checklists, and teacher-designed tasks and tests. **Structured performance assessments** are predetermined or designed to include questions or tasks that require problem solving, synthesis, and analysis. Questions are open-ended, and all students are administered the questions through similar test administration procedures.

Another perspective of the two classifications is as spontaneous and structured. Similar to Lee's definition, spontaneous assessments evolve from the teacher's natural day-to-day interactions and observations in the classroom. Structured performance assessment not only is preplanned but also must meet the standards for reliability and validity required of standardized measurement instruments. Such assessments are carefully designed and have specified scoring criteria as well as well-defined behaviors that are to be measured.

Performance assessments can also be classified as direct or indirect. On the one hand, **direct performance measures** require students to use knowledge in some type of application. On the other hand, **indirect performance measures** measure what students know about a topic. An example of an indirect measure is a paper-and-pencil test. An example of a direct measure is taking measurements of a table to determine how large to make a tablecloth to fit the table. The distinction between these performance measures is assessing knowledge versus assessing application of knowledge (Pierson & Beck, 1993).

The Role of Observation

Strategies for observation were discussed in chapter 5. Further, the importance of using observation to evaluate the development of young children was emphasized. A discussion of the role of observation within performance assessments reinforces that importance. When considering the measurement of the young child's performance, observation is the most effective strategy (Hills, 1992). Observation behaviors such as attending, examining, heeding, considering, investigating, monitoring, studying, and watching enable the teacher to understand and know the child and what the child can do in real-life circumstances and common learning situations (Hills, 1993).

Observation should occur throughout the day in all types of classroom activities. Strategies for observation, including anecdotal records, running records, observation with checklists and rating scales, and time and event sampling, can all have a role in performance assessment. To ensure that the desired performance is observed and recorded, Hills (1993, p. 27) recommends that the following components be determined prior to conducting the observation:

- **Purpose**   What do we want to know?
- **Focus**   Who or what is being observed? Exhibits what behaviors? When? Where?
- **Record/documentation**   What information is needed? How will it be recorded? How frequently?
- **Use of the observation**   What does the observed event mean for the child's progress and needs? What next steps would we take to further the child's development?

Gathering and documenting information through observation is not enough. Analysis and use of assessment data must also be facilitated as a result of the observation. Therefore, the child should be observed at different times, at different places, and using different materials before determining whether new knowledge has been developed (Bergan & Feld, 1993). In addition, teachers should spend time reflecting about the information that has been gathered. The intent of reflection is so that teachers will use assessment in an intentional manner to plan for children's future learning opportunities. To properly collect and reflect on observation data, teachers might include the following steps (Hills, 1992, p. 50): (1) establish purpose and focus, (2) observe and record, (3) compile what was recorded, both for individual children and for the group, and (4) reflect on the records and refocus teaching and learning activities.

Observation is the foundation of performance assessment. It is used with interviews when the teacher observes the child's responses and behaviors. It is integral to directed assignments as the teacher observes the child completing the assignment or task. Observation enables the teacher to understand the child's thinking and knowledge when engaging in assessment games. Observation complements other strategies used for unstructured and structured and direct and indirect performance assessments. Finally, checklists and rating scales and teacher-designed assessments of various types incorporate observation as part of or the entire process of understanding the child's performance.

ADVANTAGES AND DISADVANTAGES OF USING PERFORMANCE-BASED EVALUATION

Advantages of Using Performance-Based Evaluation

There are definite advantages in using performance-based evaluation for assessment of young children. Although performance assessment is recommended for children of all ages, it is particularly suitable for children in preoperational and concrete operational stages of development. Because young children learn best by acting on the environment, it logically follows that assessment that permits the child to demonstrate ability by performing some action is most compatible with developmental capabilities. Performance assessments, then, are fitting for the development of children in the early childhood years. Some arguments for using performance assessments for evaluation are the following:

1. Performance assessments are conducted in the context of what children are experiencing, rather than in isolation from classroom curriculum. Earlier in the chapter it was recommended that assessment be an integral part of curriculum and instruction. Whenever possible, performance assessments are conducted as part of a lesson, during center activities, or serendipitously when the teacher observes desired learning demonstrated spontaneously. Performance assessments are meaningful and timely.

2. Performance assessments take advantage of the premise that children construct their own understanding. Early childhood educators today prepare curriculum activities with the comprehension that knowledge is not transmitted by the teacher; instead, the child gradually forms or produces new knowledge through repeated encounters with concepts and information. Performance assessment provides the teacher with tools to observe and document the child's progress. This provision means that assessment goes beyond assessing whether the child has mastered the teacher's learning objectives. The child's progress toward mastery using Vygotsky's (1983) zone of proximal development can also be evaluated. The zone described by Vygotsky refers to the variability between what the child can currently do and what the child can master potentially in the future. The teacher can determine whether the child is unable to demonstrate an ability or understanding, whether the child can show some of the desired behaviors with assistance, or whether the child can perform independently (Hills, 1992). Further, the focus of the assessment is on the child, and not on the child's responding to the teacher. The teacher still plays a major role in the assessment, but the child's performance is the key and the teacher responds to what the child is doing.

3. Performance assessments provide a variety of means whereby the child can demonstrate what he or she understands or can do. The child's ongoing work examples, art products, play, conversation, emergent writing, and dictated stories are a few examples of ways children can perform. Some of the performances can be recorded as a result of the teacher's observation or interviews, whereas others can be documented by work samples. Because assessment is integrated with instruction and daily activities, the possibilities for observing and interpreting accomplishments are almost unlimited.

4. Performance assessment is continuous or ongoing. Unlike more formal assessments such as tests, end-of-chapter assessments, and reporting period evaluations, performance assessments reflect daily opportunities to be aware of the child's thinking and work.

5. Performance assessments provide meaningful information for parents to understand their child's progress and accomplishments. They also enable parents to contribute and participate in the assessment process. Teachers can use performance assessments of all types in parent conferences. Likewise, parents can become more aware of behaviors their child is using at home that demonstrate developmental advancement and share their observations with the teacher. Once parents understand the significance of the child's activities and their relationship to development and learning, they can be partners with the teacher and child in facilitating opportunities for the child.

Disadvantages of Using Performance-Based Evaluation

Performance assessments have their disadvantages or limitations. Like all informal assessments, they are subjective; teacher bias and interpretation are part of the process. Teachers must be constantly alert for the need for objectivity when evaluating young children. Also, performance assessments increase the responsibility and accountability of the teacher in administering and interpreting evaluations. This opportunity for more meaningful assessments is accompanied by the need for teachers to be skilled in the assessment process.

Although some of the strategies used to evaluate children in performance assessments are not new, the approach as the primary means to assess and give grades to students is considered to be an innovation. Like any educational innovation, problems and difficulties can cause teachers and administrators to become disenchanted with the process and to doubt the effectiveness of the practice. Therefore, it is important to be aware of and understand the implications and limitations of performance assessment, as well as the benefits. Following are some of the concerns that measurement specialists propose about the use of performance assessments.

1. Performance assessments are time-consuming. Teachers need time to conduct observations, record data, and interpret information in planning future instruction. All performance assessments require extensive involvement of the teacher. Record keeping adds to paperwork responsibilities; moreover, teachers must consider how to fit assessment into otherwise busy days. Teachers must develop the ability to do several things at once and to keep up with reflection on information and ideas they gain from studying the child's performance activities.

2. Authentic assessment can be more complex than more traditional types of assessment. Because assessment is integrated into instruction, teachers must clearly understand what they are looking for in assessment. Assessment with young children might be interdisciplinary or measure more than one type of development when it is a part of integrated curriculum and child-centered activities. The teacher must predetermine explicit standards of performance for development and learning objectives no matter how incidental or integrated the assessment process. The more complex and integrated the curriculum is, the more difficult the performance assessment process will be in terms of interpreting the implications of the child's performance (Bergen, 1994).

3. More traditional forms of assessment have had the goal of evaluating the child's achievement. Performance assessment has the goal of evaluating progress, as well as achievement. Teachers may have difficulty incorporating this new role of understanding the child's progress and implications for curriculum planning for that child. Teachers must not only develop new competencies in acquiring assessment information but also become more competent in using progress information to further the child's development. Teachers may find this requirement to be very confusing and be uncertain about how skillfully and appropriately they are using performance assessments (Bergen, 1994).

4. There are also concerns about validity and reliability of performance assessments. Schweinhart (1993) proposes that early childhood assessment tools must be developmentally appropriate, valid, reliable, and user-friendly. As described in the section above, the difficulty of using performance assessments would raise doubts about how user-friendly they are. To be valid, the tools must correlate with concurrent measures being used to assess young children. Likewise, assessments should be internally consistent and assessed similarly by various assessors. Informal procedures used in performance assessments must provide evidence of validity, reliability, objectivity, and freedom from bias if they are to be considered feasible (Goodwin & Goodwin, 1993). The probability that public school systems will understand this necessity and undertake the extensive work needed to ensure quality seems doubtful.

5. Parental involvement and education are a requirement when implementing performance-based evaluation. Parents are familiar with traditional evaluation and reporting practices. School districts must plan to educate and prepare parents before moving into performance assessments. Parents need to be knowledgeable and comfortable with how the innovative assessment process is used before they encounter it in their child's grade report or in a parent-teacher conference. Unfamiliar terminology and assessment procedures can cause a lack of confidence in and support for the school and the teachers.

Most of the disadvantages and limitations discussed above seem related to proper preparation and training for performance assessments. Too often in the past, schools have embraced and implemented curriculum and instruction innovations without training teachers and administrators properly. Some of the authors cited in this chapter consistently discuss the need for extensive training and preparation prior to using new performance assessments. Like any change or new approach to curriculum or assessment, adequate training and knowledge about performance assessments can do much to ensure that they will be a successful and appropriate alternative for assessment of young children. Because performance assessments inherently have the potential to measure young children's development and learning in a realistic and meaningful way, the limitations can become either difficult obstacles or perceptive cautions that can be used to facilitate appropriate and skilled use of new tools.

SUMMARY

> The time has come for us to adopt a new assessment paradigm: *performance assessment.* Performance assessments document activities in which children engage on a daily basis. They provide a means for evaluating the quality of children's work in an integrated manner. They are flexible enough to reflect an individualized approach to academic achievement. They are also designed to evaluate many elements of learning and development that standardized tests do not capture well. As active constructors of meaning, children analyze, synthesize, evaluate, and interpret facts and ideas (Brown, 1989, as cited in Meisels, 1993). Performance assessment allows teachers the opportunity to learn about these processes by documenting children's interactions with materials and peers in the classroom environment. In short, performance assessment puts assessment back where it belongs: in the hands of teachers and children, and in the classrooms that they inhabit. (Meisels, 1993, p. 36)

In this chapter we have discussed performance-based evaluation as an alternative or authentic method of assessing young children. Meisels, quoted above, believes that this approach to assessment makes teachers more powerful and in control of the learning-evaluation process.

A number of methods or strategies can be used to evaluate the child's development or learning through performance of what he or she understands and can do. Interviews, directed assignments, contracts, games, work samples, and portfolios are among the assessment activities that will permit young children to demonstrate their ability to understand and apply new skills and information.

Performance assessments complement each other in how they focus on the child's progress and accomplishments. In addition, informal assessment methods such as observation, checklists and rating scales, and teacher-designed assessments are used in the process of assessing through performance.

Performance assessment transfers responsibility to teachers for the instructional and assessment process. This empowerment of the teacher facilitates the teacher's opportunity to design assessment that includes all areas of development and that is appropriate for the level of development of each child. It also allows for the teacher to make a close connection between curriculum and evaluation.

Although performance assessment is more relevant and appropriate than traditional, formal methods of measuring learning, it can also be more difficult. Teachers must accept the time that is needed to organize and conduct this type of evaluation; moreover, they must overcome limitations related to validity, reliability, and accountability. Care must be exercised in planning and implementing performance assessment if it is not to become an educational fad that fades after a few years.

REVIEW QUESTIONS

1. Explain the definition of performance assessments or performance-based evaluation.

2. Why is performance assessment suited for children in the early childhood years?

3. Why do measurement specialists describe performance and instruction as closely related?

4. Interviews can be used for evaluation in several ways. Discuss three types of interviews and when they are appropriate.

5. How are interviews helpful to understanding children's thinking processes?

6. Why can it be said that directed assignments are designed by the teacher but contracts are designed by teacher and child?

7. How is assessment through games different from assessment through an interview?

8. Explain the role of observation in performance assessments.

9. What is meant by interrelated assessments? Describe two assessments that can be interrelated.

10. Explain the difference between direct performance measures and indirect performance measures.

11. How do you believe performance assessments will be advantageous to you as a teacher of young children?

12. Explain how performance assessments can be difficult to interpret.

13. How can teachers ensure that performance assessments are accurate?

14. Why is it possible that performance assessments can lack validity and reliability?

15. What role should parents have in using performance assessments? Explain.

KEY TERMS

authentic assessment
authentic performance assessment
contract
directed assignment
direct performance measure
game
indirect performance measure

interview
performance-based evaluation
portfolio
structured performance assessment
unstructured performance
    assessment
work sample

SUGGESTED ACTIVITIES

1. Visit a classroom where performance assessments are used. Identify the assessments used that demonstrate what the child *knows* and those that demonstrate what the child *can do* or *can apply.*

2. Select a learning objective suitable for a child in the first grade. Design assessments that use observation, an interview, and a game. Describe how you would conduct the observation and analyze the results.

REFERENCES

BERGAN, J. R., & FELD, J. K. (1993). Developmental assessment: New directions. *Young Children, 48,* 41–47.

BERGEN, D. (1994). Authentic performance assessments. *Childhood Education, 70,* 99, 102.

BROWN, R. (1989). Testing and thoughtfulness. *Educational Leadership, 7,* 31–33.

ENGEL, B. (1990). An approach to assessment in early literacy. In C. Kamii (Ed.), *Achievement testing in the early grades* (pp. 119–134). Washington, DC: National Association for the Education of Young Children.

GOODWIN, W. L., & GOODWIN, L. D. (1993). Young children and measurement: Standardized and nonstandardized instruments in early childhood education. In B. Spodek (Ed.), *Handbook of research on the education of young children* (pp. 441–463). New York: Macmillan.

GRACE, C., & SHORES, E. (1991). *The portfolio and its use.* Little Rock: Southern Association on Children Under Six.

HILLS, T. W. (1992). Reading potentials through appropriate assessment. In S. Bredekamp & T. Rosegrant (Eds.), *Reaching potentials: Appropriate curriculum and assessment for young children* (Vol. 1, pp. 43–64). Washington, DC: National Association for the Education of Young Children.

HILLS, T. W. (1993). Assessment in context: Teachers and children at work. *Young Children, 48,* 20–28.

KAMII, C., & ROSENBLUM, V. (1990). An approach to assessment in mathematics. In C. Kamii (Eds.), *Achievement testing in the early grades* (pp. 146–162). Washington, DC: National Association for the Education of Young Children.

KRECHEVSKY, M. (1991). Project Spectrum: An innovative assessment alternative. *Educational Leadership, 48,* 43–48.

LEE, F. Y. (1992). Alternative assessments. *Childhood Education, 69,* 72–73.

MEISELS, S. J. (1993). Remaking classroom assessment with the work sampling system. *Young Children, 48,* 34–40.

PIERSON, C. A., & BECK, S. S. (1993). Performance assessment. The realities that will influence the rewards. *Childhood Education, 70,* 29–32.

SCHWEINHART, L. J. (1993). Observing young children in action: The key to early childhood assessment. *Young Children, 48,* 29–33.

SEEFELDT, C. (1993). *Social studies for the preschool-primary child* (4th ed.). New York: Merrill/Macmillan.

VYGOTSKY, L. (1983). School instruction and mental development. In M. Donaldson, R. Grieve, & C. Pratt (Eds.), *Early childhood development and education: Readings in psychology* (pp. 263–269). New York: Guilford.

Chapter 9

Using Informal Assessment Strategies to Report Student Progress

Chapter Objectives

As a result of reading this chapter you will be able to

1. understand the limitations of report cards for reporting student progress.
2. understand the importance of developing alternative reporting systems.
3. design and use portfolios for assessing and reporting student progress.
4. write a narrative report to report student progress.
5. understand models of reporting systems.
6. understand the advantages and limitations of alternative reporting systems.

What is the best way to assess the young child's progress and develop an evaluative report for that child? In early chapters of this text we discussed standardized measures, how they are developed and used, and when they are not appropriate for evaluating young children. We also discussed some strategies for conducting informal assessments. In chapter 8 we described performance assessments and how informal strategies are a part of or complement performance assessments.

In this chapter we address how to take the data we collect by using informal or performance assessments and construct a holistic picture of a child's progress that can be reported to parents and school district administrators periodically throughout the school year. These alternative types of reporting are suggested as more suitable for reporting the development and learning of children in the early childhood years.

UNDERSTANDING THE NEED FOR ALTERNATIVE ASSESSMENT AND REPORTING SYSTEMS

We are in a period of new trends in curriculum and instruction that have implications for assessment. New curriculum models for language arts have emerged as schools move from the use of basal readers to emergent literacy, whole language, and the use of trade books for reading instruction. Thematic or integrated curriculum signals a shift from teaching isolated content areas to combining curriculum to develop meaningful connections. Teachers are more aware of the cultural, linguistic, and ability diversity in their students and are designing activities that complement the strengths that accompany the diversity. Alternative, informal, and performance assessments (discussed in chapters 4 through 8) and strategies to report performance (addressed in this chapter) are partly in response to limitations and concerns about standardized tests and partly to fulfill the need for more appropriate methods of measuring the new trends in curriculum and instruction (Glazer, 1993).

Using Alternative Assessments Appropriately

In this period of transition in curriculum and instruction and assessment, particularly with children in the preschool and primary years, the fundamental task for educators is to make a knowledgeable shift from more traditional forms of assessment and reporting to alternative strategies. Basic to any transition is first determining what method of reporting achievement and progress to parents is to be used. If the traditional report card is to be maintained, assessment records will have to be compatible with that type of report. That is, if grades or some type of scale to compare progress among students is the profile to be reported, teachers must be accountable for how they determined the child's grade. If a narrative report or portfolio, rather than a report card, is to be used to present the child's profile of progress, there must be understanding and consensus as to what the report means and how parents can share in the communication of the child's development and achievement.

Administrators and teachers must be clear about the purposes for and methods used for assessment. School districts that are moving to a whole language approach and integrated curriculum in elementary classrooms but that are expecting teachers to be accountable for letter grades, particularly in primary grade classrooms, must understand the incompatibility of methodology and assessment and reporting. In sum, the trend toward holistic, developmental, and integrated learning must be accompanied by sensible assessment and evaluation strategies provided in the alternative assessments defined as authentic and performance-based. The reporting systems should also include these strategies when the teacher is developing an evaluation profile for individual children.

Limitations of Letter Grades and Report Cards

Currently teachers in school districts all over the United States are reviewing and redesigning report cards. A primary motive for this endeavor is the difficulty teachers have in following new trends in curriculum and instruction and in trying to report the child's progress in terms of isolated skills or letter grades based on more traditional teaching methods.

Curriculum and instruction for children in the early childhood years in quality programs are shifting from an academic approach in which children are expected to learn the same information at the same time to a developmental approach. The developmental approach reflects the understanding of development and learning as a continuum along which each child progresses via an internal clock and an individual cognitive process that depends on maturation and previous experiences. Each child's understanding of new knowledge is based on the cognitive information stored from previous encounters in the environment. There is a basic incompatibility between developmental programs reflected in the emergent literacy approach in language arts that is organized to respond to the individual child's development and letter grades that require competence in skills development based on a timetable established by the teacher or the school district.

Letter grades can reward students for correct answers and discourage risk taking and experimentation. Newer trends in curriculum and instruction stress the student's willingness to use ideas and develop problem-solving strategies as part of the process of learning. Grading undermines these instructional practices because students are unwilling to take the chance of making errors and possibly receiving low grades.

Letter grades are also limited because they only measure achievement. They do not reflect the student's strengths and weaknesses or the effort made to earn the grade. Critics believe that grades tend to limit how many students can do well. Not only does the system tend to sort students into categories, but also slower students lose their motivation to learn as a result of continuing negative feedback. In addition, they get labeled as poor students, and teacher expectations are lower for them than for students who make higher grades (Willis, 1993).

Alternative systems of reporting that use authentic or performance assessments provide more than letter grades. They can include (1) a continuum of development and learning, (2) information about the whole child, not just about skills that have been mastered, (3) diagnostic information that allows the teacher to adjust instruction and activities, and most importantly, (4) examples of what the child has done to demonstrate understanding. In the following sections we discuss some assessment and reporting systems that can be developed as alternatives to traditional report cards.

Report cards themselves are changing as teachers and administrators find more flexible and meaningful types of reporting. Figure 9.1 shows a continuum or hierarchy of skills for language arts, math, science, and social studies. The report is used as a ongoing tool to report progress.. The continuum begins at the bottom of the page, and the complexity or difficulty increases as the indicators or objectives move up the page. After the child has mastered a concept or a skill, it is checked off. Progress is the important factor, rather than a letter grade given if mastery is demonstrated during a reporting period. Likewise, the child can progress along the hierarchy of objectives above or below grade level. The reporting form shown is at the piloting stage. As teachers and administrators become more knowledgeable and skilled, more indicators of development may be included along with refinements in the objectives presently listed.

Developing Alternative Assessment and Reporting Systems

Once school district policymakers, administrators, and teachers determine that performance assessments are to be included in the evaluation process, decisions are then made on how to use performance assessments and develop a comprehensive picture of the child's progress. Collection and interpretation of data relevant to the child's performance require organization of an evaluation system that permits the teacher to describe growth in a meaningful manner.

Assessments and tools to report assessment results are interwoven. Two commonly used methods of assessment and reporting are portfolios and narrative reports. A *portfolio* can be described both as an assessment tool and as a system to report the child's overall evaluation. A *narrative report* is a written description of the

FIRST GRADE

6.0

Language Arts
- ☐ Recognizes vowels
- ☐ Reads primer level simple sentences
- ☐ Understands antonyms
- ☐ Writes phrases
- ☐ Arranges events in sequential order
- ☐ Alphabetizes according to initial letter
- ☐ Acquires basic sight vocabulary
- ☐ Engages in creative dramatic activities and nonverbal communication
- ☐ Responds to nonverbal cues

Math
- ☐ Knows greater than/less than
- ☐ Writes numerals 1 - 20
- ☐ Recognizes simple color and size patterns
- ☐ Recognizes and sorts plane figures
- ☐ Finds differences by separating and comparing objects
- ☐ Solves problems involving addition and subtraction with manipulatives
- ☐ Uses numeral sentences

Science
- ☐ Acquires data through the use of senses
- ☐ Identifies careers related to theme: mayor, construction workers, business people, etc.
- ☐ Identifies internal organs and their functions (brain, heart, lungs)
- ☐ Identifies skeletal parts (skull, ribs, pelvis, spine)
- ☐ Classifies food into pyramid levels
- ☐ Classifies events in a consistent, organized fashion while making observations (plant growth)

Social Studies
- ☐ Is aware of others' needs
- ☐ Identifies kinds of work of school personnel and family members
- ☐ Knows birthdate
- ☐ Knows geography of school campus
- ☐ Identifies name of school
- ☐ Knows geographical location of home in relation to school/community
- ☐ Identifies and accepts one's classroom responsibilities
- ☐ Completes assigned tasks
- ☐ Identifies positive traits of self and others

6.3

Language Arts
- ☐ Selects topics of interest to self and others
- ☐ Understands opposites
- ☐ Understands naming words (people, places, things, animals)
- ☐ Recognizes a sentence
- ☐ Understands action words
- ☐ Identifies the main idea in speakers
- ☐ Uses basic phonics: media/message/final consonants
- ☐ Uses pronouns properly
- ☐ Contributes ideas and information in group discussion

Math
- ☐ Finds sums by combining groups and counting
- ☐ Finds differences by separating and comparing objects
- ☐ Estimates and predicts quantities
- ☐ Identifies lines of symmetry
- ☐ Measures/estimates mass using standard units
- ☐ Develops concept of conservation (measuring capacity using containers)
- ☐ Constructs picture graphs

Science
- ☐ Creates an order of events in a logical continuum while making observations
- ☐ Collects information to make reasonable interpretations
- ☐ Makes accurate measurements and uses them appropriately as descriptors
- ☐ Manipulates laboratory materials and equipment
- ☐ Uses information and observations to make reasonable interpretations

Social Studies
- ☐ Contributes to group activities
- ☐ Understands food processing
- ☐ Discusses visuals (pictures, charts)
- ☐ Knows how animals are used for clothing, food, etc.
- ☐ Understands and distinguishes animal habitats
- ☐ Uses terms concerning time (today, tomorrow, yesterday)
- ☐ Knows months of the year
- ☐ Knows the days of the week
- ☐ Knows N, S, E, W
- ☐ Knows the four seasons

Figure 9.1 (pp. 201-202)
A first-grade reporting system.

FIRST GRADE

6.6

Language Arts
- ☐ Uses homophones properly
- ☐ Reads using word attack skills
- ☐ Uses was/is properly
- ☐ Reads first-grade level
- ☐ Distinguishes long and short vowels
- ☐ Begins sentences with capital letter
- ☐ Writes brief descriptions
- ☐ Uses information and ideas from personal experiences as a source of writing
- ☐ Describes time and setting of a story
- ☐ Uses phrases in oral reading

Math
- ☐ Numbers to 20 and graphing
- ☐ Understands the operation of addition by having one more
- ☐ Understands the operation of subtraction by having one less
- ☐ Makes and reads data from a graph
- ☐ Writes number before, after, between: order 0–20
- ☐ Compares quantities of objects by counting and regrouping
- ☐ Recognizes coins
- ☐ Develops concept of place value (10's)
- ☐ Recognizes even parts
- ☐ Identifies and solves word problems
- ☐ Measures time by reading clock
- ☐ Measures time related to calendar
- ☐ Uses measurement units of time, length, and mass

Science
- ☐ Acquires data by environmental observations
- ☐ Identifies and manipulates conditions of investigation data
- ☐ Identifies cause/effect relationships
- ☐ Asks thoughtful and relevent questions
- ☐ Identifies significant similarities
- ☐ Identifies significant differences

Social Studies
- ☐ Identifies important Texas and U.S. holidays
- ☐ Recites the Pledge of Allegiance
- ☐ Identifies the state and nation by name
- ☐ Knows state and national anthems
- ☐ Understands concept of exchange
- ☐ Recognizes necessity of making economic choices among alternatives
- ☐ Can read map symbols
- ☐ Knows patriotic customs of the state and nation
- ☐ Distinguishes between producing and consuming
- ☐ Distinguishes between goods and services

6.9

Language Arts
- ☐ Becomes acquainted with a variety of selections, characters and themes of our literary heritage
- ☐ Understands cause/effect
- ☐ Uses contractions in writing
- ☐ Uses correct forms of regular verbs (oral-written)
- ☐ Uses correct singular and plural forms of regular nouns (oral-written)
- ☐ Uses conventions of capitalization and punctuation
- ☐ Follows simple written directions
- ☐ Uses context clues
- ☐ Gives short sequence of directions for others to follow

Math
- ☐ Addition facts count ones and zero
- ☐ Uses property of zero
- ☐ Uses commutative property of addition
- ☐ Identifies greater sum
- ☐ Addition facts sums of 12
- ☐ Estimates and measures length using standard units
- ☐ Estimates and measures length using inch units
- ☐ Uses ruler to measure inches
- ☐ Uses ruler to measure foot
- ☐ Orders objects by length and height
- ☐ Estimates and measures using a centimeter ruler
- ☐ Estimates and measures capacity (weight)
- ☐ Uses subtract facts
- ☐ Continues a number pattern

Science
- ☐ Makes thoughtful, accurate questions
- ☐ Transfers learning to new situations
- ☐ Constructs interesting, creative questions
- ☐ Acquires data by environmental observations
- ☐ Constructs interesting, creative models (landforms, relief maps)

Social Studies
- ☐ Learns family history
- ☐ Identifies ways people learn from each other
- ☐ Describes similarities and differences among people
- ☐ Practices rules of safety
- ☐ Recognizes safety symbols
- ☐ Completes if/then statements
- ☐ Understands the concept of scarcity
- ☐ Identifies cause/effect relationships
- ☐ Discusses graphs/tables

Language Arts	Math	Science	Social Studies

Figure 9.1 (continued)
A first-grade reporting system.

child's development and achievement that is derived from multiple assessment tools. Nevertheless, a narrative report can be part of a portfolio, and vice versa.

In this segment of the chapter we elaborate on how assessment tools and reporting systems can be developed to report student progress. Some current models for reporting systems—Project Spectrum, the Work Sampling System, and the High/Scope Child Observation Record—are discussed.

USING PORTFOLIOS FOR EVALUATION AND REPORTING

As was defined in chapter 8, portfolios are a collection of a child's work and teacher data from informal and performance assessments to evaluate development and learning. A portfolio may be kept just by and for the child, with samples of work over a period of time. It may also be organized by the teacher and contain observation reports, checklists, work samples, records of directed assignments, interviews, or other evidence of achievement. There are child portfolios, teacher portfolios, and combinations that include entries made by both the child and the teacher.

Types of Portfolios

Portfolios have become a popular trend in elementary schools in the last few years, particularly in the language arts. Although abundant literature is available on how to use the portfolio for assessment in language arts, particularly for the whole language and emergent literacy approaches, less has been offered for other developmental or content area categories. Some educators and parents thus may assume that the portfolio is limited to classes using whole language or emergent literacy methods. It is just as appropriate to use portfolios for social studies, science, and mathematics as it is to use alternative or authentic strategies for assessment for all types of curriculum and instruction.

Portfolios can be organized by content area as described above, by developmental category, or by topics or themes if an integrated curriculum is followed. As is true for curriculum design, the goals of the program and objectives for development and learning serve as the foundation for instruction and assessment. As teachers understand more about the emergent nature of cognition and development, their task is to become comfortable with using characteristics of emerging development and how that is reflected in the work they and the children can collect for assessment. In this respect, understanding the principles and characteristics of development become essential if the teacher is to comprehend how to assess the child's developmental progress. For example, the pattern of emergence of writing and reading can be organized into a checklist or other record keeping form to determine the child's progress in emergent literacy (Farr, 1993; Sulzby, 1993). See Figure 9.2 for an example of a form that can be used in a portfolio. Similar patterns of progress can be developed and used for physical and social development (McClellan & Katz, 1992). Science and mathematics can be assessed through a hierarchy of development in cognition, as well as behaviors observed in science process activities (Carin, 1993; Cliatt & Shaw, 1992). Figure 9.3

Teacher's Record of Child's Reading	

Student	

BOOKS THE CHILD HAS READ EMERGENTLY	
Date Read	Title

BOOKS THE CHILD HAS READ CONVENTIONALLY	
Date Read	Title

Other observations:

Figure 9.2
Teacher's record of child's reading.

Source: From TEACHER'S GUIDE TO EVALUATION, ASSESSMENT HANDBOOK, CELEBRATE READING! grade 1 by Elizabeth Sulzby. Copyright © 1993 by Scott, Foresman. Reprinted by permission.

	Children														
Behaviors															
Makes groups consistently when given a basis for classification.															
Names basis for classifying.															
Devises basis for classifying.															
Makes subclassifications.															
Other															

A checklist for classifying skills.

	Children														
Qualities															
Applies information.															
Conveys information clearly.															
Represents creative work.															
Neatly made.															
Clearly explained (as applicable).															
For group projects, was project work shared?															
Was work cooperative?															
Other															

A checklist for evaluating projects.

Figure 9.3
Science assessment checklists.

Source: Reprinted with the permission of Macmillan College Publishing Company from HELPING CHILDREN EXPLORE SCIENCE by Mary Jo Puckett Cliatt and Jean M. Shaw. Copyright © 1992 by Macmillan College Publishing Company, Inc.

gives two examples of forms teachers can use to evaluate student work. Regardless of the developmental, content area, or integrated components of the instructional program, teachers and administrators must establish the goals and objectives of the program, determine what types of assessment would be appropriate, and determine what types of records and work samples would be useful to collect in a portfolio for reporting progress to parents.

Uses for Portfolios

In addition to deciding how to organize portfolios so that they reflect the goals and objectives of the instructional program and complement the approach to curriculum and instruction, decisions must be made about how the portfolios will be used. Three common uses are for child reporting, for teacher and child assessment and evaluation, and for evaluation of the teacher.

Portfolios organized and maintained by the child are generally used to share progress with parents. The child makes selections of best samples of work for a period of time and takes them home to share with parents or participates in a parent-teacher conference during which the portfolio is displayed and discussed. In this context, assessment may not be the main purpose for the portfolio; rather, it may be used for the child to demonstrate general progress and to share what transpired in the classroom as reflected in his or her work.

When portfolios are used for assessment and evaluation, a more structured report of progress is intended. In this case, the likely organization is to have a section for child work and a section for teacher assessment records. If the portfolio is for a single purpose such as mathematics or language arts, all of the work would reflect examples of the child's efforts in that area. A more comprehensive portfolio would include all types of examples of the child's work. Self-evaluations made by the child are also put into portfolios. Children can engage in determining how well they did or whether they enjoyed an activity. Figure 9.4 is an example of a process of child self-evaluation.

Another purpose for portfolios is to evaluate the teacher. In addition to the child and the teacher assessing the child's achievements, the child is given an opportunity to provide feedback for the teacher. This type of assessment can be reported orally by the child or obtained by using some type of form. The teacher can do self-evaluation via the portfolio by assessing how successful activities were as reflected by the child's work samples.

Setting Up Portfolios

The first task to begin assessment with portfolios is to develop a way to store portfolio entries. Portfolios can be as simple as a manila folder or as complex as a commercial file cabinet with folders designed specifically for portfolio use. Grace and Shores (1991) recommend expandable file folders, x-ray folders for art work, or cleaned pizza boxes. Whatever type of container or storage system is selected, the teacher should plan how the portfolios can be accessed easily and arranged neatly at the same time.

Name _____ Date _____
Teacher _____ School _____

Organizing My Portfolio

I have looked at all the things in my portfolio.
1. This picture or writing tells about the thing I like best.

```
┌─────────────────────────────────────────────┐
│                                             │
│                                             │
│                                             │
│                                             │
│                                             │
└─────────────────────────────────────────────┘
```

2. Here is the work I have the most of.
   Here is my picture or writing about it.

```
┌─────────────────────────────────────────────┐
│                                             │
│                                             │
│                                             │
│                                             │
└─────────────────────────────────────────────┘
```

3. This is the work I would like to have more of.
   Here is my picture or writing about it.

```
┌─────────────────────────────────────────────┐
│                                             │
│                                             │
│                                             │
│                                             │
└─────────────────────────────────────────────┘
```

Figure 9.4
Organizing my portfolio.

Source: Farr, R. C. (1993). *Portfolio assessment teacher's guide grades K-8.* Orlando, FL: Harcourt Brace Jovanovich.

Organizing Portfolios Using a Developmental Approach

A sensible approach to organizing portfolios for preschool and primary grade children is by developmental category. Thus the teacher might provide dividers in the portfolio for motor development, social and emotional development, language development, and cognitive development. Grace and Shores (1991), citing Meisels and Steele (1991), make the following suggestions for organizing such a portfolio (pp. 21–25):

Art Activities (Fine Motor Development)

- Drawings of events, persons, and animals. The child might dictate descriptions or explanations of the drawings to the teacher or a parent or classroom volunteer. Or the child might write such explanations. (The teacher may need to make notes if the child writes his own picture caption.)
- Photos of unusual block constructions or projects, labeled and dated.
- Collages and other examples of the child's use of various media when designing a picture.
- Samples of the child's manuscript printing. (The appearance and placement of the letters on the page are evaluated in the context of a developmental continuum.)

Movement (Gross Motor Development)

- Notes recorded by the teacher or video tapes of the child's movement activities in the classroom or on the playground, which reflect the child's developing skills
- Notes, photographs, video tapes and anecdotal records which demonstrate the child's skills and progress in music activities and fingerplays
- Notes from teacher interviews with the child about his favorite active games at school

Math and Science Activities (Concept Development)

- Photographs of the child measuring or counting specific ingredients as part of a cooking activity
- Charts on which the child has recorded the planting, care, watering schedule, periods of sunlight, etc., of plants in the classroom or on the school grounds
- Work samples demonstrating the child's understanding of number concepts. An example is the numeral four formed with beans glued to a sheet of paper and the appropriate number of beans glued beside the numeral.
- Work samples, teacher notes, taped pupil interviews illustrating, in a progressive fashion, the child's understanding of mathematical concepts
- Photographs and data gathered from checklists and taped pupil interviews which document the child's conceptual understanding, exploring, hypothesizing and problem-solving. (The documentation will depend upon the child's developmental stages during the life of the portfolio.)

Language and Literacy

- Tape recordings of a child re-reading stories which she "wrote" or dictated to a parent, teacher or classroom volunteer
- Examples of the child's journal entries
- Copies of signs or labels the child constructed
- A log of book titles actually read by the child or read to the child by a teacher, parent or other adult
- Copies of stories, poems, or songs the child wrote or dictated
- Taped pupil interviews that reveal the child's increase, over time, in vocabulary and skill in use of the language

Personal and Social Development

- Teacher notes and anecdotal records that document interactions between the child and her peers. Such interactions can indicate the child's ability to make choices, solve problems, and cooperate with others.
- Teacher notes, anecdotal records, and video-recordings that document events that occurred on field trips. Such incidents may illustrate the child's social awareness.
- Notes from teacher-parent conferences.

Organizing Portfolios Using a Subject Area Approach

The teacher may prefer to organize portfolios using a subject area approach. If this approach is taken, the choice must be made whether to include all subject areas or to dedicate a portfolio to a single content area. If a comprehensive collection of the child's work, teacher assessments, and other evaluation data are desired, Batzle (1992) recommends the following contents for the portfolio:

I. **Required Tests and Accountability Measures**
- Standardized Tests
- Minimum Competency Tests
- Criterion-Referenced Tests
- Chapter or Unit Tests

II. **Samples Across the Curriculum**
- Language Arts
  Reading Responses
  Reading Logs
  Home Reading Logs
  Oral Reading Tapes
  Writing Folders
  Writing Samples
  Spelling Work
- Math
- Fine Arts
- Content Areas

III. Teacher Observations and Measures
- Kid Watching and Anecdotal Records
- Running Records
- Retellings
- Progress Checks
- Teacher-made Tests
- Rubrics
- Conference Records
- Summary of Findings

Inventories and Other Forms
- Reading Inventory
- Informal Reading Inventory
- Writing Inventory
- Parent Surveys, Comments, and Evaluations

Additional Items
- Cassette or Photo of Drama Presentations
- Oral Presentation, Booktalk
- Oral Language Inventory
- Oral "Publishing"

It should be noted that this example includes possibilities for several subject areas to be included; nevertheless, some subjects, such as social studies, are omitted. More-over, the predominant categories suggested are related to language arts. It should also be observed that inclusion of results of standardized tests is recommended.

The pamphlet "Portfolio Assessment," published by Teaching for Excellence (1992) has more complete ideas for a portfolio that include all subject areas. The ideas proposed could focus on specific subjects or integrated subject areas. Possibilities suggested are the following:

- Self-evaluation through an "All About Me" portfolio in which students choose items which express themselves, such as their likes, dislikes, hobbies, personality and family.
- Written literacy portfolios, with such works as timed writing samples, best notes, log and journal entries, essays, critiques and short stories.
- Math portfolios, with such items as statistical studies, graphic representations, diagrams of problem-solving steps, written descriptions of math investigations, and responses to open-ended questions and problems.
- Creative expressions such as art, music, dance and photography.
- Projects such as science and social studies investigations. A fun way to teach and test applications is to assign job role simulations, such as an archaeologist who must find the culture or time period of an artifact, or a policy analyst who must predict the future in a country being studied.
- Videotapes and written analysis of progress for physical skills such as soccer, gymnastics, volleyball, etc.

Organization of student portfolios can focus on a single content area, and there are options for how to organize the contents. Farr (1993, p. 13) suggests some organization patterns for student portfolios for a reading/writing system as follows:

1. **Organization by topic.** Students might put reading and writing materials on sports in one section, school topics in another, and mysteries in another.
2. **Organization by genre.** Students might arrange materials according to whether they are stories, letters, articles, songs, and other genres for reading and writing.
3. **Organization by difficulty.** One section might include those things that were easy to do; in another those that were more difficult; and in a third those that were very difficult.
4. **Chronological organization.** Students use weeks or some other time period as the organizational pattern.
5. **Organization by preference.** Students use one section for reading and writing activities they liked a great deal, another for those they felt neutral about, and a third for those they disliked.
6. **Multiple-level organization.** Students arrange materials first by topics and then within topics by genre, preference or difficulty.

Vermont undertook to establish a statewide assessment system in mathematics and writing using a portfolio system. During the 1990–91 school year, pilot schools used portfolios to assess student achievement (Abruscato, 1993). Figure 9.5 provides the specifications for writing and mathematics portfolios in the Vermont project.

Organizing Portfolios for Teacher and Child Assessment and Reporting

After the teacher has determined how the portfolio is to be organized, and before materials are collected, decisions must be made about how evaluation is to be conducted. Teaching for Excellence (1992) recommends that standards be clear and specific, that criteria be related to learning goals, and that evaluation be based on either performance compared to a standard or performance over a period of time. Such decisions are especially important when evaluating the young child's portfolio. The standard must be both consistent with the teacher's curriculum and appropriate for the children's level of development. Program objectives and developmental checklists can serve as guides to the child's developmental progress and accomplishments when compiling the evaluation profile.

When the time comes to conduct the evaluation, the teacher must draw some conclusions about the child's progress. Information is compiled about the child's strengths, weaknesses, achievements, and instructional needs. Using all data collected in the child's portfolio, the teacher describes the child's developmental status and characteristics (Grace & Shores, 1991).

Farr (1993) recommends that evaluation include process and product evaluation with students. In process evaluation, the teacher has conferences with students on a frequent basis to discuss materials in their portfolios and the progress they are making. Students as well as the teacher review portfolio contents prior to

The Writing Portfolio

THE WRITING portfolio used in Vermont schools at grades 4 and 8 includes two types of products: 1) a collection of six pieces of writing done by the student during the academic year; and 2) a "uniform writing assessment," a formal writing assignment that is given by all teachers to all students at the grade level.

Examining a student's writing portfolio reveals the following:

1. a table of contents;
2. a "best piece";
3. a letter;
4. a poem, short story, play, or personal narrative;
5. a personal response to a cultural, media, or sports exhibit or event or to a book, current issue, math problem, or scientific phenomenon;
6. one prose piece from any curriculum area other than English or language arts (for fourth-graders) and three prose pieces from any curriculum area than English or language arts (for eighth-graders); and
7. the piece produced in response to the uniform writing assessment, as well as related outlines, drafts, etc.

The Mathematics Portfolio

A STUDENT'S achievement in mathematics problem solving and communication is revealed through:

1. five to seven "best pieces"— among them at least one puzzle, one investigation, one application, and no more than two pieces of group work— listed in a table of contents and including the solution and the work involved;
2. a letter to the portfolio evaluator; and
3. a collection of other pieces of mathematics work.

Figure 9.5
The writing portfolio and the mathematics portfolio.
Source: Abruscato, J. (1993). Early results and tentative implications from the Vermont Portfolio Project. *Phi Delta Kappan, 47,* 475–476.

engaging in a conference for process evaluation. Product evaluation also involves review of portfolio materials; however, the purpose is to sum up a student's progress. One resource that can be used to compile the results of the student's progress is a rating scale that includes the pertinent categories of the evaluation. Figure 6.6 in Chapter 6 is an example of a rating scale for primary grade reading.

ADVANTAGES AND DISADVANTAGES OF USING PORTFOLIOS TO REPORT STUDENT PROGRESS

The advantages of using portfolios for assessment and reporting were discussed earlier. Portfolios permit a wide range of assessment methods and a variety of ways that children can demonstrate mastery and growth in development. They allow for flexibility in how the teacher documents student progress; at the same time, they provide parents with extensive information about the child's experiences in school that facilitate learning and accomplishments.

Portfolios provide evaluation above and beyond letter grades on a report card. Children can be tracked on a continuum of development. In addition, assessment can be used for diagnostic purposes, as well as assessment to document learning. Teachers can meet individual needs of each child by examining portfolio contents and discussing progress and problems with the child through interviews and conferences.

Portfolios include input from the child, making the child an active partner in the evaluation process. The child not only makes selections for portfolio contents but also participates in the assessment process. This participation includes discussing progress with parents during parent-teacher conferences.

The most obvious difficulty in organizing and maintaining portfolios is the issue of time. Time is needed by both the teacher and the children to implement and maintain portfolios. It is important for the teacher and the children to work regularly with portfolios, review contents, discuss progress, and make changes in what is to be kept in the portfolio. If the portfolios are to be effective, they must be kept organized and current. Time is needed to work with portfolios, and teachers who are enthusiastic about the benefits of portfolios may also be concerned about the time needed to use portfolios appropriately.

Teachers are also concerned about accountability and grading portfolios. If a school district combines the use of portfolios with the evaluation of the child's longitudinal progress, and if the evaluation of that progress is the primary purpose of reporting, teachers can become very comfortable with using portfolios. If, however, portfolios are used to assess and assign grades, the evaluation process is much more difficult when using portfolios. Teachers can be much more anxious about using portfolio assessment when they have to use them to compare the achievement of students with each other. The issue of assigning grades can be one of the biggest challenges teachers face when initiating portfolio assessment.

A major concern when using portfolios for assessment and reporting is validity of the assessment strategies used. Earlier in the chapter we discussed the need to predetermine standards and procedures that would be used to assess portfolio contents. In addition, steps must be taken to ensure that the assessment strategies have been checked for validity (Goodwin & Goodwin, 1993). Teachers are particularly concerned about their own accountability for the evaluation process. They may be insecure about using portfolio assessment because they are uncertain whether they will be able to grade the child's work appropriately.

The statewide use of portfolios in Vermont (O'Neil, 1993) gives some information about the possible difficulties in establishing reliability. Low reliability coefficients in the 1991–92 statewide assessment process led Vermont to improve the portfolio assessment process to overcome these technical limitations. Teachers who individually are trying to be accountable for the quality of their assessments are rightfully concerned about the ability to be accountable to parents and administrators about the evaluation process they use in the classroom.

Education in the United States reflects a history of embracing innovations only to discard them within a few years. Some instructional changes lack the research that can prove or question effectiveness. The introduction of portfolio assessment may suffer from this pattern. As with other innovations, teachers in some schools are asked to implement portfolios without the training needed to make the process successful. Likewise, when training is provided, it is possible that only the positive characteristics of portfolio assessment are stressed, without adequate information about difficulties and cautions that should be observed and followed. A major limitation of portfolio assessment may be this lack of competence and confidence that teachers need to implement the process successfully. It is important that the implementation of portfolio assessment and reporting be accompanied by the training, decision making, and preparation that is required for any type of assessment to be a quality method of assessing and evaluating student progress and achievement.

USING NARRATIVE REPORTS FOR EVALUATION AND REPORTING

Purposes for Narrative Reports

Narrative or summary reports are another alternative to report cards for communicating a child's progress to parents. A *summary report* is an evaluation written by the teacher to describe the child's development and learning. A **narrative report** can stand alone as the periodic evaluation of progress or be combined with other assessment and reporting strategies. A narrative report can be part of a portfolio assessment or another system of assessment and reporting. Purposes for the report are to describe a review of the child's growth over a period of time and to describe that growth in a meaningful way for parents.

A summary report can describe the child's strengths, using developmental categories or subject areas. It (1) can be organized to include projects and integrated curriculum topics, (2) is a profile of development and change over time, and (3) is written with terminology that parents can understand to draw a picture of their child. Using the results of observations, checklists, performance assessments, and other performance strategies, the teacher translates the information so that parents can comprehend what their child accomplished (Horm-Wingerd, 1992; Krechevsky, 1991; Meisels, 1993).

Writing a Narrative Report

A narrative report as described by Horm-Wingerd (1992) includes the following:

1. Descriptions of examples of the child's behaviors
2. Examples of what the child can do

3. Concerns the teacher may have about the child's progress
4. Goals and plans for the child in the future

Advocates of written summaries to report child progress express concern that teachers write reports in such a manner that parents have an appreciation of their child and value his or her progress. Strengths, rather than weaknesses, should be stressed. When the child's weaknesses are described or concerns are expressed, the teacher should be careful to not assess blame and to use a positive tone in the report. The goal is to develop reports that develop positive home-school relationships (Horm-Wingerd, 1992). Project Spectrum, described in more detail later, suggests that any home activities described for the parents for use with their child require inexpensive, readily available materials (Krechevsky, 1991).

It is important for teachers to write the narrative report carefully and accurately. It should inform the parents about the child's progress and educate them about appropriate instruction and assessment practices. Horm-Wingerd (1992, p. 14) suggests the following procedure when writing narratives:

1. Open with an overall statement describing a child's progress in a broad developmental area since the last report or conference.
2. Give a specific example of behavior to serve as evidence for your global description of change and to help parents understand exactly what you are describing.
3. State your plans.
4. If appropriate, note what the parents can do at home to facilitate their child's development.

Horm-Wingerd also provides guidelines for writing narrative reports to ensure that complete and appropriate information is shared with the parents. Figure 9.6 includes specifications, suggestions, and cautions that, if followed, help the teacher write a quality report to share with parents.

ADVANTAGES AND DISADVANTAGES OF USING NARRATIVE REPORTS TO REPORT STUDENT PROGRESS

Many of the advantages and disadvantages of using performance assessments in general and strategies for reporting the child's performance and development discussed in terms of portfolios are true for narrative reports. Advantages are that they permit the teacher to report the child's broad range of developmental characteristics over a period of time. They can incorporate information from various sources and assessment and record-keeping strategies when the child's evaluation is reported. A unique aspect of the narrative report is that the teacher can describe in writing what the child has accomplished. Unlike the portfolio, which might be the focus of verbal exchange between the parents and the teacher, the narrative report requires the teacher to think through what is desired in the report and to write it down prior to a conference. If a face-to-face conference is

Format

- Are organizing categories congruent with philosophy, goals, and curriculum?
- Does it reflect the "whole" child?
- Does it honestly encourage and facilitate parent-teacher communication?

General Content

- Does it blame the child?
- Does it blame the parent?
- How will it make the child feel?
- How will it make the parent feel?
- How will it impact parent–teacher relations?
- How will it affect parent–child relations?

Specific Content

- Does it contain information about the essential areas of development and learning?
- Does it describe patterns of typical classroom behavior over time?
- Does it describe individual growth and progress?
- Does it focus on strengths rather than weaknesses?
- Does it contain specific examples of what the child can do?
- Does it communicate real, authentic, meaningful information?
- Does it let the parents know your plans?
- Does it let the parents know that you are "on the child's side"?
- Does it educate parents about developmentally appropriate practices?

Preparation

- Is the tone conversational, personal, and positive?
- Is it clear and easy to understand?
- Does it contain educational jargon?
- Is it professionally prepared? (Grammar, spelling, handwriting)
- Has it been proofread?

Figure 9.6
Guiding questions for designing, writing, and critiquing narrative reports.
Source: Horm-Wingerd, D. M. (1992). Reporting children's development: The narrative report. *Dimensions of Early Childhood, 21,* 15.

not possible, the narrative report contains the essential information and interpretation the teacher wishes to communicate.

The obvious disadvantage of the narrative report is the time needed to write, edit, and finalize a narrative report in professional form. The teacher must not only collect pertinent information and organize it to reflect the advances made in all developmental or subject areas of the curriculum but also translate those data into a coherent, comprehensive, concise narrative. The ideal would be to combine the written summary with the portfolio so that contents of the report could be supported with contents of the portfolio; however, each additional component of an evaluation also adds time to the teacher's overall evaluation tasks. Perhaps if the written report is completed at the end of the school year or, at most, twice a year, the teacher would have the opportunity to write down thoughts and descriptions about the child.

MODEL ASSESSMENT AND REPORTING SYSTEMS

Attempts have been made in recent years to develop models of assessment and reporting systems that reflect the strengths of authentic or performance assessments. Educational leaders and measurement specialists for young children have worked toward designing and piloting methods of assessing and reporting children's evaluations in a logical and coherent manner. The goal is to guide teachers in connecting curriculum, instruction, assessment, and reporting via strategies that are natural and meaningful. Three examples of these models are Project Spectrum, the Work Sample System, and the High/Scope Child Observation Record. Each of these systems seeks to correct the mistakes in assessment that are currently being made with young children. They also focus on strategies for informal and performance assessments differently, but with the same goal of evaluating and reporting child development and learning in a meaningful and constructive manner.

Project Spectrum

Project Spectrum was initiated in 1984 at Harvard and Tufts Universities to better understand the linguistic and logical bases of intelligence. A major goal of the project was to produce a developmentally appropriate approach to assessment in early childhood. In addition to studying the child's individual cognitive style, the project emphasized the child's areas of strengths often not included in Piagetian approaches to education. The areas of cognitive ability examined in the project included numbers, science, music, language, visual arts, movement, and social development. The assumption was that by evaluating the young child's strengths in many domains, all children will exhibit performance in some domains.

Assessment is integrated into curriculum and instruction in Project Spectrum. A variety of activities is offered to the children; assessment is conducted through the child's involvement in the activities. Thus assessment is performance-based within both structured and unstructured tasks and teacher observation. Assessment is interfaced with meaningful activities provided in the classroom environment. Assessment is conducted throughout the year and documented through observation checklists, score sheets, portfolios, and tape recordings. Activities used for curriculum and assessment include games, puzzles, and other activities in learning areas such as obstacle courses for movement assessment, a child's activity in reporting for language assessment, and a bus game designed to evaluate the child's ability to make mental calculations and to organize numbers.

Assessment data collected during the year are reported through a Spectrum Profile, a summary of the child's participation in project activities during the year in the form of a narrative report. The child's areas of strength are described, along with suggestions for follow-up activities the parents can conduct with the child.

The child's active involvement in the assessment process and the wide range of developmental domains incorporated into the curriculum are considered to be strengths of Project Spectrum. A concern is that parents might focus only on the child's strengths described in project assessments and focus on those strengths prematurely, thus neglecting the development of other areas (Krechevsky, 1991).

The Work Sampling System

The Work Sampling System was designed as an alternative to the use of standardized tests for the assessment of young children. The system is based on the philosophy that performance assessments are appropriate because they (1) document the child's daily activities, (2) reflect an individualized approach to assessment, (3) integrate assessment with curriculum and instruction, (4) assess many elements of learning, and (5) allow teachers to learn how children reconstruct knowledge through interacting with materials and peers.

The first component of the Work Sampling System is teacher observation by means of developmental checklists. Because learning and instruction are integrated with assessment, the documentation of development and learning also provides information on the curriculum. Checklists cover seven domains: (1) personal and social development, (2) language and literacy, (3) mathematical thinking, (4) scientific thinking, (5) social studies, (6) art and music, and (7) physical development. Guidelines are provided for understanding the process of observation with the checklist indicators.

A second component is portfolios, which provide an assessment process that actively involves the teacher and the child. Both the teacher and the child select portfolio contents. The activity of organizing the portfolio permits the teacher and the child to review progress and to plan future activities, thus integrating the teaching/learning process. Items are selected that represent the seven domains covered by the checklist. Essential or core items of work samples are selected several times during the year, in addition to other items selected that represent all domains. The portfolio becomes a tool for documenting, analyzing, and summarizing the child's learning and development through the year (Meisels, 1993).

A third component of the Work Sampling System is the summary report completed for each child three times a year. The report summarizes the child's performance by means of specific criteria for the evaluation. Information from the checklists and the portfolios are used to communicate the child's progress to the parents. The child's overall progress is reported, as well as whether or not the child is making appropriate progress in each developmental category. Figure 9.7 is a diagram of the components of the Work Sampling System and how domains of development serve as the foundation for the assessment and reporting process.

The Child Observation Record

The Child Observation Record, too, is based on observation as the core of the assessment project with young children. The system was developed as an answer to the misassessment of young children, including those in caregiving settings during the preschool years. The goal was to produce an assessment process that is developmentally appropriate, reliable, valid, and user-friendly. Further, the purpose of the system is to observe and assess children conducting child-initiated tasks for some of the activities. Because child-centered activities integrate all cate-

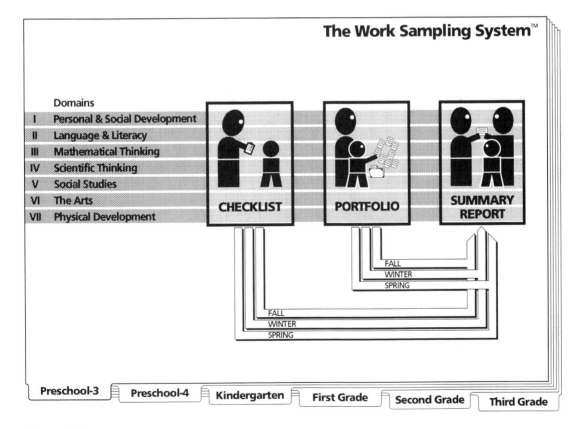

Figure 9.7
The Work Sampling System™.

Source: Meisels, S. J. (1993). Remaking classroom assessment with The Work Sampling System. *Young Children, 48*, 34–40, p. 37.

gories of development, children can be assessed during natural daily activities. Developmental checklists combined with anecdotal recordings of observations form the activities used by the teacher in the assessment process.

The Child Observation Record system (COR) was developed by the High/Scope Educational Foundation for use in all developmentally appropriate programs. The system was studied for two years to establish validity and reliability. COR assesses six areas of development: (1) initiative, (2) creative representation, (3) social relations, (4) music and movement, (5) language and literacy, and (6) logic and mathematics. The teacher rates the child several times a year on thirty COR items that have five levels of indicators. Anecdotal notes taken in an ongoing basis through observations are used to complete the ratings (Schweinhart, 1993).

SUMMARY

In this chapter we have explored some strategies for reporting student progress to parents through performance or authentic assessments. We discussed the inherent limitations in traditional report cards that report only what the child knows. In contrast, performance assessments demonstrate what the child knows and how the child applies that knowledge in a realistic context.

A major focus of the chapter was to describe some alternative methods of constructing an evaluative profile of the child's development and learning that permits the teacher and the child to communicate to the parents broad information about what the child accomplished. Two alternative systems discussed were portfolios and narrative reports. It was stressed that portfolios can contain many types of informal and performance assessment results to support what the child has learned.

Many types of examples of children's work and assessment results can be included in a portfolio. Various organizational possibilities can be used for portfolios as well.

The narrative report can likewise be incorporated into a portfolio reporting system or stand alone as a written evaluative system of performance. A narrative or summary report is another way a teacher can develop a profile of the child's total progress and report it to parents. When planning and writing the report, the teacher writes a description of the child's activities and work in such a way that the parents have a picture of their child and what he or she accomplished at school. The teacher stresses the child's positive characteristics and strengths and expresses concerns about the child carefully so that bias and judgmental statements are not included.

Currently, efforts are being made to develop comprehensive systems for reporting authentic assessment results. Project Spectrum uses children's involvement in activities for assessment. Teacher observation and structured and unstructured tasks are recorded through checklists, score sheets, portfolios, and tape recordings.

A narrative report at the end of the year summarizes the child's activities and suggests follow-up activities for the parents to conduct with the child.

The Work Sampling System likewise combines teacher observations and portfolio contents for performance assessment. A set of checklists that include all areas of development are used to document and analyze developmental progress. Portfolio contents contain essential items of the child's work that have been collected throughout the year. A summary report is completed three times a year. Each summarizes the child's performance by using specific criteria.

The Child Observation Record uses observation as the core of the assessment and reporting system. Child-initiated tasks are used for some of the assessment activities. Natural, daily activities are the source for assessment and are particularly relevant because all categories of development are integrated. Developmental checklists and anecdotal recordings of observations are used for evaluation and reporting.

REVIEW QUESTIONS

1. What are the concerns about using report cards with young children?

2. How do authentic assessments and reporting provide a broad picture of children's progress?

3. Describe why curriculum and instruction and reports of performance need to complement each other.

4. How are report cards being revised to be more compatible with current trends in curriculum and instruction?

5. How do portfolios meet the criteria for appropriate performance assessment and reporting?

6. Outline the possible components of a portfolio and briefly describe each one.

7. What types of teacher assessments can be included in the portfolio?

8. How can teachers overcome concerns they might have about initiating the portfolio process?

9. Why is some type of summary or profile needed to communicate the child's progress to parents? What topics about the portfolio and progress should be included in a parent-teacher conference?

10. How are children actively involved in the assessment process when portfolios are used? How are they a part of the process of reporting to parents?

11. Why are narrative reports a positive alternative or addition to portfolios when developing the child's evaluative report?

12. What are some cautions teachers need to consider when writing a narrative report?

13. What do the three examples of appropriate assessment systems described in the chapter have in common? How are they different?

KEY TERM

narrative report

SUGGESTED ACTIVITY

1. Design a portfolio to be used with preschool children. Include (1) sections or dividers for the portfolio, (2) the types of teacher assessments you would use, and (3) how you would report the child's progress to parents.

REFERENCES

ABRUSCATO, J. (1993). Early results and tentative implications from the Vermont Portfolio Project. *Phi Delta Kappan, 74,* 474–477.

BATZLE, J. (1992). *Portfolio assessment and evaluation. Developing and using portfolios in the k–6 classroom.* Cypress, CA: Creative Teaching.

CARIN, A. A. (1993). *Teaching science through discovery* (7th ed.). New York: Macmillan.

CLIATT, M.J.P., & SHAW, J. M. (1992). *Helping children explore science.* New York: Merrill/Macmillan.

FARR, R. C. (1993). *Portfolio assessment teacher's guide grades k–8.* Orlando, FL: Harcourt Brace Jovanovich.

GLAZER, S. M. (1993, January) Assessment in the classroom: Where we are, where we're going. *Teaching k–8,* pp. 68–71.

GOODWIN, W. L., & GOODWIN, L. D. (1993). Young children and measurement: Standardized and nonstandardized instruments in early childhood education. In B. Spodek (Ed.), *Handbook of research on the education of young children* (pp. 441–464). New York: Macmillan.

GRACE, C., & SHORES, E. F. (1991). *The portfolio and its use.* Little Rock: Southern Association on Children Under Six.

HORM-WINGERD, D. M. (1992). Reporting children's development: The narrative report. *Dimensions of Early Childhood, 21,* 11–15.

KRECHEVSKY, M. (1991). Project Spectrum: An innovative assessment alternative. *Educational Leadership, 48,* 43–48.

MCCLELLAN, D., & KATZ, L. G. (1992). Assessing the social development of young children: A checklist of social attributes. *Dimensions of Early Childhood, 21,* 9–10.

MEISELS, S. J. (1993). Remaking classroom assessment with the Work Sampling System. *Young Children, 48,* 34–40.

MEISELS, S. J., & STEELE, D. (1991). *The early childhood portfolio collection process.* Ann Arbor: University of Michigan, Center for Human Growth and Development.

O'NEIL, J. (1993). The promise of portfolios. *ASCD Update, 35,* 1, 5.

SCHWEINHART, L. J. (1993). Observing young children in action: The key to early childhood assessment. *Young Children, 48,* 29–33.

SULZBY, E. (1993). *Teacher's guide to evaluation: Assessment handbook.* Glenview, IL: Scott, Foresman.

TEACHING FOR EXCELLENCE. (1992). Portfolio assessment: A worthwhile testing alternative. *Teaching for Excellence, 12.*

WILLIS, S. (1993). Are letter grades obsolete? *ASCD Update, 35,* 1, 4, 8.

Chapter 10

Putting Measurement and Evaluation in Perspective: Looking Ahead

Chapter Objectives

As a result of reading this chapter you will be able to

1. discuss current issues in measurement and evaluation of young children.
2. explain the purposes of program evaluation.
3. understand the roles of formative and summative program evaluation.
4. describe why classroom teachers should have input in the selection and use of tests and other forms of measurement.
5. understand the role of measurement and evaluation in new and expanding programs for young children.
6. understand future trends in measurement and evaluation.

In the preceding chapters we studied the many methods used to measure young children. We examined the strategies employed to learn about young children from birth through the early childhood years: how they grow and develop, how they learn, and how we can discover problems with development and learning.

In discussing each measurement and evaluation method, we considered the information that teachers, caregivers, and parents may want or need to know. This information included the purposes of the evaluation, how it is conducted, and why it is useful. Each topic was also discussed in terms of surrounding problems or issues, as well as its strengths and limitations, particularly when used with young children.

In this chapter we go beyond these topics and consider how the programs that serve children can be evaluated. Many of the measurement strategies used to learn about children can be broadened or generalized to examine and evaluate programs. Program evaluation also includes measurement tools that do not directly involve testing children, but focus instead on evaluating how different components of the program have succeeded or need to be modified.

We also consider the status of issues and controversies related to testing and evaluating young children that may remain as significant concerns in the future. Many problems about the use of testing in the early childhood years have not been resolved. Where are we headed in addressing the issues of the misuse of testing with young children?

Finally, we look at the teacher's role in the measurement and evaluation of young children. What are the teacher's responsibilities in using various measurement tools? Should the roles and responsibilities of teachers be altered or expanded? How will future measurement trends affect teachers and how they work with young children?

PROBLEMS IN MAKING PLACEMENT DECISIONS

Mr. Kreplick is attending a meeting for parents of kindergarten children. The principal is explaining the new policy on whether children will be sent to first grade from kindergarten or placed in a transitional first grade with a developmental curriculum for those who need more time before they enter first grade.

Timmy Kreplick has had problems adjusting to kindergarten all year, and his parents have been worried about what will happen to him next year in first grade. Mr. Kreplick is relieved to hear that the children will be tested in May. If the test shows that children are better suited for the transitional class, they will be placed there, rather than in first grade. They will not experience failure.

Mrs. Standish, sitting next to Mr. Kreplick, questions the plan. What happens if a child matures over the summer? What happens if, in October, the child can do well in first grade? Will the child be moved to a regular first-grade class?

Because this is the first year of the transitional class, the principal has no answer. The school will use a wait-and-see approach, monitoring the children to see how well they do during the year. One possibility that has been considered is to retest the children when school begins in September to reassess their abilities after the summer vacation. It is possible that a child will belong in first grade instead of the transitional class. It has also been suggested that the teacher in the transitional class will have a six-week period with the children during which individual children can be reevaluated and placed in first grade if it appears that they can succeed.

Mr. Kreplick is less anxious about Timmy's progress next year. He is convinced that Timmy will need the program offered by the transitional class. Mrs. Standish is less sure about the program. She still has concerns about adding an extra year of school, whether it is a transitional class or retention in kindergarten. She is not convinced that the school district knows clearly what it hopes to achieve through the transitional first-grade classes. She also does not understand what is meant by a developmental curriculum.

CURRENT ISSUES CONCERNING MEASUREMENT AND EVALUATION OF YOUNG CHILDREN

The use of standardized tests with young children continues to be the major concern of testing specialists and educators of young children. Despite abundant literature reporting research on the negative effects of using standardized tests for placement purposes and reporting the achievement of children in the early childhood years, their use is increasing rather than decreasing (Meisels, Steele, & Quinn-Leering, 1993). In the light of this continuing trend, Goodwin and Goodwin (1993) propose that four major issues must be considered at this time as follows:

1. What is the overall value of measurement in American society? The answer seems to be that American society looks to test results to find out the truth about effective education. Test scores are studied to determine whether educational programs are successful.

2. Are the instruments used with young children fair? This issue is related to concerns about test bias. Bias concerns include language, ethnicity, gender, culture, and socioeconomic status. Test bias is seen as significant for children who are school-disadvantaged; moreover, teacher bias and teacher expectations can be related to test results.

3. Is measurement influential with early childhood educators? Early childhood educators tend to reject the use of standardized tests. They particularly question the suitability of achievement tests for children in the early grades. Teachers report pressures to teach to the test and to use teaching practices that are consistent with testing strategies.

4. Are the measurement needs of practitioners and researchers synonymous? Teachers look to measurement results to guide them in making instructional decisions, whereas researchers use measurement to determine accountability and make policy decisions. Nevertheless, standardized tests are an integral part of identifying children for intervention programs and measuring program effectiveness.

As can be seen from the issues described above, concerns about the appropriate measurement measures for young children persist. Although efforts are made to influence testing practices used with children in early childhood programs, inappropriate practices are still widespread (Anderson, 1993). The increased use of standardized tests has become more prevalent in preschool and primary grades, and curriculum changes to accommodate tests is a continuing trend. Teachers are designing their curriculum to match the focus of the test being used (Meisels et al., 1993).

Children from minority backgrounds are particularly affected by standardized test results. The bias of standardized tests and the factors that can have a negative effect on the test performance of minority students makes the use of these for achievement and placement in a grade or a program especially questionable. A complicating factor is teacher perception and expectations of poor and minority children. Research provides substantial evidence that teacher perception affects school achievement of poor and minority children; student performance on standardized tests, in turn, influences the teacher's perception. As a result, these populations of children are placed in programs for low-ability children, including transitional classrooms and special education programs (Meisels et al., 1993; Patton & Wortham, 1993).

BEYOND MEASUREMENT AND EVALUATION OF YOUNG CHILDREN: THE ROLE OF PROGRAM EVALUATION

Throughout this book, we have referred to program effectiveness. Standardized tests were discussed not only for assessing student achievement but also for determining strengths and weaknesses in the instructional program. In discussing testing of preschool children for developmental delays, we also mentioned that the selection of intervention services and the evaluation of their effectiveness are part of the overall plan for the child. Program evaluation involves these measurements to determine what works or does not work well in programs for young children. This information serves many purposes, which are discussed next.

Purposes for Program Evaluation

The purpose or purposes of evaluating early childhood programs depend on the type of program and what one wishes to accomplish. Programs funded by a state, federal, or foundation source are required to submit yearly evaluation reports affirming that the projected results have been achieved. Accountability for program quality to meet regulation or accreditation standards also requires evaluation results. Child care centers regulated by state agencies must demonstrate that they maintain the minimum requirements for licensing. Evaluations must be done periodically to ensure that standards are observed. Public schools must evaluate their instructional programs to determine whether standards for student learning have been met. They may also use program evaluation results to validate instructional quality for parents.

Program evaluation is performed to assist in the management, planning, and development of the program; for decision making and policy formation (Royce, Murray, Lazar, & Darlington, 1982); and for program assessment and improvement (Decker & Decker, 1992). Two types of evaluation—formative and summative—are used to determine whether the program is functioning effectively or has achieved its purpose.

Formative Evaluation

When a program is designed, the planning process includes the development of objectives for each program component, such as the administration, curriculum, and budget. After the program has been implemented, formative evaluations are done to assess progress and provide ongoing improvement (Royce et al., 1982). Formative evaluation is used to determine whether the program is meeting its objectives and to discover any weaknesses.

The effectiveness of curriculum experiences provided for young children can be monitored by studying such factors as equipment and materials, curriculum activities, and teacher behaviors. The *Early Childhood Environment Rating Scale* (Harms & Clifford, 1980) provides ongoing assessment of personal-care routines, equipment and furniture, language and reasoning experiences, fine and gross motor activities, creative activities, social development, and adult needs. Another measurement tool, the *Instrument Based Program Monitoring Information System* (Fiene, 1985) is designed to help early childhood centers meet state day care regulations, and the *Day Care Environmental Inventory* (Prescott, 1975) provides a system for gathering information about physical space and descriptions of children's experiences. The staff can study the information to decide whether the activities observed met their expectations for the children and make adjustments in the program.

Administration and budget goals can also be monitored throughout a program. Program goals for administration may include the establishment of a computerized record-keeping system for payment of fees and expenses. Periodic monitoring during the year can be conducted to determine whether the goal is being met and what needs to be done if the system is not being developed adequately and on time. The yearly budget can be examined throughout the year to ensure that expenditures are not exceeding income and that funds are being spent for the purposes intended.

Each type of formative evaluation is designed to improve the program and to make corrections when objectives are not being achieved. Formative evaluation allows developers to investigate the program on a continuing basis. They are directed to be attentive to the progress of the program during the year, rather than to discover at the end that certain changes should have been made.

Summative Evaluation

Whereas formative evaluation is used to make adjustments so that program objectives can be met, summative evaluation is used to measure the outcomes of a program (Decker & Decker, 1992). Summative evaluation is used to determine program effectiveness at the end of a set period by measuring overall program success and quality.

Federally funded programs are held accountable for reaching their objectives by the end of a funding year. Program developers must report program outcomes to the funding agency. Achievement tests may be administered to determine whether students benefited from the program (Zigler & Valentine, 1979). In a nationally funded program such as Head Start, positive findings from summative evaluations may affect congressional decisions on future funding (Comptroller General of the United States, 1979).

Summative evaluation can also be used to assess research projects associated with early childhood programs. Evaluations are used to answer research questions about program effectiveness. Guralnick (1982) was interested in whether young children with disabilities benefited more from mainstreamed programs than from segregated programs. Warger (1988) cited public school early childhood programs that have been validated as effective through research of program outcomes. Phillips (1987) reported on research conducted with child care centers that provided indicators of quality programs.

The Future of Program Evaluation

Program evaluation will continue to have a significant role in education. Awareness of the importance of programs for all populations of young children is growing at the local, state, and national levels. Program evaluation will expand as new programs are developed and as the quality of existing ones is improved by the many individuals, groups, agencies, and institutions involved in implementing early childhood programs.

As more parents seek child care, as well as educational programs, for their infants and preschool children, providers of these services become more competitive. Day care centers, churches, public schools, and private preschools are beginning to recognize that they must provide quality programs for both care and learning. Day care programs are moving from caregiving to more comprehensive services. Thus centers providing daily care for young children now call themselves child enrichment centers or early learning centers, rather than child care centers.

Public schools also recognize that working parents need care for their children beyond regular school hours. Many schools now provide care before and after school to accommodate family needs. Parents will increasingly look for quality in the programs they select for their children. They will also be concerned about convenience. Many parents prefer to have their child remain at one location for the entire day. The overall quality of both care and learning will be a factor in deciding where to place their child. If early childhood programs wish to compete, they must constantly monitor the quality of their program as compared with that of others in the area or community.

Whereas public schools will use locally or state-designed program evaluation, other early childhood settings will seek validation of the quality of their programs through other means. The National Association for the Education of Young Children (NAEYC) has developed a process whereby providers of early childhood programs and care can gain recognition for the quality of their program. Using the *Accreditation Criteria and Procedures of the National Academy of Early Childhood Programs* (NAEYC, 1984), early childhood centers can attain accreditation through a national organization. As more programs seek accreditation, program evaluation will become a continuing process for centers and schools that previously did not conduct periodic assessments.

At the end of the 1980s, state and federal funding for early childhood programs began to expand after a cutback for several years. Expansion of future programs for children who have disabilities, are gifted and talented, or are at risk for learning deficits in the early childhood years will include provisions for accountability. Evaluation will be required to validate the quality of existing and new programs (Jennings, 1988). An example is the Head Start program. The longitudinal success of the program is well documented; nevertheless, there are concerns about the consistency in quality in programs from one community to another. The original exemplary models and services designed and implemented in the 1960s and 1970s have not been maintained. Cautions about expanding the Head Start program are related to the inconsistent quality and how the program is to be evaluated (Kantrowitz, 1992). A new developmental assessment system has been designed to replace the standardized tests used previously (Bergan & Feld, 1993); however, plans to improve program quality are yet to be realized.

As the need for programs and subsequent program evaluation increases, issues surrounding the testing of young children will continue to be a concern. The methods of measuring and testing young children will continue to be examined as educational reforms and new program development call for program evaluation strategies including the use of standardized testing and other measurement strategies.

RESOLVING THE ISSUES: FUTURE TRENDS

In the 1990s, no one is certain of the trends that will develop in the measurement of young children and early childhood programs. Unresolved issues of the 1980s will remain as the education reform movement continues to affect children of all ages, both in school and in preschool years. These issues will include how to improve the quality of programs for young children, the developmentally appropriate curriculum for young children, the correct use of testing and measurement with young children, and the continuing need for research on program effectiveness.

Providing Quality Programs for Young Children

As the push to accelerate learning in response to calls for improved instruction clashes with efforts to ensure that young children are placed in classes with a developmentally appropriate curriculum, the struggle between the two forces is escalating. The problem of providing the best possible programs for young children within current restrictions is likely to continue for some time, with implications for how children will be tested and how frequently tests will be administered.

Part of the conflict focuses on developmental programs versus academic programs, sometimes referred to as the "push-down curriculum." Warger (1988) describes the problem as follows:

> Curriculums once intended for 1st grade have been moved to kindergarten and
> now are being moved into preschool. The assumption is that mastering a
> preschool academic curriculum will give young children an early jump on the
> academic curriculum they will face later on. (p. viii)

Day (1988) states that we have accepted the proposition of fitting the child to the curriculum, rather than designing the curriculum to meet the developmental needs of the child. Although research clearly indicates differently, the Early Childhood and Literacy Development Committee of the International Reading Association (1985) lamented that a heavy emphasis on children's academic development in kindergarten is replacing a more balanced curriculum. Katz (1988) comments on the emphasis of the first-grade curriculum in kindergarten classrooms: "This appears to me to be doing earlier and earlier what we don't do very well later" (p. 36). Despite efforts to counter the increased academic emphasis in early childhood programs, this trend seems destined to continue in the foreseeable future.

The increased academic pressure on preschool and primary school students has resulted in a parallel increase in early school failure. Because preschool programs, particularly kindergartens, are not based on the development of young children, more children are failing. In an effort to prevent early school failure, educators are using alternatives, such as delaying entry into kindergarten, retention in kindergarten or first grade, and placement in a transitional class before or after kindergarten. Decisions about placement in the appropriate program result in screening and testing of children for developmental maturity, readiness, and school achievement (Meisels et al., 1993). In *Kindergarten Policies: What Is Best for Children?* Peck, McCaig, and Sapp (1988) observe that "children are being tested before, during, and after kindergarten to determine whether they will be permitted to enter school, which class they will be placed in, and whether or not they will be 'promoted'" (p. 7). This practice is labeled "high-stakes testing" (Meisels et al., 1993) because of the power that tests are accorded in decisions affecting young children.

The issues of retention and placement in transitional classes were discussed extensively in earlier chapters. The fact remains that as long as we expect preschool children to learn primary school objectives by using primary school strategies and materials, children will fail to fit the curriculum. Efforts to help children do better in school will involve increased testing. This change in concern from "continuity of development to a concern for continuity in achievement" (Spodek, 1981, p. 179) will have far-reaching effects on many young children in the future.

The increased use of testing, especially standardized testing, is another trend, at least for the near future. Many states have instituted state assessment systems to guide them in making educational reforms. Cohen (1988) asserts that states should design assessments to meet their own needs. He also believes that state assessments might help identify effective programs and indicators of quality in state schools.

Two major factors will fail to halt the downward spiral of elementary curriculum and the use of standardized testing. One factor is related to funding of preschool programs. Because many preschools are funded through sources that require accountability, standardized tests are necessary. The curriculum of the program becomes defined by the test so that good test results will ensure funding for the next year. Because the standardized tests available for use with children measure academic skills, the curriculum taught must prepare the child for success on the test (Karweit, 1988; Meisels et al., 1993).

The other factor is the continuing effect of educational reform. Shepard and Smith (1988) state that the downward shift of curriculum demands is likely to continue because many see the academic emphasis in preschool classes as evidence of the success of educational reforms. As school districts and states broaden the use of standardized tests to evaluate the effect of educational reforms, the tests will continue to encroach on the kindergarten curriculum (Hiebert, 1988). Because existing tests such as the *Iowa Tests of Basic Skills* (Hieronymous, Hoover, & Lindquist, 1986) and the *Metropolitan Readiness Test,* (Nurss & McGauvran, 1976) which are most frequently used, focus on academic skills, kindergarten programs will continue to stress instruction in those skills.

Using standardized testing to help in making decisions about promotion and retention seems destined to continue as a side effect of school reform efforts. However, some states are reconsidering this practice with younger children. Ezra Bowen (1988) reported in *Time* that 61 percent of children in the Norwood-Norfolk central school district in the state of New York failed a standard readiness test used for entry into kindergarten. The test was determined to have a 50 percent margin of error after the children had been assigned to a two-year kindergarten program. Peck et al. (1988) remind us that research evidence indicates that readiness tests do not predict whether a child will succeed in kindergarten.

Increased attention likely will be paid to the problem of placing children in transitional classes or retaining them in kindergarten because they are not considered to be ready for first grade. Shepard and Smith (1988) urge educators to find alternatives to labeling unready children as deficient. They propose that continuing to screen children for school entry will deny public education to children who need it the most.

Karweit (1988) suggests that we must consider more viable alternatives to retaining children in kindergarten or assigning them to a junior first grade. She proposes that the preprimary school years be broken into smaller time units or that children be allowed to enter school during the quarter of the school year in which their birthday occurs. Both of these practices would introduce flexibility into the school year that might help accommodate developmental variations. Nevertheless, regardless of what methods are used to assign children to classes, wide variations still will occur in development and preparation for academic learning. It is hoped that increased efforts will be made to stop labeling children as deficient because they do not fit a prescribed level of development; rather, school districts will focus on modifying preschool programs to best instruct their young students.

Some states are heeding the warning that formal instruction and standardized tests are not developmentally appropriate for kindergarten children. In an article in *Education Week,* Gold (1988) reported that Mississippi was discontinuing the use of standardized tests with kindergarten children. He also reported that North Carolina, Arizona, California, and Georgia were eliminating or modifying the use of standardized tests for kindergarten and, in two of the states, for first- and second-grade children as well. The Georgia legislature mandated and then rescinded the Quality Basic Education Act requiring standardized testing for all children seeking promotion to the first and fourth grades ((Meisels et al., 1993). Changes in testing practices may increase as educators respond to information about problems with standardized tests. Hiebert (1988) reports that changes in future tests will reflect an emergent literacy perspective. Teale (1988) and others will continue informing teachers about how informal techniques can provide effective alternatives for assessing and evaluating young children.

The trend to use performance or authentic assessments reflects the search for appropriate assessments. The growing popularity of whole language and emergent literacy has been accompanied by portfolio assessment and observation as important tools for assessing development and learning (Grace & Shores, 1992; Hills, 1993). The use of integrated learning through thematic curriculum also encourages the use of relevant assessment practices. The conflict between school reform and standardized tests and child-centered instruction based on developmental characteristics has not been resolved; however, a growing number of teachers are attempting to sort out the differences between the two opposing approaches and to determine how they can resolve the problem for the benefit of their students.

Indications are that advocates of developmentally appropriate early childhood programs will also be heard. Peck et al. (1988) cite twenty position statements concerning the need for developmentally appropriate kindergartens compiled from national and state organizations and agencies. These position statements are strong indicators that policymakers are being alerted to the problem and, it is hoped, will respond in a manner that will benefit children in kindergartens and other early childhood programs.

Expanding Programs for Children with Disabilities in the Early Childhood Years

Public Law 94-142, the Individuals with Disabilities Education Act, guarantees a free and appropriate public education for all children with disabilities between the ages of 3 and 21, regardless of the type or severity of their disability. This law made sweeping changes in public schools. It is perhaps the most important law affecting the young child with disabilities. In previous chapters we discussed how the law contributed to the development and use of measurement instruments for preschool children. Some of the tests designed and constructed in response to the law were described.

In the years to come, PL 99–457 (Education of the Handicapped Act Amendments), passed in 1986, will have an equal impact on children in the early childhood years. The new law partially corrects some limitations of PL 94–142 and adds new services for young children.

Although PL 94–142 brought comprehensive services to children beginning at age three, many were not served. Obviously, children from birth to age three were not covered by the law. In addition, states were required to provide services between the ages of three and five only if they provided services to children of those ages who did not have disabilities. If a state only provided kindergarten or did not have a kindergarten program, public program services for preschool children with disabilities might not be available.

Under PL 99–457, states applying for funds under PL 94–142 must demonstrate that they are providing a free public education to all children with disabilities between the ages of three and five. Beginning with the 1990–91 school year, states no longer had the option of serving or not serving preschool children with disabilities.

A federal Early Intervention Program, also part of PL 99-457, established services for infants and toddlers with disabilities from birth to two years of age. The program provides early intervention services for infants and toddlers who are developmentally delayed. Because each state determines what constitutes developmental delay, there are significant implications for the development and use of additional tests for developmental screening and diagnosis of deficits. These services may also vary in quality from state to state.

Family services also a part of PL 99-457 program options serving infants and toddlers with disabilities include part-day, home-based programs and part- or full-day center- or school-based programs. Individualized Family Services Plans (IFSP) must be designed by a team that includes the parents. A broad range of services must be provided to meet the child's developmental needs (Diener, 1993; Morrison, 1988). The IFSP includes a multidisciplinary assessment developed by the team and the parents. Caregivers, parents, and professionals will use observation and other informal assessments with standardized instruments to determine the child's developmental status. Checklists and rating scales will be used to help identify the characteristics that are developing normally. Once developmental delay is established, professionals on the team will conduct more intensive diagnostic tests before designing a plan for the child and the family.

PL 99-457 is intended to expand services to preschool children with disabilities. With the new interest in early childhood years, it is hoped that services for preschool children through improved funding for Head Start, day care, and preschool programs for gifted and talented children will be expanded. When funding is available, such programs will probably have to document their effectiveness through evaluation.

A new dimension to programs serving young children with disabilities is the practice of integrating these children within regular classrooms. Sometimes called "inclusion," the effort is to include the child in a regular classroom within the intervention program. Research studies into the effectiveness of this practice for both the child with disabilities and children without disabilities provide evidence that populations of young children benefit. Integrated programs include young children with disabilities in the regular early childhood program with individualized consideration for the child's disability. The inclusion process goes beyond mainstreaming and provides for ongoing interchanges between the classroom for children with disabilities and classrooms for children developing normally. The philosophy of inclusion is that the child with a disability should be able to participate in the classroom where he or she would have been placed if a disability had not been present (Diener, 1993; Diamond, Hestenes, & O'Conner, 1994).

Providing Quality Programs for Children with Diverse Backgrounds

Children attending preschool programs have always represented different ethnic, language, and socioeconomic groups; nevertheless, diversity in children's backgrounds is increasing, and this trend will continue. The traditional family with a working father, a mother who works in the home, and an average of two children represents only 6 percent of families today. While the percentage of traditional families is shrinking, the nonwhite population is expanding. By the year 2000, the nonwhite population will represent one-third of the total population. The middle class is also shrinking as poverty and the lower-class expand (Raymond & McIntosh, 1992).

Attention to the diversity in children is of importance in the development and expansion of early childhood programs. Regardless of whether the setting is child care, a private preschool, or a public school program, curriculum and assessment must embrace the opportunities and challenges that accompany the variety of children enrolled. One implication is that the curriculum developed for the children represent the cultures and ethnic groups present in the classroom. Because each classroom is different, the content is adapted to the individual needs of the children in the class (Derman-Sparks, 1992).

The use of a variety of strategies for measurement and evaluation will be needed in the future if young children with diverse abilities and backgrounds are to be served well in educational programs.

Appropriate assessment of children from diverse backgrounds is especially important. Because standardized tests are even less likely to reflect the development and learning of children from backgrounds that are culturally, linguistically, or economically different from the majority culture, informal and performance-based evaluation strategies should be used. It is essential for the teacher to assess the individual needs and potential of each child in the classroom; moreover, the teacher must become familiar with the child's culture and family (Raymond & McIntosh, 1992). Unlike procedures and measures developed to identify and serve children with disabilities, the responsibility for determining the individual needs of children from diverse backgrounds is the teacher's. The teacher will need to become skilled in the assessment possibilities and use them appropriately to develop an accurate profile of each child.

THE ROLE OF TEACHERS IN THE SELECTION AND USE OF TESTS AND MEASUREMENT USED WITH YOUNG CHILDREN

What is to be the role of classroom teachers in the selection and use of tests and other forms of measurement? Will teachers have more authority and responsibility for the measurement tools that will be selected for use in their classes?

In previous chapters we discussed the design and construction of informal and formal measurement strategies, believing that teachers, caregivers, parents, and other school personnel involved with young children should be knowledgeable about the characteristics of various tests. In the case of standardized tests, we discussed how to evaluate and select tests for use with young children.

Some of the tests discussed are used by teachers. Others, particularly psychological tests such as IQ tests, require extensive professional training and are administered only by psychologists, counselors, or diagnosticians. Teachers use observation, checklists and rating scales, and screening tests, as well as standardized tests such as achievement tests. They also design and use their own assessment tools. In evaluating children with disabilities and in providing the necessary services, teachers work within a team of providers conducting screening and testing.

The important point is that, in the case of some standardized tests that teachers administer, teachers have no part in the decisions that are made when the tests are selected. When achievement tests are chosen for a school district, teachers are rarely included in the decision-making process. Readiness tests and other instruments used with preschool children are administered by teachers but are rarely selected by them.

This situation leads to questions about the selection and use of tests. Should teachers who administer tests to young children be informed about the tests' quality? Should they have a voice when the decision is made to test their students?

These questions may become issues in the future as testing with preschool and primary-age children becomes more controversial and receives more publicity. As parents become more informed about questions concerning the tests used to help make decisions about grade placement, they will expect teachers to explain the rationale for such tests. Will teachers themselves expect to be included when a decision is made about a testing procedure or instrument that affects the future of their students?

As school reform decisions increase the use of testing of preschool and primary grade children for placement, promotion, and retention, teachers will increasingly believe that they are accountable for their role in the decisions made about their students. If they disagree with the grading procedures they are required to use, for example, do they have a responsibility to voice their concern? When they have research-based information that an instrument is being used for the wrong purpose or lacks reliability, should they so inform the personnel who selected the tests? Should teachers press for more informal methods of evaluation as alternatives to standardized testing? Teachers should be encouraged by administrators to be informed and to share that information so that appropriate testing methods and instruments will be used with the young students in their district or institution.

Parents will want teachers to explain the use of performance assessments and changes in student progress reports that accompany the use of these assessments. Teachers will want to have input when the decision is made to move to this type of assessment. In addition, they will need to be confident that they have the skills to use and interpret performance assessments appropriately.

Teachers may seek to be included in program evaluation. Research cited about retention and placement in transitional classrooms in earlier chapters demonstrated that there is little evidence that children placed in transitional classes do better than children who are promoted. Recent research (Jones, 1985; Shepard & Graue, 1993; Shepard & Smith, 1987) supports the same conclusion. In addition, children retained in a grade do not generally do better than those who are promoted. Regardless of this research, however, school districts are continuing to establish more transitional classes (Meisels et al., 1993). Should teachers be informed of the research on the effectiveness of transitional classrooms? Should school districts and states implementing additional transitional classrooms conduct ongoing research on the effectiveness of these programs, which seem to be a trend for the future? Should teachers question their role in these programs and expect to be accountable to the parents that their instructional program has proven its effectiveness and quality through well-designed evaluation?

SUMMARY AND CONCLUSION

Measurement and evaluation of young children, which started at the turn of this century, have broadened and intensified over the decades as more has been learned about how young children develop and learn and how variances in development may cause young children to encounter difficulties when they enter school. Movements to provide services for preschool children such as Head Start, PL 94–142, and PL 99–457 have used the advances of the child study and testing movements to evaluate children for developmental delays and disabilities. Tests and measures for the early childhood years have been developed in response to the need to identify young children who will benefit from intervention services and preschool programs to enhance their academic success when they enter the primary grades.

Other measures have been developed to evaluate or assess the progress and achievement of children in preschool and primary programs. Procedures have been established to evaluate not only the children but also the programs and schools that serve them.

The development and use of a variety of approaches to teaching and measurement of children in the early childhood years has many problems. Because of the nature and rapidity of development of young children, it is difficult to design measures that are dependable and that accurately measure personal characteristics and other needed information. Each kind of measure designed for use with young children has pluses and minuses. Users of each type of measure must be informed about the strengths and limitations of the strategies they plan to use. With young children especially, a combination of measurement approaches, rather than a single instrument or method, is indicated.

No crystal ball reveals future trends in the measurement of young children. There are certain indicators, however. School reform, which is a national phenomenon, will continue to affect early childhood education. At the same time that the importance of the early years is again being emphasized, the school reform movement is establishing restrictive parameters on the education of young children. The push for quality programs that are developmentally appropriate for young children is in conflict with efforts to raise academic standards. As a result, academic policies that are counter to the best educational programs for children in the early childhood years are being forced on early childhood educators. Measurement and evaluation of young students and preschool children are and will continue to be both a cause and an effect of the forces that will characterize future early childhood programs. As the makeup of early childhood classrooms changes to reflect the presence of more children with disabilities and representing diverse backgrounds, competence in selecting and using appropriate types of assessment assumes even more importance.

The issues that surround the measurement and evaluation of young children will not be resolved soon. If present trends continue, a parallel increase will occur in the measurement of young children in the effort to improve their potential for optimum development and learning. The ongoing improvement in measurement methods and instruments should have a positive result for children in the early childhood services and programs yet to be designed.

REVIEW QUESTIONS

1. How do program evaluations affect the teacher's decisions about the classroom curriculum?
2. How can program evaluation results help improve instruction?
3. How can tests used for program evaluation control the teacher's method of instruction?
4. Why will program evaluation become more important in the future?
5. Why will the emphasis on academic skills in preschool classes continue to increase in the 1990s?
6. How can parents affect the types of early childhood programs that will be available in the 1990s?
7. Why are retention and transitional classes not the best alternatives for accommodating developmental differences in young children?
8. How will programs for children with special needs under PL 99–457 help more children than were served under PL 94–142?
9. How are parents more involved with the services provided to children under PL 99–457?
10. What implications for measurement and evaluation are reflected in the expanding presence of children from diverse backgrounds in early childhood programs?
11. Will measurement and evaluation of young children increase or decrease in future years? Why?

REFERENCES

ANDERSON, S. R. (1993, June). Trouble with testing. *American School Board Journal*, pp. 24–26.

BERGAN, J. R., & FELD, J. K. (1993). Developmental assessment: New directions. *Young Children, 48,* 41–47.

BOWEN, E. (1988, April 25). Can kids flunk kindergarten? *Time*, p. 86.

COHEN, M. (1988). Designing state assessment systems. *Phi Delta Kappan, 69,* 583–588.

COMPTROLLER GENERAL OF THE UNITED STATES. (1979, February 6). *Early childhood and family development programs improve the quality of life for low-income families.* A report to the Congress. Washington, DC: General Accounting Office.

DAY, B. D. (1988). What's happening in early childhood programs across the United States? In C. Warger (Ed.), *A resource guide to early childhood programs* (pp. 3–31). Alexandria, VA: Association for Supervision and Curriculum Development.

DECKER, C. A., & DECKER, J. R. (1992). *Planning and administering early childhood programs* (5th ed.). New York: Merrill/Macmillan.

DERMAN-SPARKS, L. (1992). "It isn't fair!" Antibias curriculum for young children. In B. Neugebauer (Ed.), *Alike and different: Exploring our humanity with young children* (pp. 2–10). Washington, DC: National Association for the Education of Young Children.

DIAMOND, K. E., HESTENES, L. L., & O'CONNER, C. E. (1994). Integrating young children with disabilities in preschool: Problems and promise. *Young Children, 49,* 68–73.

DIENER, P. L. (1993). *Resources for teaching children with diverse abilities*. Fort Worth, TX: Harcourt Brace Jovanovich.

EARLY CHILDHOOD AND LITERACY DEVELOPMENT COMMITTEE OF THE INTERNATIONAL READING ASSOCIATION. (1985). *Literacy development and pre-first grade. A joint statement of concerns about present practices in pre-first grade reading instruction and recommendations for improvement*. Newark, DE: International Reading Association.

FIENE, R. (1985). The Instrument Based Program Monitoring Information System and the indicator checklist for child care. *Child Care Quarterly, 14,* 198–214.

GOLD, D. L. (1988, August 3). Mississippi to end standardized tests for kindergartners. *Education Week, 39,* 1, 32.

GOODWIN, W. L., & GOODWIN, L. D. (1993). Young children and measurement: Standardized and nonstandardized instruments in early childhood education. In B. Spodek (Ed.), *Handbook of research on the education of young children* (pp. 441–463). New York: Macmillan.

GURALNICK, M. J. (1982). Mainstreaming young handicapped children: A public policy and ecological systems analysis. In B. Spodek (Ed.), *Handbook of research in early childhood education* (pp. 456–500). New York: Free Press.

GRACE, C., & SHORES, E. F. (1992). *The portfolio and its use: Developmentally appropriate assessment of young children*. Little Rock: Southern Early Childhood Association.

HARMS, T., & CLIFFORD, R. (1980). *The Early Childhood Environment Scale*. New York: Teachers College Press.

HIEBERT, H. E. (1988). The role of literacy experiences in early childhood programs. *Elementary School Journal, 89,* 161–171.

HIERONYMOUS, A. N., HOOVER, H. C., & LINDQUIST, E. F. (1986). *Iowa Tests of Basic Skills*. Chicago: Riverside.

HILLS, T. W. (1993). Assessment in context: Teachers and children at work. *Young Children, 48,* 20–28.

JENNINGS, J. F. (1988). Working in mysterious ways: The federal government and education. *Phi Delta Kappan, 70,* 62–65.

JONES, R. R. (1985). *The effect of a transition program on low achieving kindergarten students when entering first grade*. Unpublished doctoral dissertation, Northern Arizona University, Flagstaff.

KANTROWITZ, B. (1992, January 27). A head start does not last. *Newsweek,* pp. 44–45.

KARWEIT, N. (1988). Quality and quantity of learning time in preprimary programs. *Elementary School Journal, 89,* 119–134.

KATZ, L. G. (1988). Engaging children's minds: The implications of research for early childhood education. In C. Warger (Ed.), *A resource guide to public school early childhood programs* (pp. 32–52). Alexandria, VA: Association for Supervision and Curriculum Development.

MEISELS, S. J., STEELE, D. M., & QUINN-LEERING, K. (1993). Testing, tracking, and retaining young children: An analysis of research and social policy. In B. Spodek (Ed.), *Handbook of research on the education of young children* (pp. 279–292). New York: Macmillan.

MORRISON, G. S. (1988). *Education and development of infants, toddlers, and preschoolers*. Glenview, IL: Scott, Foresman.

NATIONAL ASSOCIATION FOR THE EDUCATION OF YOUNG CHILDREN (NAEYC). (1984). *Accreditation criteria and procedures of the National Academy of Early Childhood Programs*. Washington, DC: Author.

NURSS, J., & MCGAUVRAN, M. (1986). *Metropolitan Readiness Test* (5th ed.). San Antonio, TX: Psychological Corp.

PATTON, M. M., & WORTHAM, S. C. (1993). Transition classes, a growing concern. *Journal of Research in Childhood Education, 8,* 32–42.

PECK, J. T., MCCAIG, G., & SAPP, M. E. (1988). *Kindergarten policies: What is best for children?* Washington, DC: National Association for the Education of Young Children.

PHILLIPS, D. A. (Ed.). (1987). *Quality in child care: What does research tell us?* Washington, DC: National Association for the Education of Young Children.

PRESCOTT, E. (1975). *Assessment of child-rearing environments: An ecological approach*. Pasadena, CA: Pacific Oaks College.

RAYMOND, G., & MCINTOSH, D. K. (1992). The impact of current changes in social structure on early childhood education programs. In B. Neugebauer (Ed.), *Alike and different: Exploring our humanity with young children* (pp. 116–126). Washington, DC: National Association for the Education of Young Children.

ROYCE, J. M., MURRAY, H. W., LAZAR, I., & DARLINGTON, R. B. (1982). Methods of evaluating program outcomes. In B. Spodek (Ed.), *Handbook of research in early childhood education* (pp. 618–652). New York: Free Press.

SHEPARD, L. A., & GRAUE, M. E. (1993). The morass of school readiness screening: Research on test use and test validity. In B. Spodak (Ed.), *Handbook of research on the education of young children* (pp. 293–305). New York: Macmillan.

SHEPARD, L. A., & SMITH, M. L. (1987). Synthesis of research on school readiness and kindergarten retention. *Educational Leadership, 24*, 346–357.

SHEPARD, L. A., & SMITH, M. L. (1988). Escalating academic demand in kindergarten: Counterproductive policies. *Elementary School Journal, 89*, 135–146.

SPODEK, B. (1981). *The kindergarten: A retrospective and contemporary view.* Urbana, IL: Clearinghouse on Elementary and Early Childhood Education (ERIC Document Reproduction Service No. ED 206375).

TEALE, W. (1988). Developmentally appropriate assessment of reading and writing in the early childhood classroom. *Elementary School Journal, 89*, 173–184.

WARGER, C. (Ed.). (1988). *A resource guide to public school early childhood programs.* Alexandria, VA: Association for Supervision and Curriculum Development.

ZIGLER, E., & VALENTINE, J. (Eds.). (1979). *Project Head Start: A legacy of the war on poverty.* New York: Free Press.

A Selected Annotated Bibliography of Evaluation Instruments for Infancy and Early Childhood

1. Title: *AAMD Adaptive Behavior Scale, School Edition*
   Authors: N. Lambert, M. Windmiller, and L. Cals
   Publisher: American Association on Mental Deficiency
   Publication Date: 1981
   Type of Test: Behavior rating scale

Uses for which the test is recommended: Assesses behavioral and affective competencies of individuals from three to sixty-nine years. It is intended to be used with individuals with mental retardation and emotional maladjustment.

2. *Battelle Developmental Inventory*
   Authors: J. Newborg, J. Stock, L. Wnek, J. Guidubaldi, and J. Svinicki
   Publisher: DLM Teaching Resources
   Publication Date: 1984
   Type of Test: Early Childhood Screening and Diagnosis

Uses for which the test is recommended: Identification of the developmental strengths and weaknesses of children with and without disabilities in infant, preschool, and primary programs. Because it also has a screening test component, it can be used for general screening of preschool and kindergarten children "at risk" for developmental delays.

3. Title: *Bayley Scales of Infant Development*
   Author: M. Bayley
   Publisher: The Psychological Corporation
   Publication Date: 1969
   Type of Test: Infant development

Uses for which the test is recommended: Measures infant development and includes a mental and motor scale of development. An infant behavior record also provides a systematic way of assessing and recording observations of the child's behavior when examined.

4. Title: *Boehm Test of Basic Concepts*
    Author: A. Boehm
    Publisher: The Psychological Corporation
    Publication Date: 1986
    Type of Test: Individual or group screening test of concepts

Uses for which the test is recommended: Intended for use in kindergarten through second grade for screening and teaching. It measures knowledge of various concepts that are thought to be necessary for achievement in the first few grades of school.

5. Title: *The Brigance Inventories*
    Author: A. Brigance
    Publisher: Curriculum Associates
    Publication Date: *Brigance Diagnostic Inventory of Basic Skills,* 1976; *Brigance Diagnostic Inventory of Early Development,* 1977
    Type of Test: Informal diagnostic and screening inventories

Uses for which the test is recommended:
    Brigance Diagnostic Inventory of Basic Skills: Designed for use with children in kindergarten through grade six to assist teachers in adjusting curriculum and instruction for mainstreaming the disabled.
    Brigance Diagnostic Inventory of Early Development: Designed for the developmental period from birth to six years. Assesses psychomotor development, self-help skills, speech and language, general knowledge and comprehension, and early academic skills.

6. Title: *California Achievement Tests, Forms E and F*
    Publisher: CTB/McGraw-Hill
    Publication Date: 1985
    Type of Test: Norm-referenced achievement tests

Uses for which the test is recommended: Provides information for use in making educational decisions leading to improved instruction in the basic skills. Measures prereading, reading, spelling, language, mathematics, and reference skills.

7. Title: *Circus*
    Publisher: CTB/McGraw-Hill
    Publication Date: 1979
    Type of Test: Standardized achievement test battery for early childhood

Uses for which the test is recommended: To assess both knowledge and developmental skills of young children. The test publisher lists three uses for the test: program evaluation, individual assessment and pretesting/posttesting, and both normative and criterion-referenced score interpretations.

8. Title: *Denver Developmental Screening Test—Revised*
   Authors: W. Frankenburg, J. Dodds, J. Fandal, E. Kazuk, and M. Cohrs
   Publisher: University of Colorado Medical Center
   Publication Date: 1975
   Type of Test: Developmental screening

Uses for which the test is recommended: Measures development—gross motor, fine motor, language, and personal-social. Used to identify children from birth to six years of age with serious developmental delays.

9. Title: *Developmental Indicators for the Assessment of Learning—Revised*
   Authors: C. Mardell-Czudnowski and D. S. Goldenberg
   Publisher: American Guidance Service
   Publication Date: 1983
   Type of Test: Individual screening

Uses for which the test is recommended: Assesses motor, concept, and language skills for children aged two to six years. It is intended to screen the range of abilities from severe dysfunction to potentially advanced.

10. Title: *Gesell School Readiness Test*

    Author: Gesell Institute of Human Development
    Publisher: Programs for Education
    Publication Date: 1978
    Type of Test: School readiness

Uses for which the test is recommended: To determine whether children are ready to begin kindergarten and to answer questions about appropriate grade placement.

11. Title: *Kaufman Assessment Battery for Children*
    Authors: A. Kaufman and N. Kaufman
    Publisher: American Guidance Service
    Publication Date: 1983
    Type of Test: Individual intelligence, achievement

Uses for which the test is recommended: Intended for use in schools and clinical settings to measure intelligence and achievement for children aged two to six through twelve to fifteen years.

12. Title: *McCarthy Scales of Children's Abilities*
    Author: D. McCarthy
    Publisher: The Psychological Corporation
    Publication Date: 1972
    Type of Test: Cognitive abilities

Uses for which the test is recommended: Measures the cognitive abilities of children from 2½ to 8½ years. Can be used for the assessment of young children with learning problems or other exceptional conditions. Measures intellectual functioning, including verbal ability, nonverbal reasoning, number aptitude, short-term memory, and coordination.

13. Title: *Metropolitan Readiness Test*
   Authors: J. Nurss and M. McGauvran
   Publisher: The Psychological Corporation
   Publication Date: 1976
   Type of Test: School readiness

Uses for which the test is recommended: To evaluate a child's readiness for school and to help develop the skills necessary for success in school. To assess readiness for formal school learning from kindergarten to early first grade.

14. Title: *Miller Assessment for Preschoolers (MAP)*
   Author: L. J. Miller
   Publisher: The Psychological Corporation
   Publication Date: 1984
   Type of Test: Preschool screening test

Uses for which the test is recommended: To screen preschool children, aged two to nine and five to eight years, for developmental delays. MAP includes guidelines for observation of behavior during the testing. Higher scores only represent average performance; therefore, it does not identify children who are functioning at a higher level.

15. Title: *Mullen Scales of Early Learning*
   Author: E. M. Mullen
   Publisher: T.O.T.A.L. Child, Inc.
   Publication Date: 1984
   Type of Test: Developmental test

Uses for which the test is recommended: To assess a young child's learning abilities and patterns. It is intended for evaluating toddlers and preschool children aged fifteen to sixty-eight months. It assesses developmental skills in specific neurosensory and expressive areas of children who may be suspect for learning disability or who have evidence of maturational or developmental delay in one or more areas. Young children of various ethnic backgrounds can be evaluated to determine relative effects of cultural, sensory, or socioeconomic deprivation.

16. Title: *Neonatal Behavioral Assessment Scale*
   Author: T. B. Brazelton
   Publisher: Education Development Center

Publication Date: 1973
Type of Test: Neonatal rating scale

Uses for which the test is recommended: To identify mild neurological dysfunctions and variations in temperament. Measures temperamental differences, nervous system functions, and the capacity of the neonate to interact.

17. Title: *Peabody Picture Vocabulary Test—Revised*
Authors: L. Dunn and L. Dunn
Publisher: American Guidance Service
Publication Date: 1981
Type of Test: Receptive vocabulary

Uses for which the test is recommended: To evaluate the hearing vocabulary or receptive knowledge of vocabulary of children and adults.

18. Title: *Stanford-Binet Intelligence Scale* (4th ed.)
Authors: R. Thorndike, E. Hagen, and J. Sattler
Publisher: Houghton Mifflin
Publication Date: 1986
Type of Test: Intelligence

Uses for which the test is recommended: To assess the cognitive ability of young children, adolescents, and young adults. Subtests may be used to identify children with learning disabilities, to assess brain damage, and to measure the cognitive skills of children with hearing impairment or visual-spatial or mathematical talents.

19. Title: *Wechsler Intelligence Scale for Children—Revised*
Author: D. Wechsler
Publisher: The Psychological Corporation
Publication Date: 1974
Type of Test: Intelligence

Uses for which the test is recommended: For clinical and psychoeducational work. Useful in the assessment of brain-behavior relationships. Intended to evaluate children's intellectual ability.

20. Title: *Wechsler Preschool and Primary Scale of Intelligence*
Author: D. Wechsler
Publisher: The Psychological Corporation
Publication Date: 1967
Type of Test: Intelligence

Uses for which the test is recommended: To assess the cognitive abilities of preschool children. Includes developmental data that can be used for program planning.

Glossary

Achievement test A test that measures the extent to which a person has acquired information or mastered certain skills, usually as a result of instruction or training.

Alternate-form reliability The correlation between results on alternate forms of a test. Reliability is the extent to which the two forms are consistent in measuring the same attributes.

Anecdotal record A written description of an incident in a child's behavior that can be significant in understanding the child.

Aptitude test A test designed to predict future learning or performance on some task if appropriate education or training is provided.

Attitude inventory An instrument that measures a person's interest in a certain area or vocation. It is not used with very young children.

Attitude measure An instrument that measures how an individual is predisposed to feel or think about something (a referent). A teacher can design a scale to measure students' attitudes toward reading or mathematics.

Authentic assessment An assessment that uses some type of performance by a child to demonstrate understanding.

Authentic measure A measure that uses authentic assessments that include performance and application of knowledge

Behavioral objective An educational or instructional statement that includes the behavior to be exhibited, the conditions under which the behavior will be exhibited, and the level of performance required for mastery.

Checklist A sequence or hierarchy of concepts and/or skills organized in a format that can be used to plan instruction and keep records.

Concurrent validity The extent to which test scores on two forms of a test measure are correlated when they are given at the same time.

Construct validity The extent to which a test measures a psychological trait or construct. Tests of personality, verbal ability, and critical thinking are examples of tests with construct validity.

Content validity The extent to which the content of a test such as an achievement test represents the objectives of the instructional program it is designed to measure.

Contract An agreement between teacher and child about activities the child will complete to achieve a specific objective or purpose.

Correctives Instructional materials and methods used with mastery learning that are implemented after formative evaluation to provide alternative learning strategies and resources.

Criterion-referenced test A test designed to provide information on specific knowledge or skills possessed by a student. The test measures specific skills or instructional objectives.

Criterion-related validity To establish validity of a test, scores are correlated with an external criterion, such as another established test of the same type.

247

Developmental checklist   A checklist that emphasizes areas and levels of development in early childhood.

Developmental screening   Evaluation of the young child to determine whether development is proceeding normally. It is used to identify children whose development is delayed.

Diagnostic evaluation   An evaluation to analyze an individual's areas of weaknesses or strengths and to determine the nature and causes of the weaknesses.

Directed assignment   A specific assignment to assess a child's performance on a learning objective or skill.

Direct performance measure   A performance measure that requires the student to apply knowledge in an activity specified by the teacher.

Enrichment activity   In the context of mastery learning, the enrichment activity is a challenging activity at a higher cognitive level on Bloom's Taxonomy than the instructional objective described on a table of specifications.

Equivalent form   Forms of a test that are parallel. The forms of the test measure the same domain or objectives, have the same format, and are of equal difficulty.

Event sampling   An observation strategy used to determine when a particular behavior is likely to occur. The setting in which the behavior occurs is more important than the time it is likely to occur.

Formative evaluation   Evaluation conducted during instruction to provide the teacher with information on the learning progress of the student and the effectiveness of instructional methods and materials.

Formative test   A test designed to evaluate progress on specific learning objectives or a unit of study.

Game   In the context of authentic assessment, a game is a structured assessment whereby the student's performance progress is evaluated through engagement with the game.

Grade equivalent   The grade level for which a given score on a standardized test is the estimated average. Grade-equivalent scores, commonly used for elementary achievement tests, are expressed in terms of the grade and month.

Grade norms   Norms on standardized tests based on the performance of students in given grades.

Graphic rating scale   A rating scale that can be used as a continuum. The rater marks characteristics by descriptors on the scale at any point along the continuum.

Group test   A test that can be administered to more than one person at a time.

Inclusion   The process of including children with disabilities into a classroom where they would have been placed if they had not experienced a disability.

Indirect performance measure   A measure that assesses what a student knows about a topic. The teacher's assessment is accomplished by observing a student activity or examining a written test.

Individual test   A test that can be administered to only one person at a time. Many early childhood tests are individual tests because of the low maturity level of the examinees.

Individualized instruction   Instruction based on the learning needs of individual students. It may be based on criterion-related evaluation or diagnosis.

Informal tests   Tests that have not been standardized. Teacher-designed tests are an example.

Instructional objective   See *behavioral objective.*

Integration   Relates to facilitating the participation of children with disabilities into the classroom with peers who do not have disabilities. The child is integrated with other children and the needs of all children are met without treating some children as "special."

Intelligence quotient (IQ)   An index of intelligence expressed as the ratio of mental age to chronological age. It is derived from an individual's performance on an intelligence test as compared with that of others of the same age.

Intelligence test A test measuring those developed abilities considered to be a sign of intelligence. Intelligence is general potential independent of prior learning.

Interest inventory A measure used to determine interest in an occupation or vocation. Students' interest in reading might be determined by such an inventory.

Internal consistency The degree of relationship among items on a test. A type of reliability that indicates whether items on the test are positively interrelated and measure the same trait or characteristic.

Item analysis The analysis of single test items to determine their difficulty value and discriminating power. Item analysis is conducted in the process of developing a standardized test.

Interview A discussion that the teacher conducts with a child to make an assessment.

Learning disability A developmental difference or delay in a young or school-age child that interferes with the individual's ability to learn through regular methods of instruction.

Mainstreaming A process of placing children with disabilities into regular classrooms with children who do not have disabilities for part of the school day. Mainstreaming is being replaced by inclusion or integration, in which the child with disabilities is not singled out as being different.

Mastery testing Evaluation to determine the extent to which a test taker has mastered particular skills or learning objectives. Performance is compared to a predetermined standard of proficiency.

Mean The arithmetic average of a set of test scores.

Minimum competency testing Evaluation to measure whether test takers have achieved a minimum level of proficiency in a given academic area.

Multiple choice A type of test question in which the test taker must choose the best answer from among several options.

Narrative report An alternative to report cards for reporting a child's progress. The teacher writes a narrative to describe the child's growth and accomplishments.

Neonatologist A physician who specializes in babies less than one month old.

Normal distribution The hypothetical distribution of scores that has a bell-shaped appearance. This distribution is used as a model for many scoring systems and test statistics.

Norm-referenced test A test in which the test taker's performance is compared with the performance of persons in a norm group.

Norms Statistics that supply a frame of reference based on the actual performance of test takers in a norm group. A set of scores that represents the distribution of test performance in the norm group.

Numerical rating scale A series of numerals, such as 1 to 5, that allows an observer to indicate the degree to which an individual possesses a particular characteristic.

Obstetrician A physician who specializes in pregnancy and childbirth.

Outcome-based assessment Similar to a performance assessment, this assessment is based on the outcome of a specific performance by a child.

Pediatrician A physician who specializes in the development, care, and diseases of young children.

Percentile A point or score in a distribution at or below which falls the percentage of cases indicated by the percentile. The score scale on a normal distribution is divided into 100 segments, each containing the same number of scores.

Percentile rank The test taker's test score, as expressed in terms of its position within a group of 100 scores. The percentile rank is the percentage of scores equal to or lower than the test taker's score.

Performance assessment An assessment in which the child demonstrates knowledge by applying it to a task or a problem-solving activity.

Performance-based evaluation An evaluation of development and/or learning that is based on the child's natural performance rather than on contrived tests or tasks.

Personality test   A test designed to obtain information on the affective characteristics of an individual (emotional, motivational, or attitudinal). The test measures psychological makeup rather than intellectual abilities.

Portfolio   A format for conducting an evaluation of a child. Portfolios are a collection of a child's work, teacher assessments, and other information that contribute to a picture of the child's progress.

Psychological test   A test for measuring human characteristics that pertain to observable and intraindividual behavior. The test measures past, present, or future human behavior.

Rating scale   A scale using categories that allow the observer to indicate the degree of a characteristic that the person possesses.

Raw score   The number of right answers a test taker obtains on a test.

Readiness test   A test that measures the extent to which a student has the prerequisite skills necessary to be successful in some new learning activity.

Reliability   The extent to which a test is consistent in measuring over time what it is designed to measure.

Running record   A description of a sequence of events in a child's behavior that includes all behaviors observed over a period of time.

Scaled score   The score obtained when a raw score is translated into a score that uses the normal curve for points of reference. Examples of scaled scores are IQ scores, percentiles, T scores, and Z scores.

School diagnostician   A school staff member trained to administer psychological tests for screening and diagnostic purposes.

School psychologist   A psychologist who specializes in testing and in the learning and emotional problems of school children.

Scope (sequence of skills)   A list of learning objectives established for areas of learning and development at a particular age, grade level, or content area.

Specimen record   Detailed observational reports of children's behavior over a period of time that are used for research purposes.

Split-half reliability   A measure of reliability whereby scores on equivalent sections of a single test are correlated for internal consistency.

Standard deviation   A measure of the variability of a distribution of scores around the mean.

Standard error   An estimate of the possible magnitude of error present on test scores.

Standard score   A transformed score that reports performance in terms of the number of standard deviation units the raw score is from the mean.

Standardized test   A test that has specified content, procedures for administration and scoring, and normative data for interpreting scores.

Stanine   A scale on the normal curve divided into nine sections, with all divisions except the first and the last being 0.5 standard deviation wide.

Structured interview   A preplanned interview conducted by the teacher for assessment purposes.

Structured performance assessment   A performance assessment that has been preplanned by the teacher to include specific tasks or activities.

Summative evaluation   An evaluation obtained at the end of a cycle of instruction to determine whether students have mastered the objectives and whether the instruction has been effective.

Summative test   A test to determine mastery of learning objectives administered for grading purposes.

T score   A standard score scale with a mean of 50 and a standard deviation of 10.

Table of specifications   A table of curriculum objectives that have been analyzed to determine to what level of Bloom's taxonomy of educational objectives the student must demonstrate mastery.

Test-retest reliability   A type of reliability obtained by administering the same test a second time after a short interval and then correlating the two sets of scores.

Time sampling   Observation to determine the frequency of a behavior. The observer records how many times the behavior occurs during uniform time periods.

True score   A hypothetical score on a test that is free of error. Because no standardized test is free of measurement error, a true score can never be obtained.

Unstructured interview   An assessment interview conducted by the teacher as the result of a naturally occurring performance by a child. The interview is not preplanned.

Unstructured performance assessment   An assessment that is part of regular classroom activities.

Validity   The degree to which a test serves the purpose for which it is to be used.

Work samples   Examples of a child's work that include products of all types of activities that can be used to evaluate the child's progress.

Z score   A standard score that expresses performance in terms of the number of standard deviations from the mean.

Index

Sue Clark Wortham is Professor of Early Childhood and Education at the University of Texas at San Antonio. Prior to beginning a teaching career in higher education in 1979 at UTSA she taught prekindergarten through second grade in the public schools, worked as a school district administrator, and was a consultant at an education service center. She is married to Marshal R. Wortham and has three sons, George, Miles, and Benjamin, and two grandchildren, Elizabeth and Miles Wortham.

In addition to this text she authored *Early Childhood Education: Developmental Bases for Learning and Teaching* for Merrill in 1994. Earlier titles include *Organizing Instruction in Early Childhood* (Allyn & Bacon, 1984) and *Childhood 1892-1992* (Association for Childhood Education International, 1992). In 1990 she coedited *Playgrounds for Young Children: National Survey and Perspectives* with Joe L. Frost (American Alliance for Health, Physical Education, Recreation and Dance).

In 1992 she served as a Fulbright Scholar in Chile and was elected President Elect of the Association for Childhood Education International in 1994.